LIBR

Mental Health, Race and Culture

Also by Suman Fernando:

Race and Culture in Psychiatry

Mental Health in a Multi-ethnic Society (editor)

Forensic Psychiatry, Race and Culture with D. Ndegwa and M. Wilson

Mental Health, Race and Culture

Second Edition

Suman Fernando

Consultant Editor: Jo Campling

First edition 1991
Reprinted eight times
Second edition 2002
Published by
PALGRAVE
Houndmills, Basingstoke, Hampshire RG21 6XS and
175 Fifth Avenue, New York, N.Y. 10010
Companies and representatives throughout the world

PALGRAVE is the new global academic imprint of
St. Martin's Press LLC Scholarly and Reference Division and
Palgrave Publishers Ltd (formerly Macmillan Press Ltd).

ISBN 0–333–96026–2 paperback

This book is printed on paper suitable for recycling and
made from fully managed and sustained forest sources.

A catalogue record for this book is available
from the British Library.

Library of Congress Cataloging-in-Publication Data
Fernando, Suman.
    Mental health, race, and culture / Suman Fernando; consultant editor,
Jo Campling.—2nd ed.
    p. cm.
    Includes bibliographical references and index.
    ISBN 0–333–96026–2 (pbk.)
    1. Psychiatry, Transcultural.   I. Campling, Jo.   II. Title.

RC455.4.E8 F468 2001
616.89—dc21

                                                          2001036098

10 9 8 7 6 5 4 3 2 1
11 10 09 08 07 06 05 04 03 02

Printed in China

To the memory of my mother and father

Contents

Acknowledgements

I am indebted to many works of scholarship in the fields of psychiatry, psychology, anthropology and religion, especially those works that cut across these disciplines. However, this book would not have been possible without the stimulation I derived from discussions with numerous colleagues of various disciplines, the insight I gained through talking to people I met as patients or clients, and, most of all, the forbearance and patience shown by my wife and daughter.

In revising the book for its second edition, I drew on discussions I had over the years with users of services and workers in the field of mental health in Sri Lanka, Canada, The Netherlands and England, and from recent publications.

SUMAN FERNANDO

Introduction

The *World Health Report* (WHO, 2000) defines the objective of good health as twofold: 'the best attainable average level – *goodness* – and the smallest feasible difference among individuals and groups – *fairness* (2000: xi). But the picture of health care in the world today is characterised by a number of paradoxes. Intensive care units in hospitals in Western cities struggle to save individual premature babies using all the techniques available to modern science, while hundreds of healthy children in Asia, Africa and South America die from the lack of basic health care. European doctors try to combat the diseases of overeating while relief workers in some parts of Africa try to combat starvation. The Western diagnosis of depression is promoted in Africa along with antidepressants manufactured by Western drug firms, while Indian mysticism is marketed in North America. The second half of the twentieth century saw a plethora of ethnic wars, often traceable to the ravages of colonialism during the heyday of European imperialism; yet, is this imperialism really over or just taken a new guise as 'globalisation'? In any case, the latter decades of the twentieth century saw a massive movement of people across continents, many seeking asylum from areas of conflict and sometimes persecution. Europe, which had been a continent of emigration for centuries, has become a continent of immigration. It is on this world stage that the current meaning of mental health has to be worked out.

So what is mental health in a world context? Is it about intervening with therapies for personal illness or the alleviation of distress in populations? Is it about each individual person in his/her own internal world or about relationships in families – or in societies as a whole? Is it about minimising violence and hatred between people and intervening with conflict resolution so that people of diverse backgrounds, cultures and races can live in peace, or just about dealing with the consequences of violence and hatred? And where does justice

1

come into all this? In any case can the health of the individual be separated from that of society? Finally, can it be mentally healthy for people to persecute minorities or refuse asylum to those in need? Is it mentally healthy for nations to condone endemic disparities of wealth and health care? Perhaps health, especially mental health, is not so much a personal matter but 'the aftertaste of a society's other activities, the residue of all its policies' (Karpf, 1988).

In the West, the individual human being, in terms of a self-centred, self-conscious entity, is valued highly as a person in comparison to the value set on ideas, philosophies and religions; this lends itself to a narrow view of what is health. Materialism and a distaste for spiritual considerations characterise today's Western values, further limiting the perception of what constitutes the person. But yet, the concept of 'mental health' has become a valued goal in the West. And awareness has grown that 'mental health' is not restricted to separate aspects of individual behaviour and experience but rather involves the functioning of human beings as whole individuals, family groups and communities. Although the notion of holism is alien to Western conceptions of human behaviour and experience, new approaches to ill health, such as 'holistic medicine' and 'systems theory', indicate dissatisfaction with the traditional reductionist approach in the West to health, illness, psychiatry and psychology. Although the West prides itself on its scientific sophistication and an advanced system of medical treatment to combat ill health, the question of mental health is somewhat different, especially when considered cross-culturally. As White (1982) states:

> The notion of 'mental health' derives from a particular tradition of medical research and practice which does not provide a neutral stance from which to analyse or represent the way 'other cultures' conceptualise disorders of the person and social behaviour. To begin with, the boundary between disorders of the mind (the province of psychiatry and neurology) and of the body (the province of internal medicine) is itself a cultural construction which underlies the segmentation of a class of illness we refer to as 'mental'.

White, an anthropologist, goes on to argue: 'The relation of cultural conceptions of "mental disorder" to cultural conceptions of "illness" or to "social deviance", etc. are empirical questions to be answered by ethnographic research.' Scientific and lay conceptions of mental health show similarities due 'in part to implicit understandings about the nature of persons and social behaviour which influence both formal and informal theories of illness'.

In the West, the recognition of mental illness as an undesirable state of mind predated the idea of mental health as a desirable state. The development of psychiatry and psychology during the eighteenth and nineteenth centuries and the early part of the twentieth was closely linked to theories of 'mind' prevalent in European thinking at the time and to the definition of mental illness as an expression of abnormalities of mental functioning. In other words, the culture of psychiatry and psychology is rooted in worldviews, attitudes and beliefs characteristic of Western culture as it was during the years when these disciplines developed. Psychiatry and psychology have not been influenced to any significant extent by systems of culture that were not specifically 'European'; they are highly ethnocentric disciplines with a limited perspective but yet assumed to have universal relevance. Once this assumption was questioned in the early part of the twentieth century, a movement within psychiatry – 'cultural psychiatry' – developed incorporating anthropological and psycho-analytic viewpoints. Meanwhile, psychiatric studies comparing Europeans and non-Europeans were called 'cross-cultural psychiatry' or 'comparative psychiatry' – a term first used by Kraepelin (1904). Neither approach, however, addressed racial issues, especially the fact that beliefs and myths about race in European culture have been ignored or taken into psychiatry and psychology. More recently, the term 'transcultural psychiatry' has been applied to both cultural psychiatry and cross-cultural/comparative psychiatry. But it is only during the past 20 or so years that transcultural psychiatry has begun to recognise and explore the significance of the encounter between psychiatry, with its ethnocentric cultural basis and its racist ideology on the one hand, and, on the other, people whose cultural background is not 'European' (in its nineteenth-century sense) and whose 'racial' origins are seen as non-white. The first edition of this book developed and broadened this field of study and exploration by placing psychiatry in a framework of mental health while examining issues around race and culture.

This second edition of the book has the same basic structure as the first, but has been revised and updated throughout with some reordering and/or retitling of chapters. The discussions of racism and of culture have been expanded to take on board recent developments. With the proliferation recently of 'cultural studies', the word 'culture' is used now in a variety of interrelated senses that are difficult to keep track of. Hence, difficulties inherent in using the term 'culture' (which was alluded to in the first edition of this book) have been further addressed. While acknowledging the usefulness of the postmodern views on the relativity of the concept 'culture', the author has kept to his original viewpoint that delineating 'cultural groups' is useful for practical purposes. Also terms such as 'Western culture', 'African culture', 'Eastern culture', etc. carry some meaning when used for the purposes of the discussions in the book. However it should be noted that these broad terms refer to traditional roots of culture (as 'Western', 'African', etc.) rather than the cultures of modern (or postmodern) societies where cultural forms are essentially hybrid.

The term 'psychiatry' is used consistently in this book to mean a body of knowledge and set of practices peculiar to Western culture in that the combination of influences characteristic of psychiatry did not occur in any other medical or religious tradition. Thus, Chapter 3 no longer refers to 'Western Psychiatry' but to 'Psychiatry'; and Chapter 6 refers to 'Asian and African Therapies' rather than 'Different Forms of Psychiatry' (as in the first edition of the book). The situation in the case of 'psychology' is somewhat different. Some non-Western traditions include studies akin to the (Western) study of 'mind'. Hence although the term 'psychology' used without any qualifying prefix refers to the study of the human 'mind' within a Western cultural tradition, terms such as 'Asian psychology', 'Buddhist psychology', etc. are used in the book to refer to similar studies within other cultures.

The first part of this book considers theory and tradition. Since race, culture and ethnicity are often confused by both professionals and the lay public and the meaning of racism is often misunderstood, these terms are discussed and, more importantly, a basis is laid down for the discussions to follow. Also, notions of mental health are explored, examining in particular the influence of racism in the development of Western psychology and psychiatry. Chapter 1 considers the concept of race in a historical context, noting that the powerful force of racism ensures the perpetuation of the biological myth that mankind can be divided into genetically discrete entities called races, based on skin colour and other physical characteristics. The notion of racism is explored, its historical derivation described and its psychological and socio-political dimensions are evaluated. In Chapter 2 the theory and traditions underlying conceptualisations of mental health and mental disorder are explored in the context of differing worldviews in various cultures. The culture of psychiatry is described in Chapter 3, contrasting its (Western) ethos and philosophical basis with those of other traditions that have a much wider acceptance globally. And then Chapter 4 explores the racist ideology that fashions Western concepts of mental health and mental disorder by considering the racism inherent in psychology and psychiatry – the two disciplines that underpin mental health services.

The second part of the book addresses practice and innovation. To start with, Chapter 5 considers the universal application of (Western) psychiatry – its use and abuse. The situation in Western multiracial and multicultural societies is explored by considering racial bias in the practice of psychiatry in Britain and the United States, resulting, for example, in racial differences in diagnostic patterns. The drawbacks of a (Western) medical model of illness leads on to a discussion of psychiatric imperialism involved in the international use of psychiatry in the context of Western domination and the ethos of white superiority. Although systems of 'therapy' and 'healing' indigenous to Asian, African and (pre-Columbian) American cultures have been seriously underdeveloped – and still marginalised or even suppressed as a result of the power and influence of psychiatric imperialism – they still function albeit under adverse conditions. Current healers who practise what may be called 'psychological medicine' in the Indian subcontinent – e.g. traditional physicians, such as the *vaids* of the Hindu Ayurveda and Siddha systems and the *hakim* of the Islamic Unani tradition, and the 'spiritual' therapists such as babas, bhagwans and swamis – are very different from their Western counterparts in both theory and practice (Kakar, 1984). African witch doctors and American shamans cure their patients by traditional means that sometimes incorporate Western ideas and methods. It is against this background that Chapter 6 examines what to Western audiences may be innovative – even exotic – ways of maintaining mental health in the current world context. Although hampered by the sparsity of reliable and unprejudiced English literature on the topics, the chapter considers some indigenous systems of medicine and spiritual therapies in African and Asian cultural traditions. While pointing out that descriptions of these therapies are distorted when analysed in terms of Western concepts and presented in Western idioms, some lessons are drawn about their potential usefulness. Finally this chapter considers issues around cross-cultural collaboration between practitioners of different systems.

The last two chapters are speculative. In Chapter 7, the feasibility of taking deculturalised technologies of psychiatry and similar 'bits' of other cultures for transportation cross-culturally is considered.

This chapter is a pragmatic, tentative venture rather than a specific plan for action. It presents an approach that may lead to the sort of cultural interchange that may be mutually beneficial at a practical level. And Chapter 7 leads on to the final chapter which addresses the possibility of a basis for incorporating ideas from all cultures in developing an approach to mental illness and mental health that is universally applicable. Chapter 8 develops the argument that programmes for mental health care must take on board the cultural diversity of humankind; address the fact of racism; and incorporate a spiritual dimension. If this can be done, it may be possible to look beyond race and culture towards a mental health for all.

In attempting to cover a wide field, this book is necessarily limited in the depth of discussion of any one aspect of it; also, it is selective in the material and views that are presented. Although his roots are in an Asian cultural tradition of Sri Lanka, the author's personal experience of work in the mental health field is restricted to that of a professional psychiatrist and researcher – albeit with a strong bias towards social psychiatry and community work – and a participant in the transcultural psychiatry movement in Britain; the author is not an anthropologist or sociologist. The literature covered in the book is confined to that in the English language available in the United Kingdom. The word 'Western' used to qualify cultures, thinking, etc. refers to 'the West' meaning (traditional) European in contrast to Asian, African, etc. The language used in the book tries to avoid phrases and descriptions that may be offensive because of their racist implications; but the words 'non-white', 'non-European' and 'non-Western' are used in order to emphasise differences between dominant and non-dominant races and cultures. Technical or mystifying terms from both social and biological sciences are avoided – except to make a special point – because the book itself is aimed at a wide readership.

PART I

Theory and Tradition

1

Race, Culture and Racism

The term 'race' entered the English language in the sixteenth century at a time when the Bible was accepted as the authority on human affairs, and was used originally in the sense of lineage, supposedly ordained at the creation of the world (Banton, 1987). From then, well into the nineteenth century, race as lineage referred to groups of people connected by common descent or origin. Later, as Darwinian concepts were accepted in European thinking, race was seen as subspecies, and finally sociological theories of race led to the notion of races as populations. Today, all these ideas exist together, giving rise to considerable confusion in current thinking about race since the corollaries of these different notions are very different. For example, race as lineage explains why people are both physically and culturally different, but race as population does not do so very clearly; it may be a satisfactory explanation of physical differentiation of populations that are relatively isolated from each other, but cannot interpret cultural differentiation except by assuming that ecological forces governing unconscious behaviour determine human culture in the way they determine social life of animals.

One of the original meanings of 'culture' was 'husbandry' (Eagleton, 2000) – the verb 'cultivate' derives from 'culture' – and this meaning persists (for example) in references to 'cultured pearls' or 'tissue culture' (the technique of growing tisses *in vitro*). But over the years the word 'culture' was transformed from being an activity to become an entity – almost an abstract concept (Eagleton, 2000). At one time being cultured was synonymous with being civilised, but then anthropology, in association with nineteenth-century colonialism, gave culture its modern meaning of 'a unique way of life' (2000: 26) initially applied to people designated (by anthropologists) as 'uncivilised' or

9

racially inferior, but later applied to all societies. The word 'culture' is now used in several ways representing its changes of meaning. Today cultured people are those who indulge in 'cultural' activities, generally activities in the field of the arts, rather than the sciences. The term 'culture' applied to an individual usually refers to a mixture of behaviour and cognition (in a wide sense) arising from 'shared patterns of belief, feeling and adaptation which people carry in their minds' (Leighton and Hughes, 1961: 447). The allusion to family culture or the cultures of whole communities extends the meaning of the word 'culture' further. Therefore, referring to a multiplicity of cultures (say in a multicultural society) implies (cultural) differences between groups of people – 'communities' with different backgrounds, traditions and worldviews. However, when reference is made to the culture of an institution or a group – for example to 'police canteen culture' or 'the culture of psychiatry' – the word 'culture' means the ethos or ways of functioning of a system or a group of people in a particular context.

A concept that builds on ideas within both race and culture, but with a personal dimension indicating a sense of belonging, is 'ethnicity'. Naturally, ethnicity overlaps in meaning with both race and culture; it is sometimes used as an alternative to 'race' or 'culture' but more often used to indicate both these concepts. But overriding all these terms is the term 'racism' which refers to attitudes and to practices. It is closely connected with the idea of 'race' discussed earlier but also connects with 'culture' when this is seen (erroneously) as a static entity applied to an individual or group and inherited or passed on from generation to generation – in other words when 'culture' is confounded with 'race' – a matter discussed later in this chapter. Racism is difficult to define satisfactorily partly because it has a diversity of meanings. Graham Richards (1997) attempts to get over this problem by using the word 'racialism' to refer to 'a theoretical or ideological belief in the reality of races' (1997: xi) and limiting the use of the word 'racism' to 'attitudes and practices which are explicitly hostile to and denigratory towards people defined as belonging to another "race"' (1997: xi). However, Richardson and Lambert (1985) use the word 'racialism' to mean the acting out of personal prejudice and racism to mean an ideology. The approach taken in this book is that attitudes and practices are difficult to separate from beliefs and theories held in people's minds as assumptions and stereotypes, and so it is simpler and more realistic to use the word 'racism' generally to cover all these.

Culture and race

Culture as a unique way of life common to a group represents an accumulation of knowledge among people constituting the group, of 'conceptual structures' that determine the total reality of life within which people live and die, or of social institutions such as the family, the village, and so on. It generally subsumes all features of a person's environment, but specifically refers to the non-material aspects of everything that he/she holds in common with other individuals forming a social group – child-rearing habits, family systems, and ethical values or attitudes common to a group. In anthropological writings, culture was seen originally as 'something out there', a social concept, but later as something 'inside' a person – a psychological state (D'Andrade, 1984). Linton (1956) defines culture as 'an organised group of ideas, habits and conditioned responses shared by members of a society'; Brody (1964) provides a short definition of culture as 'a pattern of shared behaviour characteristics of a society', and, Kluckholm (1944) an even shorter one, 'a blueprint for living'.

Following on the writings of Foucault (1967, 1977, 1988), there has been an increasing awareness of the relationship between discourse (fields of knowledge, statements and practice, including medical, psychiatric and psychological practice) and power. And categories which lump peoples or experiences together have become suspect. Today culture is explored on a 'postmodern' terrain; it is no longer seen as something static inside or outside a person, but as something variable and relative depending on historical and political viewpoints in a context of power relationships. *The Location of Culture* (Bhabha, 1994) emphasises the hybridity of the concept in today's world; *Culture and Imperialism* (Said, 1994) unravels the intimate connections between the understandings of culture presented in Anglo-American literature and European domination – nowadays called 'globalisation'. In general, culture is seen today as something that cannot be clearly defined, as something living, dynamic and changing – a flexible system of values and worldviews that people live by, a system by which they define identities and negotiate their lives. Although this postmodern concept of culture cannot be captured properly in terms of polarities such as East and West, traditional and modern, etc., it is the view of the author that broad categories, such as Eastern, Western, Asian, African and European, have to be constructed and used in the interests of brevity. Thus, in spite of the

limitations of doing so, these rough categorisations are used in
discussing cultural variations throughout the book.

It would be seen from the earlier discussion that the term 'culture'
lacks precision and its meaning is both variable and dynamic. As a
result, culture is often confused with race. People seen as being
racially different are assumed to have different cultures, and value
judgements attached to 'race' are transferred to 'culture'. Moreover,
racism has distorted European views of culture and laid the basis for
skin colour, designating race, being an important dimension in all
group interactions – and possibly all personal relationships too – in
which Western people or Western ideas play a part. 'Culture', as an
immutable, fixed property of social groups, has become confounded
with 'race', and racism is articulated in cultural terms. For example,
when in 1979 the (then) leader of the British Opposition in the House
of Commons, Mrs Margaret Thatcher, warned the electorate of
being 'swamped' by alien cultures (quoted by Fitzpatrick, 1990:
249), she meant 'races' and not 'cultures'. In psychiatry and mental
health services in general too racist ideas are expressed in cultural
terms. So in considering discourse about 'culture' one has to be
mindful of the impact of racism.

Ethnicity

Ethnicity is a term that alludes to the definition of both cultural and
racial characteristics – and perhaps much more. Sociologist Stuart
Hall (1992) states: 'The term ethnicity acknowledges the place of
history, language and culture in the construction of subjectivity and
identity, as well as the fact that all discourse is placed positioned,
situated, and all knowledge is contextual' (1992: 257). However the
bonds that bind together people of an ethnic group are often not
clear-cut; they are not definable in terms of physical appearance
(race) or social similarity (culture) alone – although both may be
involved; and subjective feelings may be determined by a variety of
influences. In practice, the overriding feature of an ethnic group is
the sense of belonging together that the individuals feel; it is basically
a psychological matter. This feeling may be promoted, or even
initiated, by the way society at large perceives people. If certain
persons are seen as belonging together – whatever the reason – and
are treated as such, a sense of being part of a group may develop. If
the bonds that seem to bind them together are seen as 'cultural' or

'racial', or both, an ethnic group is identified. Thus, cultural similarity, real or imagined, may engender or even determine a sense of belonging that determines ethnicity. But this sense of belonging may well arise for different reasons: for example, a sense of belonging that emerges in a racist society is likely to be based on race as perceived by society at large, rather than culture as experienced by the group members. Yet a sense of belonging to a particular religious tradition (for example) may override all others.

In practical shorthand (for the purpose of ethnic monitoring or census designation) the term 'ethnic' is taken to mean (at least in Britain) a mixture of cultural background and racial designation, the significance of each being variable. It is essentially about self-perception – how people see themselves. A British government paper (in this case about collecting health statistics) sees ethnicity as a mixture of culture, religion, skin colour, language and family origin (NHS Management Executive, 1993). So if racism is felt as a powerful force in society, people from various backgrounds and cultures may see themselves largely in racial terms (e.g. as 'black people') but also (or alternatively) identify in 'cultural' terms of religion or parental origin (e.g. as 'Muslims' or 'Asian'). The main broad ethnic groups referred to in British health surveys and research are African-Caribbeans, Africans, Asians and whites, the two largest minority ethnic groups in the UK being South Asians and African-Caribbeans. In Britain, the term 'black people' is applied quite often to mean all ethnic minorities or more specifically Africans and African-Caribbeans, but in other places (e.g. USA and Canada) the term 'people of colour' or 'visible minorities' is preferred and in many European countries the pejorative term 'migrant' is still used (Fernando, 1991). However, it should be noted that the meaning of ethnicity (as described above) may well change – and so the categories for the census and for ethnic monitoring too may need to change.

Connections between race, culture and ethnicity

Race, culture and ethnicity are difficult to disentangle in practical situations; confusion between them is rife in many areas of thought – from politics to scientific research. In short, race is primarily physical, culture is sociological and ethnicity is psychological (Figure 1.1). Although physical difference, skin colour in particular, is the basis of perceived racial difference, culture and ethnicity may be more

	CHARACTERISED BY	DETERMINED BY	PERCEIVED AS
RACE	Physical appearance	Genetic ancestry	Permanent (genetic/biological)
CULTURE	Behaviour Attitudes	Upbringing Choice	Changeable (assimilation, acculturation)
ETHNICITY	Sense of belonging Group identity	Social pressures Psychological need	Partially changeable

Figure 1.1   Race, culture and ethnicity

important in some circumstances and for some people. Since the definition of culture is so variable, race and ethnicity may often be used to define boundaries on the assumption that culture is associated with one or the other. It is race that was used to enforce racial discrimination through apartheid in South Africa and ethnicity that is now used in the course of ethnic monitoring in order to locate discrimination in British employment practices. Race, culture and ethnicity are interrelated in complex ways depending on historical, political and social factors. For example, the experience, post-slavery, of black people in the United States has shaped a black consciousness – a sense of belonging to a group – as well as a recognisable black culture (Richardson and Lambert, 1985). In post-empire Britain, black people sometimes found themselves trapped under a system of 'internal colonialism within cities' (Pryce, 1979); and these 'internal colonies' provided the material base for a cultural revival of (for example) a 'West Indian consciousness' extending into a more generalised 'black consciousness' (Hall *et al.*, 1978) or an 'Asianness'. These black or Asian 'colonies' (for example in Brixton and Southall in London) have sometimes been referred to as 'ghettos', although they have never been ghettos in the sense of the word 'ghetto' used for Jewish ghettos in pre-war Eastern Europe or even the ghettos in some cities like Chicago and Washington in the United States.

In a multiracial and multicultural society the concept of ethnicity, identified by a sense of belonging, emerges through various pressures, social, political, economic, etc., as well as cultural ties and perceptions of racial identity, the strength of which too may be influenced by these same pressures. Among the social forces in many societies is the pressure arising from racism that drives together people perceived as being racially similar to each other. The ethnicity that is promoted and crystallised by social forces has been called an emergent ethnicity (Yancey *et al.*, 1976). This is the ethnicity that is of practical importance in most communities where there is racial and cultural diversity. Thus sociologists refer to 'new ethnicities' derived from African, Caribbean and Asian cultures in a context of complex social and cultural changes that have emerged in Britain's black and Asian communities during the past 20 years (Cohen, 1999). The ways in which ethnicity develops in British society depend on the significance of racism; if racism diminishes, the interplay of cultural diversity is likely to achieve increasing importance in determining ethnicity. But while racism continues, as it does in most Western societies, racial difference will play an important part in determining ethnicity.

Racial groups and ethnic groups

The practical importance of the concepts of race and ethnicity is in their application to people; and this is usually done by assigning people to 'groups' described as racial or ethnic. Unfortunately, a person so categorised is likely to be labelled and seen henceforth, not as an individual, but as a carrier of various qualities assumed to be consistent with the category. This is the danger of stereotyping and of labelling. Therefore, however useful and convenient racial and ethnic categorisation may be – not least for identifying racial discrimination – one important fact must be borne in mind at all times: individuals within a racial or ethnic category are all different and individual differences may outweigh group differences in extent and importance. Although, as emphasised earlier, members of a racial group do not share a distinctive aggregate of genes that differentiates such a group from other racial groups, people perceived as belonging to a racial group are assumed to share a common ancestry. But more than that, they must look similar in terms of traditional racial criteria, in particular, and often exclusively, skin colour, or else they must be perceived as having ancestral links that imply such similarity. Hence, the statement about the people included within a racial group is a social statement about their perceived ancestry and/or physical appearance. Thus racially 'black' people may include those of varying skin colours or degrees of pigmentation; some may indeed appear to be lighter skinned than people who may be included in a 'white' group. This statement about the race that they belong to is essentially political, not biological.

Ethnic attachments between people are seen as arising in various ways (Rex, 1986): first, people develop close relations with others having similar cultural behaviour to themselves; secondly, cultural and physical characteristics bring about a 'consciousness of kind' – the 'sense of belonging' noted earlier in this chapter; thirdly, cultural similarity is taken as a sign of common ancestry. When someone is perceived as a member of an ethnic group, it is the behaviour denoting a sense of belonging and/or cultural similarity that is considered. However, the terminology that is used, i.e. the definition of a particular group as 'racial' or 'ethnic', is often determined by popular misconceptions and institutionalised attitudes as well as political expediency and historical prejudice.

The distinction between racial and ethnic groups (outlined above) gives rise to certain corollaries (Figure 1.1). While they are both recognised by actual behavioural and physical characteristics, the basis of racial behaviour is perceived as being very different from that of ethnic behaviour. The former is seen as unchangeable, predetermined and unaffected by social pressures, while the latter is assumed to be flexible, amenable to change under social and other pressures, and subject to the volition of its members. Thus, ethnic groups are viewed as potentially changeable and assimilable into other ethnic groups, and racial groups as being for ever separate from other racial groups. The use of the terms 'racial' and 'ethnic' is affected by these differences: for example, a group that is clearly an ethnic group may be termed a 'race' by those who wish to isolate and oppress it; a group which is recognisable as a race may nevertheless be termed an 'ethnic' group by liberal-minded people wishing to absorb it into a larger social group (Rex, 1986).

In Nazi Germany, the Jews were declared to be a race; subsequently most writers suggested that they were 'only' an ethnic group. In the United States, earlier practice was to refer to ethnic differences between new European immigrants and longer settled white Americans, but to acknowledge that difference between blacks and whites was racial. Later there was a tendency to regard all minorities, whether black, Mexican or Native American and whether European, Latin American or Asian immigrants, as 'ethnic'. In the United Kingdom, the meaning of 'migration' was distorted (for racist reasons) when black and Asian people were regarded as 'immigrants', whereas actual immigrants from Europe, Ireland and the white Commonwealth were not; consequently, the word 'immigrant' became a pejorative term. As more positive attitudes towards black and Asian people were adopted, they were referred to as 'ethnic minorities', along with other visible groups (like the Cypriots).

Finally with the influx in the 1990s of Muslim refugees from Bosnia and Kosovo, clearly 'white' people were included within the 'ethnic minority' category. Thus, what is 'ethnic' and what is 'racial' changes from time to time, depending on circumstances and attitudes of the majority communities. Hence, the context of the situation in which groups of people are 'named' in this way must be examined and the consequences of naming considered before the types of name given to them are accepted: political, social and personal factors enter into such an evaluation, which must always be seen in the context of power structures in society at any given time. Further, the picture is complicated by racism. Both 'racial' and 'ethnic' carry racial connotations; merely renaming a racial group as 'ethnic' does not eliminate racial persecution of that group, but using ethnic, rather than racial, labels for groups may, in certain circumstances, permit the investigation of discrimination, etc. Thus it may be preferable to undertake 'ethnic' rather than 'racial' monitoring (of, say, employment practices or health service provision), although the aim is to detect racism. However, it is counterproductive to talk of a multiethnic society when the aim is to promote racial acceptance in the society of people of all colours, for, by doing so, the racial element is concealed and, therefore, not confronted.

Cultural and ethnic identity

The concept of an 'identity crisis' has been used to explain various diverse problems; when a person is seen as black or different in some way from the majority of people considered important in the society, a crisis in that person's life is often assumed to be related to a problem in ethnic identity (or racial identity or cultural identity). It is in this setting that, during the past 20 or 30 years, there has been much talk of racial identity, ethnic identity and cultural identity.

The term 'identity' refers to a person's sense of uniqueness – of knowing who one is or is not. It represents the importance given in Western culture to the individual as distinct from – perhaps opposed to – the family or community. So it is often assumed – and this is an ethnocentric assumption – that identity is a basic 'fact' about a person; and the development of a stable sense of personal (individual) identity is thought of as central to personality development during childhood and adolescence. A sense of identity that involves a concept of culture or ethnicity could be termed cultural or ethnic identity. However, this implies a static, unchanging view of identity. But, just as culture and ethnicity are not static, cultural and ethnic identity too cannot be seen as static. However, racial identity may be different since the concept of 'race' implies permanence (Figure 1.1). Although the eurocentric view of identity refers to a unique quality, a less individualistic worldview would see identity as a part of group solidarity. This is too large an issue to pursue in this book but the point to note is that there is a political dimension to identity.

A person's cultural or ethnic identity depends largely on context, emerging through a mixture of social pressures or influences (e.g. experienced racial discrimination, generalised racism in society, political movements, religious movements), family pressures or influences (e.g. to conform to certain practices), and perceived (or felt) cultural or ethnic similarities with others. For example, the growth of identification as Serbian, Bosnian and Kosovan in the former Yugoslavia as the communist state itself disintegrated had obvious political dimensions, although based on historic identities, family ties and religious affiliations. Political forces are less obvious in Western European countries and in North America – although they do undoubtedly exist. What appears to happen in the United Kingdom is that if a person feels and recognises the effects of racism, an ethnic identity as 'black' may be strengthened; if certain family, community or subgroup (e.g. religious subgroup) pressures are strong, identification as (for example) Indian, African, Jewish or Muslim may be strengthened; a historical sense of colonial imperialism in Europe may strengthen identity as Irish among people in the UK who are of Irish ancestry; and so on.

The analysis of the damaging psychological effects of racism on the individual identity of black people and the way out for them psychologically are significant aspects of the writings of Frantz Fanon. Although many of Fanon's writings have not been translated into English and so not directly accessible to the author, the translations of his main work *Black Skin, White Masks* (Fanon, 1952) and the subsequent *The Wretched of the Earth* (Fanon, 1961) provide sufficient material for the purposes of this section. Fanon's thinking developed from his own experiences as a black man from the French colony of Martinique who practised as a psychiatrist in France and the (then) French colony of Algeria before becoming a freedom fighter in Algeria. Although influenced by existentialism and psychoanalysis, Fanon's thinking extended into the social and political arenas. For Fanon, the internalisation of a belief system imbued with racism damages the psyche of a black person causing alienation; but the process of alienation is inextricably linked to, and arises from, a socio-economic political system that denies black people the opportunity to confirm their self-worth. In Fanon's view, the freedom from oppression is equivalent to the freedom to develop self-worth and so overcome alienation. And both the imposition of oppression and the retrieval of freedom are violent processes; they cannot be given but must be taken. Fanon's work highlights the connections between the psychological and the political; the struggle that black people must go through in order to divest themselves of the violence of racism is thus not just within themselves but intimately connected with the political world around them.

The 1960s saw positive aspects of black identity being emphasised in the USA and UK as a counterbalance to the harm that was perceived as having being done to black people as a result of their identifying with white norms and thereby internalising racism. The classic studies were the doll preference studies (Clarke and Clarke, 1947) that seemed to identify black self-hatred; although these studies were criticised for methodological faults, the thesis of black self-hatred became widely accepted because it resonated with the discourses of the civil rights movement that was then emerging (Mama, 1995). The 'black is beautiful' movement came about and the term 'black' itself changed in its meaning – at least for many black people. However, the psychological insights of Frantz Fanon (1952) on the effects on black people of living in a white-dominated society are as relevant today as they were in the 1950s.

Myths and realities of race

The classification of people into racial types on the basis of physical appearance has a long history in Western culture. And from the very beginning, skin colour was the most popular physical characteristic used for this purpose. In the eighteenth century, Linnaeus (1758–59) divided *Homo sapiens* into six varieties: *americanus, europaeus, asiaticus* and *afer* identified in terms of being red, white, yellow and black, and *ferus* and *monstrosus* identified on general characteristics. Later in that century, Blumenbach, a German physician and anthropologist, classified humans into Caucasian, Mongolian, Ethiopian, American and Malayan – again using skin colour as the main criterion for so doing but adding hair form, facial characteristics and the shape of skull (Blumenbach, 1865). According to Molnar (1983), Blumenbach believed that the shape of the skull was highly resistant to change and therefore a significant 'racial' trait; having studied a large number of skulls from all over the world, Blumenbach decided that a skull recovered from the Caucasus Mountains, in an area near Mount Ararat, came closest to fitting his image of the skulls of a particular 'race' of people. 'Caucasian' eventually became a term applied to people from Europe, North Africa and the 'Middle East', but is now used loosely to mean 'white-skinned'.

Cuvier, a French anatomist and one of the dominant figures in French science at the time of Napoleon, believed that the three major races, the white, the yellow and the black, were subspecies of *Homo sapiens* and descended from groups of people who escaped in different directions after a catastrophe; and his conception of human varieties was hierarchical – whites at the top and blacks at the bottom (Coleman, 1964). Morton (1839), an American doctor, reported on measurements of the interior capacities of skulls of the five races (as designated by Blumenbach) which suggested that people called 'Caucasians' (which included some 'Hindoos') had the biggest brains, so-called 'Ethiopians' ('unmixed Negroes' and 'Africans') had the smallest, and the other groups were in between. When these skulls were re-examined in 1977 by Gould (1981), the findings were very different. Also, Morton made several errors by selecting some skulls and excluding others, with the net result of increasing the Caucasian average while lowering that of other groups (Banton, 1987). Gobineau (1853), who has been called the father of racist ideology, took up Morton's alleged findings in the context of wide reading in German literature to devise the theory that a superior white-skinned 'Aryan race' had given rise to all civilisations. These Aryans are supposed to have either destroyed other races or else, by mixing with them, brought out latent powers in others to produce various civilisations (Buenzod, 1967). It should be noted that the term 'Aryan' was misused by Gobineau, for its proper use is to describe a group of languages – also known as 'Indo-European' – including Sanskrit, Persian, Latin, Greek and languages derived from them. Even at the time of Gobineau, Muller (1888), a specialist in Aryan languages, wrote:

> When I say Aryas (Aryans) I mean neither blood nor bones nor hair nor skull; I mean simply those who spoke an Aryan language. When I speak of them I commit myself to no anatomical characteristics. To me an ethnologist who speaks of Aryan

race, Aryan blood, Aryan eyes and hair, is as great a sinner as a linguist who speaks of a dolichocephalic (narrow-headed) dictionary or a brachycephalic (broad-headed) grammar.

Robert Knox, a medical practitioner and teacher of medical students at Edinburgh, was a strong propagandist for racial theories in Britain and his influence was considerable (Banton, 1987). In *Races of Man*, Knox (1850) maintained that external characteristics, mainly skin colour, reflected internal ones such as intelligence and propensity for cultural pursuits; that dark races were generally 'inferior'; and that 'hybrids' were eventually sterile. The view of race as a human type had been taken to an extreme to give rise to the concept of humankind being divisible into 'pure' races that do not mix.

Darwin's theory of evolution in the mid-nineteenth century gave rise to a different concept of 'race'. By analogy with his description of numerous 'races' within each species, the idea developed that, while human beings as a whole were a 'species' with fertile mating within it, individual (human) 'races' were 'varieties' or 'subspecies' with partial reproductive isolation from each other (Banton, 1987). In this model, Nordics and Africans (for example) were seen to have maintained their distinctiveness because mating was predominantly within each group, possibly for geographical reasons. Each race was seen as being subject to continual modification and development rather than to a static set of inherited characteristics. Although the Darwinian idea of race as a subspecies promoted the concept of geographical race, it did not exclude the view that races may become separate types: it was held that a subspecies may evolve to a point where it is no longer able to interbreed with other forms and hence become a species. This new view of race was a flexible and egalitarian approach compared to that of Gobineau and Knox. But in *The Descent of Man* Darwin (1871) appeared to have succumbed to the temper of his times in writing about the likely extinction of 'savage races' because of their inability to change habits when brought into contact with 'civilized races'; and he then joined his cousin Francis Galton in calling for eugenic measures to maintain the integrity of the latter (Banton, 1987).

As the knowledge of genetics grew in the twentieth century, the distributions of genetically simple traits, such as blood groups, were used to study race. Thus, different races were described in terms of the percentages of the four blood types, A, B, AB and O, and the rhesus (Rh) factor. Although the proportions of each type were different in different races, no one race was found to lack any one blood type and the same groups were found in the blood of all races. Moreover, the distribution of blood groups in every population studied (e.g. an African tribe or a European nation) was found to be different from every other population on the average; and the level at which a difference was designated as a 'racial' difference was entirely arbitrary. The genetics of skin colour and other physical characteristics, noted earlier as racial criteria, are extremely complex – much more so than that of blood types. If the distribution of each separate skin colour gene were mapped, 'race differences would probably be resolved into gene frequency differences' (Dobzhansky, 1971). Geographical variation in gene frequency may be used to identify genetic relationships between population groups, and diagrammatic 'trees' have been constructed to show them. But there are no means of deriving genetically differentiated discrete races from them. At one time, evidence from skeletal (bone) study seemed to contradict that from biochemical study because the effect of climate on skull configurations was not appreciated. Once climatic effects are allowed for, both skeletal and biochemical measures lead to similar conclusions. It is now clear that racial differentiation on traditional criteria of skin colour, etc. is scientifically untenable as an indication of biological difference between groups of people. However, genetic connections between geographically located populations may be estimated by examining gene frequencies; for example, they 'show that Africans and Europeans are more closely related to each other than either are to Amerindians or to Australasians' (Guglielmino-Matessi *et al.*, 1979).

Recent scientific advances have enabled geneticists to identify human genes that code for specific enzymes and other proteins. It is now possible to use information on the distribution of polymorphic proteins (i.e. proteins that have alternative forms that exist in varying frequencies in the human species) in order to calculate differences between individuals and between defined populations. A geneticist from University College London, writing in *Nature* (Jones, 1981), notes that the proportion of genes which two randomly chosen individuals have in common may be measured by means of an index using 18 polymorphic gene loci from 180 different human populations from each of six racial groups corresponding to European, African, Indian, East Asian, New World and Oceanian. Using this measure, it has been shown that 84 per cent of all genetic variation results from genetic difference between individuals belonging to the same tribe or nationality, 6 per cent from differences between tribes or nationalities, and 10 per cent from genetic divergence between 'racial' groups. 'In other words, the genetic differences between the classically described races of man are on the average only slightly greater than those which exist between nations within a racial group, and the genetic differences between individual human beings within a population are far larger than either of these' (ibid.). Thus the genetic differences between, say, indigenous populations of France and Spain, or between different tribes of Africa, are similar to those between so-called races. The inclusion together in one 'race' of everyone who has a particular skin colour or hair type or some other aspect of physical appearance, assigning borderline cases according to traditional ideas (e.g. that 'white' skin colour is pure and 'non-white' is caused by an admixture that corrupts that purity) is no longer biologically acceptable or useful in scientific practice.

Clearly, genetic studies have strengthened the view that the popular racial categories are spurious and scientifically invalid. But the historic ideas about race persist. Although 'pure' races are no longer identified with any confidence, the view persists that persons resembling each other in obvious physical characteristics, such as skin colour, belong to a 'race' that represents a genetically differentiated human type. The myth of race has been exploded, but the reality of race persists for historical, social and psychological reasons – in fact for all the reasons that result in racism. Thus, in popular lore, and even in medical and scientific circles, racial differences are still seen as biological differences – or at least physical ones that are inherited genetically. Although skin colour remains the most popular basis for distinguishing one race from another, a whole range of physical characteristics are used as racial criteria. Ruth Benedict (1942: 30–1), an anthropologist, divides these into six groups, namely skin colour, eye colour and eye form, hair colour and hair form, shape of nose, stature and cephalic index, but notes the problems that this approach presents to physical anthropology:

Whether the physical anthropologist measures Swedes or Algerians or Chinese or Greeks, the same difficulty presents itself. Over and over again he discovers the obvious consequences of the great intermixture that has occurred, or he discovers that the universality of the 'ideal' type he set out to investigate in a given group is an illusion. If he compares his findings in his own group with those of another investigator in a different group – comparing, for example, Swedes with Sicilians – he finds that none of his traits are utterly lacking in individuals of the other group. The statistical distribution is different; that is all. He set out to isolate an

anatomical variety of mankind as he would isolate a species of birds, but the facts
he has gathered prove only that the human situation does not correspond to the
situation among birds.

The problem is that when anthropologists, biologists and medical
people classify human beings into races, usually using skin colour as
the main marker, they treat races as species (of animals) and this
approach – this myth – continues to influence popular and professional thinking. It is necessary, therefore, to emphasise the fact that the
human species has been a single evolutionary unit, at least since the
mid-Pleistocene epoch (Ice Age), and this 'genetic oneness of mankind
has been growing steadily since the development of material culture
has made travel and communication between the inhabitants of
different countries progressively more rapid and easier' (Dobzhansky,
1971).

Husband (1982: 11) suggests that one reason for the 'continuing
vitality' of racial classification is

that beneath its apparently simple reduction of complex individuals and societies
to self-evidently basic units there lies a highly complex body of emotive ideas.
These are ideas which reach out in their reference and significance beyond the
immediate forms of racial categorization as such. Rather they invoke a rich
matrix of values and images referring to purity–pollution, Christianity–Heathen,
national–alien, amongst others.

Thus social forces, subsumed under the title 'racism', generate an
emotional impetus to the perpetuation of racial classification. Clearly,
economic and political factors feed into this; and psychological needs
of the people who stand to gain from racial classification play a part
too. Race thinking persists because racism is required by many individuals and social groups for psychological and political reasons in
order to dominate and control others.

The illusory nature of race as a basis for identifying genetic difference does not deny its importance as a marker – although not a
genetic one. It is a social marker for racism; for the assignment of
rights to individuals, for oppression and for exploitation. It may be said
that race is only one of several markers used for these purposes; and
indeed religious affiliation, social class and gender are the bases of
'isms' similar to racism. One difference is that, in the case of race,
the criterion used (i.e. skin colour) is inflexible and unremitting and
that race carries with it a vast historical 'baggage' – a very heavy burden
for the people affected by racism. The reality is that race is important
as a sociological concept because of racism and that the use of skin

colour as a marker for racial classification is a (sociological) fact – although based on a biological myth. People of different races are perceived as 'different', and more importantly, different in being inferior or superior to others. It should be noted in passing that, while the assumption of racial groups being biologically distinct from each other is not correct in scientific terms, race as a marker might be useful in a very limited way. For example, certain genetically transmitted conditions, such as Tay-Sachs disease (infantile amaurotic idiocy), sickle cell trait or sickle cell disease, and cystic fibrosis may be suspected when there is evidence of East European Jewish, West African and North European ancestry respectively (Molnar, 1983), and race may be used as an initial indicator to detect people who may be vulnerable to these conditions. But this use of 'race' in no way challenges the overall conclusion that scientifically, 'as a way of categorising people, race is based upon a delusion' (Banton and Harwood, 1975). Although clearly a biological myth, race continues to be a social reality.

Racism

The doctrine of racism developed in Western culture in conjunction with ideas about race. Today, racism is fashioned by racial prejudice and underpinned by economic and social factors; when implemented and practised through the institutions of society, it is called 'institutional racism'. Although race prejudice and racism are related concepts (Figure 1.2), they should be distinguished from each other. Race prejudice is basically a psychological state, a feeling or attitude of mind, felt and/or expressed as 'an antipathy based upon a faulty and inflexible generalisation' (Allport, 1954); at a deeper level it may be likened to a superstition (Fryer, 1984). Racism, however, is a doctrine or ideology – or dogma. Race prejudice and racism often go together but racism, unlike prejudice, is recognised by the *behaviour* of an individual and/or the way an institutional system works in practice, although (racially prejudiced) attitudes of mind that are recognisable and consciously held may be present also. And racism is associated with power – the power of one racial group over another. Further, Wellman (1977) argues that an attitude such as prejudice must be seen within its 'structural context' – the distribution of power within the society, political constraints arising from external influences, rivalries between social classes, etc. And once racial prejudice is

	BASIC DEFINITIONS	LIKELY ASSOCIATIONS	POSSIBLE CAUSES
RACIAL PREJUDICE	Feeling	Misperception	Malevolence/ immorality
		Personal antipathy	
	Attitude	Rejection of outsider	Insecurity/illness
	Belief	Racism Ignorance	Human nature/ instinct
RACISM	Ideology	Assumptions about inferior/ superior races	Political/economic advantage
		Value judgement about people	
	Dogma	Power/domination	Social conditioning
	Political stance	Racial prejudice	Tradition/history

Figure 1.2   Racial prejudice and racism

embedded within the structures of society, individual prejudice is no longer the problem, it is *racism* that is the active principle. Racism is then essentially about 'institutionally generated inequality' based on concepts of racial difference; although it affects the behaviour of individuals, 'prejudiced people are not the only racists'. Institutional racism based on colour of skin pervades many aspects of Western society – including psychology and psychiatry (see Chapter 4). Sometimes other similar terms are used to describe institutional racism: an official report into the deaths of black patients in a forensic hospital in the UK used the term 'subtle racism' (Special Hospitals Service Authority, 1993). In commenting upon the reality and implications of institutional racism in London's police, the report of an inquiry into the response of the police to a racist murder of a young black man, Stephen Lawrence, defined institutional racism thus (Home Department, 1999: 28):

> The collective failure of an organisation to provide an appropriate and professional service to people because of their colour, culture or ethnic origin. It can be seen or detected in processes, attitudes and behaviour which amounts to discrimination through unwitting prejudice, ignorance, thoughtlessness and racist stereotyping which disadvantages minority ethnic people.

History of racism

The classifications of races devised in Europe in the eighteenth and nineteenth centuries (referred to earlier) were largely based on skin colour. They occurred in a context where the words 'black' and 'white' were associated in the English language with heavily charged notions of good and bad and went hand in glove with race prejudice from the very beginning. Then came the Atlantic slave trade. As Winthrob Jordan (1968) states in *White over Black*, qualities associated with black skins which 'had for Englishmen added up to savagery' denoted that 'sense of difference which provided the mental margin absolutely requisite for placing the European on the deck of the slave ship and the Negro in the hold'. Together with colonialism, slavery of blacks by whites became a bedrock of European society and an axiom of Western culture (Kovel, 1984). The bias in Europe that promoted an unfavourable view of people seen in negative terms as 'non-white', in classificatory terms as black, brown, yellow and red, and in openly derogatory terms such as niggers and wogs, was reinforced by the economic advantages accruing from their exploitation. Slavery and colonialism fed into racial prejudice and vice versa; the result was the emergence of a consolidated dogma of racism. As the foremost slaving nation and, later, the most aggressive coloniser of non-European nations, Britain led the world in applied racism. The plunder of America and the genocide of its natives, the enslavement of Africans, the economic and cultural destruction of India, the imposition of opium on to an unwilling China, the devastation of Africa, and the genocide of Native Australians were all justified in the name of racism.

   While colonial exploitation was in full swing, scientific 'justification' for racism emerged in the eighteenth and nineteenth centuries. Physical anthropology developed 'methods' for classifying skulls to indicate intelligence – procedures that invariably placed Europeans at the top (Jordan, 1968). In documenting the pseudo-scientific racism of the eighteenth and nineteenth centuries, Fryer (1984: 177) quotes the following tenets of anthropology summarised by Hunt (1863) in his presidential address to the Anthropological Society of London which he founded:

> 1. That there is good reason for classifying the Negro as a distinct species from the European, as there is for making the ass a distinct species from the Zebra: and if, in classification, we take intelligence into consideration, there is a far

greater difference between the Negro and European than between the gorilla and chimpanzee. 2. That the analogies are far more numerous between the Negro and the ape than between the European and the ape. 3. That the Negro is inferior intellectually to the European. 4. That the Negro becomes more human-ised when in his natural subordination to the European than under any other circumstances. 5. That the negro race can only be humanised and civilised by Europeans. 6. That European civilisation is not suited to the Negro's require-ments or character.

Anatomists, biologists and physicians joined in with 'proof' of the superiority of white races over all others. The writing of history was distorted in line with racist notions of black inferiority. Bernal (1987) shows how the Afro-Asiatic origin of Greek civilisation (accepted as historical fact until the nineteenth century) was replaced by the myth of a migration into Greece of white people from the north of Europe; and the image of China was changed 'from one of a refined and enlightened people to one of a society filled with drugs, dirt, corruption and torture'. The continuity of ancient Egypt with the rest of Africa was denied and Egyptian civil-isation was downgraded; theories about 'Aryans' and 'Semites' as superior white races emerged. The achievements of African cul-tures were sidetracked by, for example, attributing the twelfth-century ruins in Zimbabwe (central Africa) to white non-Africans (!) or ignoring the 'glowing accounts' of material culture carried by Portuguese explorers of central Africa and sailors shipwrecked on the coast of South Africa (Fuller, 1959).

   As the sciences developed, racism became integrated into sci-entific thinking. Although arguing against the 'races of man' being 'distinct species', Darwin (1872) saw the domination of white races as a natural development: 'when civilised nations come into contact with barbarians the struggle is short, except where a deadly climate gives its aid to the native race'. The application of 'Social Dar-winism' led to the eugenic movement later taken on by European fascism in the 1930s. Physical anthropology was 'inextricably linked to the functioning of empire', its efforts being 'chiefly devoted to a description and analysis – carried out by Europeans, for a European audience – of non-European societies dominated by the West' (Kabbani, 1986). Fryer (1984) observes that 'virtually every scientist and intellectual in nineteenth-century Britain took it for granted that only people with white skin were capable of thinking and governing'. And this applied to the whole of Europe and white America.

Just as the wealth extracted by slavery and colonialism enriched all social classes and nations of Europe and white America, racist ideology has pervaded all their political and social systems. But the ways in which racism manifests itself assumes a specific form 'which arises from the present – not the past – conditions and organisation of society' (Hall, 1978). Joel Kovel (1984) has observed that, with the breakdown of direct racial domination and physical oppression in the United States during the 1960s, institutionalised racism has become implemented through technocratic means so that the economic position of black Americans in relation to that of their white compatriots actually dropped between 1970 and 1980. And the trend has continued so that many American cities now have a black underclass that is increasingly criminalised (through racism). Stuart Hall and colleagues in Britain (Hall *et al.*, 1978) observed how 'mugging' was constructed by the media and public agencies in such a way that, by the 1980s, convicting black muggers became synonymous, at least partly, with policing the British (social) crisis. Now, at least 46 per cent of the inmates of American prisons are black men (Poussaint cited by Kovel, 1984), and 12 per cent of the British prison population (as compared with 1.5 per cent of the general population) are classified as 'black' of African-Caribbean origin (Penal Affairs Consortium, 1996).

The association of blacks with falling educational standards, a decline in moral values and street crime had found a place in popular thinking in Britain even before the so-called riots erupted in various British cities in the 1980s (Ben-Tovim *et al.*, 1986). On both sides of the Atlantic, vicious circles have developed with myths about degeneracy of blacks becoming 'facts' of diagnosed psychoses through the collaboration of psychiatry.

Explanations of racism

Racism is often confused with racial prejudice, and when this happens, it may be attributed naively to a mere personal quirk or ignorance; or it may be seen simply as a mistake made in European history and perpetuated by misinformation and ignorance. When socially unacceptable as a form of behaviour, racism is seen as crime, immorality or sickness (Watson, 1973). When acceptable, for whatever reason, it is defended as 'human nature' – even an inherent instinct (Thomas, 1904) or a natural feel for self-preservation; then colour may be excused as a mere marker for the outsider, and racism as an expression of a natural or 'normal' rejection of the outsider. A relatively novel justification for racism has emerged in new forms of Darwinism popularised by some ethologists and socio-biologists (Barker, 1990), in suggesting that 'it is biologically fixed that humans form exclusive groups, and that these groups succeed internally in so far as they close up against outsiders' (1990: 18). Robert Ardrey (1967), arguing that 'aggression' is '*innate*', postulates that its exhibition towards outsiders is a natural condition because 'the biological nation is the supreme natural mechanism for the security of a social group' (1967: 253). Richard Dawkins (1976) writes that 'racial prejudice could be interpreted as an irrational generalisation of a kin-selected tendency to identify with individuals physically resembling oneself and to be nasty to individuals different in appearance' and that this tendency 'could have positive survival value' (1976: 8).

In considering ways of analysing the causes of racism, Cashmore and Troyna (1983) contrast the view of racism, on the one hand, as a part of an economic system of exploitation (Cox, 1948), and, on the other, as a problem located in the mind, a personal problem of whites encouraged by nationalism and Christianity (Myrdal, 1964); they find both notions as insufficient explanations individually. Racism is often seen as having originated in the political need for exploitation of resources and/or labour during slavery and colonialism. Although there is no doubt that political and economic factors reinforced racism, they are insufficient explanations for the strength of racism in the present day.

In the view of the author, racism has been socially constructed over hundreds of years and its origins are lost in the history of Western culture. As Banton and Harwood (1975) state:

> Current notions of race are an integral part of the history of Western Europe, drawing upon many aspects of that story. These notions cannot be separated from the rest of that history and attributed to single 'factors' like capitalism, colonialism, biological error or personal prejudice. The sources of popular imagery concerning race are very diverse and the interrelationships between their growth and contemporary political affairs are far too complex for the whole historical sequence to be explicable in simple terms.

Racism in the here and now is not explicable by any particular factor or event either historically or in the present; it is reinforced by different forces in different places. Further, it is not a unitary concept in that it manifests itself according to circumstances. It may be seen as having both psychological and social components – the latter to do with power and the former with the mixture of ideas, feelings and beliefs subsumed by the term 'race-thinking' (Barzun, 1965), described by Charles Husband (1982) as being composed of certain basic propositions: the categorisation of people is associated with physical characteristics transmitted 'through the blood'; mental and moral attributes of human beings are related to physical structure and a racial label denotes a satisfactory account of the behaviour; individual personality and capabilities as well as culture, morality, etc. are products of social entities termed race, nation, class, family, etc. without further definition. The power within racism ensures that the application of race-thinking invokes assumptions of inferiority–superiority, justifying exploitation and the allocation of individuals, their cultures, etc. to positions on a hierarchy. And racism, integrated with ideas about race in Western culture, has been exported all over the globe by means of power – at first, purely military, and later, both military and economic.

It should be noted at this point that racism, in a broad sense, is not confined to relations between white people and populations perceived as not being white. Anti-Semitism in Europe is a type of racism, too, although not associated with skin colour; race relations in the southern United States, characterised by racism, may have similarities to relations between 'untouchables' and other castes in India (Berreman, 1960); conflicts between groups of people in various parts of the world, such as Tamils and Sinhalese in Sri Lanka, Catholics and Protestants in Northern Ireland, or Serbs and Bosnians in former Yugoslavia may stem from perceptions akin to racist ones. But the racism that is based on skin colour and power relationships where white people dominate others, either as individuals or as groups, overrides other forms of racism in its importance across the globe. It is this that is referred to generally in this book as racism.

An analysis of racism must address several interrelated issues. First, the fact that it is based on a delusion embodied in popular ideas about race classification referred to earlier. Hence, 'race' should not be accorded identical analytical status with factors such as class or gender (Miles, 1982); 'race relations' is not analogous with class relations, nor sexism with racism. The subject matter of 'race relations' is the nature of relations between people of different physical appearance and diverse ancestry in a setting where social significance is attributed to physical appearance – and the problems addressed in 'race relations' are to do with racism (Dummett, 1973). In the case of sexism, unlike that of racism, real (rather than 'delusional') bio-logical differences are given social significance. Secondly, there is the contention that racism is essentially about value judgement about people based on an a priori basis; the doctrine that people of a certain 'race' are inherently different from others in qualities that are ordered hierarchically leads on to the assumption that some races as a whole are superior to others. Thirdly, there is the issue of the close involvement of racism with power. It is the association of value judgement with power that is fundamental to racism. Hence, racism is a means of domination, exploitation and enslavement, at a personal, political and economic level. Finally, although racism was created by, and is perpetuated by, various psychological, economic and political factors, it has to be understood historically as an integral part of the history of Western Europe (Banton and Harwood, 1975).

Manifestations and effects of racism

Although the ways in which racism is manifested may be fundamentally similar in all Western societies, there are differences in detail from society to society, often related to historical and general social differences. For example, in the United States, the traditions derived from slavery represent a very direct and obviously vicious racism in relation to the descendants of African people who were taken there by force – the present African Americans. The genocide and suppression of Native Americans were no less vicious in their day but the derision towards the 'American Indians' is now being associated in the northern part of the American continent with colonial-type paternalism. But in South America a new spate of genocide is being practised with the connivance of the United States through its economic interests and its missionaries (Lewis, 1989). The United States today is proud of its tradition of being a land of (voluntary) immigrants from many parts of the world; in this context, immigrants are viewed with respect and Oriental Americans from Japan, China, India, Vietnam, etc. may not be seen as different in terms of status from other (immigrant) Americans. But Hispanic Americans appear to face considerable racial hostility.

The background to British racism is somewhat different from that in America. Although traditionally welcoming European refugees fleeing persecution, the British have never held a favourable attitude towards the immigrant who chooses to migrate to Britain. Moreover, immigrants to Britain from parts of the world that used to form the British Empire are viewed with the sort of racism that thrived in that empire, but without the imperial paternalism that existed there towards the 'native'. British racism today is seen in the derision implied in the term 'immigrant', often used to describe all black people wherever they were born rather than to describe real immigrants from (say) Ireland, and the contempt implied when people are referred to as 'coloureds' or 'Pakis'. Racist practice in Britain today tends to include everyone denoted on the basis of skin colour as not being 'white' in one large group of 'blacks', only slightly separated into Asians, Afro-Caribbeans, Cypriots, etc. Since the strengthening of immigration rules in the 1970s by the British government, most immigrants to Britain in the new millennium are refugees and asylum seekers – essentially 'refugees from globalism' (Sivanandan, 2000) and from the consequences of 'five hundred years of occidental expansion and hegemony' (Pieterse, 1992). And in the late 1990s into the new millennium, it is these refugees and asylum seekers who face most overt hostility for their 'alienness', their 'culture', their 'race'.

Recent changes in the way racism is manifested in Western societies have been commented upon by various writers. Gilroy (1993) believes that racism now 'frequently operates without any overt reference to "race" itself or the biological notions of difference which still give the term its common-sense meaning'(1993: 23). 'Culture', seen as an immutable, fixed property of social groups (which it is not), has become confounded with 'race', and racism is articulated in cultural terms. In analysing the historical representations of European racism, Pieterse (1992) states:

> 'Race' discrimination has increasingly yielded to discrimination along cultural lines, bringing with it different sets of images and discourses. ... Culture as a new basis for differentiation is much more diffuse in its ideological claims than race theory, but is in some ways equally effective in establishing boundaries and demarcations.

In such a context, the promotion of multiculturalism and the question of national identity have become the main frontiers of friction and conflict both in Europe and the United States (Pieterse, 1992). Although 'multiculturalism' itself may be seen as an anti-racist measure – its promotion in a colour-blind way (i.e. without addressing racism) where 'culture' is understood as something static, passed on from generation to generation, merely results in strengthening racism. As a result, in the British scene – and possibly in Europe as a whole – national identity tends to be defined in 'racial' terms, articulated in cultural language, sometimes with little attempt to disguise the racist message.

Conclusions

At the beginning of the twentieth century, W. E. B. Du Bois (1903) in his classic *The Souls of Black Folk*, forecast: 'The problem of the twentieth century is the problem of the color line – the relation of the darker to the lighter races of men...' (1903: 9). Du Bois was writing at time when slavery based on colour lines in the Atlantic slave trade had been abolished but colonial exploitation of Asia by European powers was well established (Panikkar, 1959) and their unseemly 'scramble for Africa' in full swing (Pakenham, 1991) with murderous slavery of black Africans this time in Africa itself – in the Belgian Congo and to a lesser extent in adjoining British, French and German colonies (Hochschild, 1999).

Although the first half of the twentieth century gave little cause for optimism, the social and political changes that took place after the defeat of Nazi Germany, namely the political liberation (decolonisation) of many parts of Asia and Africa, and the American civil rights movement, should have led one to expect the demise – or at least the serious containment – of racism. But, at the beginning of the twenty-first century, racism continues as strong as ever although its manifestation may have changed: the divide between the increasing poverty of the 'Third World' and the affluence of the 'West' is becoming larger, pointing to an 'economic imperialism that [has] ensured that the United States and former European colonial powers become richer, while, with a tiny scattering of exceptions, their ex-colonies have become poorer' (McClintock, 1995: 393); the civil rights movement of the 1960s in the United States may have resulted in legal changes and the emergence of a black middle class, but 'the bitter irony of integration' (West, 1994: 24) is that American society remains divided along racial lines – as Andrew Hacker (1992) states in the title to his bestseller *Two Nations. Black and White, Separate, Hostile, Unequal*; the rise of extreme right-wing political parties in several countries that comprise the European Union (EU) is supplemented by notions of defending 'European civilisation' from 'other cultures' by building a 'Fortress Europe' (Marfleet, 1999). In all these situations, the fault line has been represented by colour. But major demographic changes expected to occur in the twenty-first century may well have a significant effect on racism. The UN's *State of the World's Population 1999* quoted in the British newspaper *The Observer* (Browne, 2000) predicts that 98 per cent of the growth in the world's population by the year 2025 will occur in the lesser developed regions, principally Africa and Asia: 'In 1900 Europe had a quarter of the world's population, and three times that of Africa; by 2050 Europe is predicted to have just 7 per cent of the world's population, and a third that of Africa' (2000: 17). Such changes in 'race demography' may well lead to changes in the nature and extent of racism – or even result in the diminution of race-thinking itself. In other words by the advent of the twenty-second century the world may see the end of colour-based racism as a significant force in human relationships.

Summary

The classification of race based on visual observations of people, particularly their skin colour, has a long history in Western Europe. The types of classification centred around three main groups or races, namely, Negroid, Mongoloid and Caucasoid – black, yellow and white. As theories about racial differences were tested against scientific observations, particularly in genetics, racial classification on traditional criteria, such as skin colour, has been shown as scientifically untenable. Osborne (1971) summarises the scientific findings: first, differences *within* races are greater than the differences *between* races on important physical characteristics apart from those used to define race. Secondly, there is no evidence for designating any race(s) as 'superior' or 'inferior' in terms of ability in any particular sphere or in adaptability to environment. Thirdly, there are no 'pure' races that have genetic characteristics that are unique. Fourthly, 'primitive' (physical) characteristics, such as thin lips, flat nose and straight hair, are found in all races. The main lesson from genetic studies is that the differences between any particular groups of people, however defined, are insignificant in comparison with the vast and complex genetic potential arising from the genetic diversity of *Homo sapiens* together with the (genetic) endowment of each person. Further, patterns of behaviour and psychological attributes of an individual are generated by complicated interactions of factors that cannot possibly be limited to groups of genes inherited by races however defined (Spuhler and Lindzey, 1967; Fried, 1968; Jones, 1981). The biological differentiation of people on the basis of race has been exploded as a myth: 'Human "racial" differentiation is indeed only skin deep. Any use of racial categories must take its justification from some other source than biology' (Rose *et al.*, 1984). However, the tendency to think of people in terms of their 'race', 'race-thinking' (Barzun, 1965), persists partly at any rate because of racism.

'Culture' is an imprecise term in research but a useful concept for defining the non-physical influences on individuals that determine their behaviour, attitudes and ways of life. It is often confused with race both in common parlance and in professional thinking, mainly because people who are seen as racially different are conceptualised as having different cultures, and the term 'culture' is used to conceal racism. The concept of ethnicity in social science literature and in popular thinking has replaced, to some degree, both race and culture as a basis for defining, meaningfully, groups of people who feel themselves to be separate in multiracial and multicultural societies. Ethnicity has both racial and cultural connotations, but its main characteristic is that it implies a sense of belonging. However, the differences between ethnic groups are not always clear and not always of the same type in all situations. Ethnicity may 'emerge' in a society through pressures and alliances arising from racial discrimination, cultural similarity or other forces that induce people to feel a sense of belonging to an 'ethnic' group. In a racist society, such an 'emergent ethnicity' may be determined largely by racism; then, the ethnic groups in that society may correspond to those seen within that society as 'racial' groups.

Although the terms 'race', 'culture' and 'ethnicity' are interrelated, they should be distinguished from each other. The choice of the term by which a particular group is described must be sensitive to the various issues that are active in the society concerned; the one to be used depends on the style and degree of racism in the society at the time, the extent to which people in power appreciate the situation, and the particular purpose for which classification is required. In monitoring for racial discrimination in employment practices in Britain, the present approach is to use 'ethnic' labels. If racial classification was understood as a biological myth, then perhaps a more direct approach via racial labels can be used without the risk of exacerbating racism. The use of labels in the course of race awareness training and anti-racism education is likely to be of crucial importance. Whenever a group or person is described in racial or ethnic terms, the choice of label must be governed by sensitivity and awareness of all aspects of the particular context in which it is used.

Racism has a long history in Western culture but the ways in which it is manifested has changed over the years and even then varies according to context. Racism should be distinguished from (racial) prejudice. When racism is implemented and practised through the institutions of society, often without people involved even being aware that they are being racist, it is called 'institutional racism'. Another name given to institutional racism is 'subtle racism'. Many sociocultural systems fashioned in the West, such as psychiatry, social work, clinical psychology and counselling, show aspects of institutional racism. In the early twenty-first century, in post-slavery, post-colonial, Europe, racism shows little sign of losing its hold. Clearly, economic and political factors feed into racism, and the psychological needs of the people who stand to gain from institutional racism play a part too. Modern racism in Western countries, often deeply embedded in its institutions, is frequently expressed in cultural language, 'culture' being seen as a static concept passed on from generation to generation. Thus the promotion of multiculturalism, without addressing racism, may actually exacerbate racism by reinforcing the notion that people should be subjected to different treatment because of cultural difference. Anti-racist strategies need to take cognisance of the current language of racism and the context in which it is manifested.

2

Mental Health and Mental Disorder across Cultures

The boundary between mental health and mental disorder is concerned with the question of normality – a subject of much controversy (Offer and Sabshin, 1966) even within the limited domain of (Western) psychiatry, without taking on considerations of cultural difference. Sabshin (1967) has described four approaches to the term 'normality' as used by psychiatrists in the United States: normality meaning health as the absence of illness; an ideal state of mind; the average level of functioning of individuals within the context of a total group; and a process that is judged by the functioning of individuals over a period of time. These ideas need to be seen in context – in this case the context of the American way of life and worldview. Once questions of culture and race are introduced, not only does one need to look at the picture through a perspective of cultural 'norms', but the distortion of these cultural norms by racist perceptions inherent in Western thinking has to be corrected. In short, not only do we need to recognise that each culture has its own norms for health, for ideal states of mind and for the functioning of individuals in society, but that these norms are perceived through race-tinted spectacles.

This chapter will discuss first, general issues of health, illness and madness, including the question of 'culture-bound' disorders; then the interconnections between psychology, religion and mental health in the worldviews implicit in various cultures and finally, emotional expression, idioms of expression and ways of coping with stress. However, these discussions are limited by one major problem: in all the fields considered, the discussion is limited by what goes for 'knowledge' by virtue of the language used to express it and the cultural viewpoints – not to speak of the racist assumptions – implicit in the underlying models and frameworks, which tend to be by necessity 'Western'.

Health, illness and madness

Health is not merely the converse of illness and mental health is generally conceptualised as something wider than the absence of mental illness. Kakar (1984) states that the term 'mental health' is 'a rubric, a label which covers different perspectives and concerns, such as the absence of incapacitating symptoms, integration of psychological functioning, effective conduct of personal and social life, feelings of ethical and spiritual well-being and so on'. But culture determines both the perception and level of concern in the case of each of these qualities. For example, varieties of inner experience acceptable as desirable states of consciousness within the cultures of Asia, Africa and pre-Columbian America may be perceived in the West as 'abnormal' experiences, even as 'illness'; Western culture, in comparison to that of non-Europeans, may place a special value on individuals exercising absolute control over their social activities and engaging in a variety of relationships, unhindered by obligations to other people. In general, most views of mental health are likely to incorporate a person's sense of fulfilment and identity, not just as an individual but also as a part of a group or society, but the extent to which this occurs may be very different in different cultures. Further, the 'group' or 'society' that is given significance may be very different too – it may refer to family, immediate or extended, or spread much wider to include community, nation, race or ethnic group, a system of ancestors or god(s), or even the extensions of 'self' in time to previous births. Hence, spiritual beliefs, ethical values and identity are all associated with mental health, not just as individual aspects of mental health but also as an integrated whole. And the concept of mental health must be seen in the relevant political and social context. In writing about African Americans, Akbar (1981) identifies mental health as the affirmative identification and commitment to an African identity; the lack of such an identity is a deficiency in the presence of racism but may not be so if racism is absent, for meaningful identities can then cross racial boundaries. Although religion, psychology and the spiritual dimension of life are as relevant to mental health as the concept of illness, the discussion in this section commences with a consideration of health as a function of illness or disease.

Although ideas about health and illness may vary across cultures on various parameters, every culture has a conceptualisation referring to departure from health (McQueen, 1978). In other words, the concept of health is generally related to the concept of illness (or disease) and vice versa. The Western medical model of illness regards the mind as distinct from body, defining 'mental illness' and promoting psychiatry as a medical specialty. But in non-Western cultures, medical belief systems, conceptualisation of mind and body and ideas about illness have developed differently. In Eastern traditions, health is seen as a harmonious balance between various forces in the person and the social context. In the Chinese way of thinking, illness is an imbalance of *yin* and *yang* (two complementary poles of life energy), to be corrected by attempts to re-establish 'balance' (Aakster, 1986). The Indian tradition emphasises the harmony between the person and his/her group as indicative of health (Kakar, 1984). In African culture, the concept of health is more social than biological (Lambo, 1964):

> Health is not an isolated phenomenon but part of the entire magico-religious fabric; it is more than the absence of disease. Since disease is viewed as one of the most important social sanctions, peaceful living with neighbours, abstention from adultery, keeping the laws of gods and men, are essentials in order to protect oneself and one's family from disease.

Not only is the concept of illness different across cultures but also the ways in which illnesses are perceived – the explanatory models for illness (Kleinman, 1980). In Western culture, insanity is 'set apart' as a special type of illness; although this may apply in many other cultures, too, the understanding of what insanity is and the way in which it is set apart may be very different. Boundaries between health and disease, and between mind and body, are drawn in different ways in different cultural traditions. As a result (for example), the major causes of 'mental illness' (in Western terms) may appear to be somato-psychic when classical Ayurvedic theories of Indian medicine are studied using Western concepts (Obeyesekere, 1977); and some forms of human distress that are conceptualised in the West as 'illness' may be seen in religious or philosophical terms in the Indian tradition. In Tibetan thinking, based on Buddhist culture, the most crucial psychological factor involved with insanity is the same as that essential for pursuing enlightenment, namely, the recognition of impermanence (Clifford, 1984). In other words, both insanity and enlightenment have the same basis: 'It all depends on whether or not it is accepted and comprehended and ultimately worked with as the key to liberation.

If it is not, it becomes, because the realization is still there uncon-sciously, the cause of denial, repression and, ultimately, mental illness' (ibid.). Although the Western model of illness has developed in a Christian culture, it has no place for Christian concepts such as 'salvation' or 'damnation', because, in the West, religion and illness are now in separate cultural compartments. This secular approach to illness is not seen in other cultural traditions. The overall worldview within a culture, appertaining to health, religion, psychology and spiritual concerns, determines the meaning within that culture of 'madness', mental illness and mental health.

The anthropological literature and early writings on transcultural psychiatry present two basic approaches to the relationship between culture and health/illness (Fernando, 1988) – cultural relativity and cultural invariance (or universality). The former states that an under-standing of health and illness is relative to each culture – each culture has its own health and its own illness; the latter that concepts of health and illness are universal, although culture determines the way illness is presented and problems of language, etc. lead to misunderstandings. A variation on the universalist viewpoint is that of evolutionism (Shweder and Bourne, 1982) where non-Western perceptions of health and illness are seen as less adequate stages in the develop-ment of (what will eventually become) 'correct' understandings. The conflict between the cultural universalism (invariance) and cultural relativism continues in current thinking usually in the form of an impasse. In the author's opinion neither view is acceptable. First, biological, social and psychological influences determine the nature of what emerges as 'illness' in a particular cultural setting. Social construction of illness within a cultural context is important but not the only consideration. And second, cultures are not distinct and unchanging and there is constant interchange between cultures, although powerful forces influence the nature of these changes – economic pressures, racism and even military might, to name just a few – all intertwined together.

'Culture-bound' disorders

When psychiatrists, using the medical model of illness, come up against syndromes of emotional disorder – or rather what appear to them to be classifiable as emotional disorder – that do not fit easily into psychiatric classifications, the usual approach is to feed in this knowledge so that the classification incorporates their observations. If the 'new' syndrome were relatively common, it would enter into the mainstream of the classificatory system; if the syndrome is rare, a distinct but acceptable condition is described. Thus, over the years, various phobias have become accepted as illnesses, while rare conditions such as that described by Gilles de la Tourette (1885) in the nineteenth century, continue as entities more or less separate from the main illness nosology, but well accepted as illnesses in the medical model. But, when a 'new' condition is noticed in a non-Western society, or more accurately among people perceived as being alien to Western culture, the syndrome itself is perceived as alien to nosology – something exotic, unclassifiable, culture-reactive, etc. And gradually, the term 'culture-bound syndrome' (CBS) has become established to describe some, at least, of these 'exotic' conditions. The fact that they may occur quite frequently makes no difference; if they are limited – or apparently limited – to *other* cultures they are not admitted into the mainstream classification of psychiatric illness. And 'other cultures', in this context, are usually those associated with people seen as alien in racial terms. The concept of a CBS is therefore one that has been generated by an ideology (of psychiatry) that sees psychopathology in the West as culturally neutral and that among people designated as 'non-Western' as 'culture-bound' unless it can be subsumed within a Western category.

This situation has come about through collusion between psychiatrists and anthropologists. Anthropologists study (by tradition) what are termed 'primitive societies' usually designated in racial terms. Psychopathology in these societies is interpreted ethnographically and anthropologists tend to see all psychiatric illness as culture-specific, if not culture-bound *in the peoples they study*. But anthropological methods have not been applied to Western societies – at least not until recently and even now only tentatively. The ideology that developed within anthropology is to see a dichotomy between modern/scientific psychiatry and traditional/ ethnopsychiatry (Gaines, 1982), the former being authentic and the latter contaminated or distorted (by culture). And this approach feeds into psychiatry where symptom constellations identified in the West are regarded as the standard and those in *other* cultures as anomalies (Bebbington, 1978). And when a symptom constellation cannot be pushed into a 'Western' illness category, a CBS is identified.

The term CBS, having arisen in the context described above, has a distinct racist connotation. Some writers and practitioners have tried to change the scene. For example, Littlewood and Lipsedge (1987) have argued that a cultural understanding of psychiatric illness is as important in the West as it is in other societies: 'Some general features of those ritual patterns usually classed as "culture-bound syndromes" are applicable to Western neurosis.' It has been suggested that anorexia nervosa (Prince, 1983) and premenstrual syndrome (Johnson, 1987) may be culture-bound syndromes of the West. A major problem in revising *DSM-III* (American Psychiatric Association, 1980) was the presence of 'culture-bound disorders' (of non-Western cultures) and a vigorous debate arose (Prince and Tcheng-Laroche, 1987; Kleinman, 1987; Kapur, 1987; Beiser, 1987) around an attempt to incorporate them into the DSM system. However the difficulties were not resolved and *DSM-IV* (American Psychiatric Association, 1994) merely lists 'culture-bound syndromes' in an appendix. Similarly, *ICD-10* (World Health Organisation, 1993) lists 'culture-specific disorders' in an annex to its criteria for research written by an anthropologist.

So is there a place for the term CBS in a global scene? Clearly, accepting it as useful is not to say that other syndromes, including those commonly diagnosed as schizophrenia and depression, are unaffected by culture; all diseases are culturally patterned. Also it does not mean that culture, and culture alone, provides a total explanation for a 'culture-bound' syndrome; a CBS, like any other illness, arises in a whole individual with bodily and mental dimensions. If all psychiatric illness – and indeed the definition of mental health – is bound up with culture, it seems misleading to designate some behaviour patterns as 'culture-bound', implying that others are not. However, it may be useful in practical terms to see certain types of 'disturbance' as culture-bound in the context of a particular health care system (Kleinman, 1978), and the term CBS should be limited to those extremes of behaviour identified by a society as deviant *and* not explicable, or understandable, without an in-depth knowledge of the culture. In other words, the term CBS should be a shorthand for identifying a condition where a cultural understanding – ethnographic analysis in anthropological terms – is a sine qua non for bringing any practical help to the individual that is identified as 'suffering' from the syndrome. But first, the racist connotation attached to the concept of a CBS has to be removed and the importance of a cultural understanding of anyone presenting as emotionally disturbed accepted.

Worldviews: psychology, religion and health

The current Western medical model of psychiatric illness is one that is relatively, if not completely, free from religious, ethical and spiritual aspects of the culture in which it is based. However, cultural traditions of Africa, (Native) America and Asia are different. In these cultures, religion, medicine and ethics (as understood in the West) are integrated and a sharp dichotomy between mind and body (in the Western sense) is not evident. Further, the distinctions between psychology, philosophy and religion are not of the same order as that in Western thought systems. For example, in Hindu culture, philosophy and psychology are combined to provide a basis for 'knowing, analyzing, and learning to use our inner potentials' (Rama, 1985); although Greek civilisation had Afro-Asiatic roots (Bernal, 1987), its philosophy developed very differently from that in African and Asian cultures, mainly because Greeks excluded religion and morality in forming a 'secular worldly science' (Diop, 1967). Thus the current 'scientific' approach in the Western ethos that has emerged from these Greek origins is at variance with the ethos underlying non-Western cultures, except in so far as they have been influenced by Western culture. In modern Western thinking, psychology, religion and medicine are clearly demarcated. Hence, in describing these subjects in this book (within a culture in which the divisions between them are not inherent), an artificial structure derived from Western thinking is inevitably being imposed; the descriptions are thereby distorted and the understanding of the conceptualisations within these cultures – the way these other cultures work – is very limited. These limitations must be borne in mind by the reader when considering the following accounts.

Few, if any, cultures have grown up in isolation from others. All the major cultural groups have influenced each other historically and continue to do so in the present. Although generalisations inevitably oversimplify and do not do justice to the cultural variety in human society, four broad cultural patterns can be distinguished for our purpose of considering a cultural worldview of relevance to a discussion of mental health. Although Western culture is the newest of these, it has developed a worldview that can be distinguished from those of the older, non-Western traditions arising originally in Africa, America and Asia – referred to here as the African, Native American and Eastern cultures. The Islamic culture that developed in the geographical area called by Europeans the 'Middle East' (mainly Western Asia) is, for the purpose of this chapter, included within 'Eastern' culture although admittedly its influence has spread into the African continent and parts of Europe. The cultures of indigenous Australians, the Maoris of New Zealand and various other peoples, such as the Polynesians, are not considered in the interests of brevity. Since it is difficult to gener-alise about the thinking of (Native) Americans, either in the past or the present, the main concerns in the discussions about worldviews in this chapter are about cultures emanating from Africa and Asia, on the one hand, and Western (traditional European) culture, on the other. In generalising about cultures, the overall differences between non-Western and Western cultures are emphasised in order to establish the importance of cultural differences. But all cultures are essentially dynamic systems that are changing all the time.

The following sections will consider worldviews in African, Eastern and Native American cultures. In order to provide a background, a short account is given first of some salient points appertaining to the 'illness' concept in Western culture. In each case, selected ideas will be drawn together to give the reader a feel of the culture, as far as possible, in terms of traditional thinking mainly. In the section entitled 'Conclusions', the effects of recent history in shaping their current worldviews will be incorporated and the overall impres-sions will be used to make some generalisations about Western and non-Western concepts of mental health derived from their world-views.

Western culture

The worldview of a people derives from both its historic past and its current functioning vis-à-vis other groups of people. Ancient Greece is the fountainhead of Western culture but its original tenets have undergone changes over the years. Very early on, the mystic vision of the ancient Greeks became distorted and fragmented (Graham, 1986):

> Maintaining a sense of proportion or right measure came to be central to the world view of the Greeks and to their way of life, for according to Platonic doc-trine, human experience could best be described in terms of pairs of opposites,

the balance or harmony between which constituted the soul or psyche.... Gradually, however, the notion of measure lost its mystical significance.

By the time it was transformed into Western civilisation, via the Romans, measure came to denote 'mainly a process of comparison with some arbitrary external standard', so that knowledge or *scientia* meant objective fact; such facts are accepted in Western science as the only valid knowledge of the world. The intellectual heritage of Western culture 'has its foundations in a linear model of knowledge, implicit in which is the notion of absolute truth or fixed reality, and from its concepts of measure and ratio it also derives its emphases on measurement and standardisation, rationality and reason, all of which involve dissection' (ibid.) – the reduction of problems into the smallest possible components.

The fundamental belief in Western culture that underpins its illness models is what Ryle (1949) calls the 'official doctrine derived from the theories of Descartes' – the 'dogma of the ghost in the machine': 'It maintains that there exist both bodies and minds; that there occur physical processes and mental processes; that there are mechanical causes of corporal movements and mental causes of corporal movements.' In separating mind from matter, Descartes enabled scientists to study matter without reference to themselves as human beings. Then, Newtonian physics led to a mechanistic worldview. The natural world became a mechanical system to be manipulated and exploited; living organisms were seen as machines constructed from separate parts, each part being broken into further divisions. Finally, there emerged the view of mind as an objective 'thing' to be studied by objectified methods. Scientists, 'encouraged by their success in treating living organisms as machines, tend to believe that they are *nothing but* machines' (Capra, 1982). It is this scientific viewpoint that now rules Western thinking and its worldview – a worldview that is in conflict with those of other cultures in crucial areas. For example, in contrasting the activity of introspection in Western culture with that of its counterpart in the Indian tradition, Kakar (1984) notes that, in the former, definitions of self and identity are contingent upon 'the scrutiny of the life in terms of a ruthless examination of motives and feelings', while in meditative procedures of 'self realisation', introspection dwells on the 'self' of Indian philosophy 'uncontaminated by time and space'. Nobles (1986) notes that, 'unlike the mathematical illusion of normality found in the West, normality which would be consistent with African thought is a normal which is equivalent to one's nature'.

African culture

A reliable body of information on the background and traditions of Africa is not available for several reasons (Karenga, 1982): the subject is vast and relatively unresearched; the sources of history in most parts of Africa were 'griots', a class of professional oral historians who 'acted as the collective memory of an ethnic group, nation or empire' – a vulnerable form of record keeping; and European conquest led to the destruction of many documents and evidence of African achievement and to the distortion of history to fit into racist models of African primitiveness. Before the appearance of Cheikh Anta Diop's *African Origin of Civilization* (Diop, 1967), African culture was expounded by Western scholars enveloped in an ideology that distorted history and 'cast a fog over cultural understanding of the African people' (Asante and Asante, 1985). African studies that attempt to avoid racist assumptions and examine the evidence objectively are a recent phenomenon. The real story of Africa and its culture is incomplete.

It is clear that the origins of African tradition are intimately connected with the wisdom of ancient Egypt, called originally 'Kemet', the black settlement, inhabited by Kemites, the black people (Carruthers, 1986). Egyptian civilisation itself was derived from other black peoples to the south of Egypt (Williams, 1976) and 'what emerges clearly from the evidence is that indigenous Black Africans developed *the whole* Nile valley including Egyptian civilization' (Hilliard, 1986). Egyptian and Yoruba culture of West Africa have links in terms of religion, language and customs (Lucas, 1948). M. K. Asante (1985) writes that the Wolof, the Yoruba, the Asante and the Ogiso of Benin are among the many tribes that have aspects of culture derived from ancient Egypt: 'The continent [of Africa] is replete with evidences of the influence of Egypt.' There is evidence for a close relationship between the Egyptian language and languages to the south of Egypt (Wimby, 1986); and, although widely separated from each other on the African continent, the languages of the Zulu (of South Africa) and the Yoruba (of West Africa) belong to the same language family, the Niger–Congo group of languages (Lawson, 1984). Wimby (1986) reckons that Egyptian may be seen as the classical African language, equivalent to Latin as the classical language of Europe, with Swahili, Walaf and Hausa as the main contenders for being the lingua franca for African people.

Although Egyptian civilisation has ceased to exist in its ancient form, it lives on in African culture. And African culture is not just in Africa, it extends across the Atlantic (Clarke, 1985):

> 'Africa-consciousness', in varying degrees good and bad, has always been a part of the psyche of the African people, in forced exile in South America, the Caribbean Islands, and in the United States. There has always been a conflict within the Black American's 'Africa-consciousness'. This conflict was created early and was extended beyond all reasonable proportions by the mass media of the twentieth century through jungle movies, elementary textbooks on geography and history, and travel books written to glorify all people of European extraction – in essence, white people. These distorted images have created both a rejection of Africa and a deep longing for the Africa of our imagination, the Africa that was our home and the first home of what man has referred to as 'a civilization'.

James (1954) has compiled strong evidence to show that Greek philosophy derives from Egyptian socio-religious philosophy. In the book *Black Athena*, Bernal (1987) shows in great detail how historical facts indicating the Afro-Asiatic roots of Greek civilisation were 'ignored, denied and suppressed since the eighteenth century – chiefly for racist reasons'. However, the Greek philosophical tradition that underlies Western culture is very different in terms of worldview from Kemetic wisdom. According to Diop (1967), Kemetic knowledge was stripped of its moral values and religion (by the Greeks) to be secularised into becoming the European discipline of philosophy. But many Egyptian ideas were clearly absorbed into Greek civilisation and continue in the modern religions of Western Europe. For example, the doctrine of 'One God' and the concept that 'the Kingdom of God is within you' were taught in Egypt by Akhenaton around 1350 BC (Rogers, 1972). The thinking of ancient Egypt gave pre-eminence to the notion of soul or spirit; and 'the Ka was the divine spirit which endowed all things and which survived past the physical life of the individual' (Nobles, 1986). The Ka was thought to have magical powers that could cause the dead to live again in the thoughts of the survivors and could animate a mummified being. Egyptian notions of God live on in the African tradition which 'in all [African] societies, without a single exception' sees God as the Supreme Being (Mbiti, 1969).

Karenga (1982) believes that religion has always been a vital part in the lives of African people in both Africa and the United States.

He identifies four general themes in traditional African religion. 'First, there is the belief in one Supreme God: Oludumare among the Yoruba, Nkulunkulu among the Zulu and Amma among the Dogon. This god is the Father in most societies, but also appears as Mother in matriarchical societies like the Ovambo in Namibia and the Nuba in Kenya'. Secondly, Africans engage in daily interaction with divinities, who are seen as God's intermediaries, 'both similar to and different from Jesus, angels and Catholic saints as intermediaries and assistants to the Supreme Being'. Thirdly, there is a stress on veneration of ancestors as the guardians of family traditions and ethics, and intermediaries between people and God. Fourthly, African traditional religion emphasises a balance 'between one's collective identity and responsibility as a member of society and one's personal identity and responsibility'. In comparing contemporary Zulu and Yoruba religions, Lawson (1984) finds that both show some similarities in their emphasis on ancestors as a source of power and the significance of sorcery and witchcraft. Other traditional themes in African religion noted by Karenga (1982) are the profound respect for nature and a belief in a collective immortality 'achieved through the life of one's people and through what one means to them'. Death is seen as 'reflective of cosmic patterns, i.e. the rising and setting of the sun, and often graves are dug east and west to imitate this pattern'.

In emphasising the spiritual dimension of African religions, Richards (1985) describes the (traditional) African worldview:

> The African universe is conceived as a unified spiritual totality. We speak of the universe as *cosmos*, and we mean that all being is organically interrelated and interdependent. The Swahili speak of *utaratibu wa kutizama dunia* (the way of the world). The Western/ European materialized universe does not yield cosmos. The essence of the African cosmos is spiritual reality; that is its fundamental nature, its primary essence. But realities are not conceived as being in irreconcilable opposition, as they are in the West, and spirit is not separate from matter. Both spiritual and material being are necessary in order for there to be a meaningful reality. While spiritual being gives force and energy to matter, material being gives form to spirit. Enlightenment and the acquisition of wisdom and knowledge depends to a significant degree on being able to apprehend spirit in matter.

Although a belief in life after death is found in all African religions, 'this belief does not constitute a hope for the future and a better life. To live here and now is the most important concern of African religious activities and beliefs.... There is no paradise to to be hoped for nor hell to be feared in the hereafter' (Mbiti, 1969).

Western Christianity came to influence Africans through the conversion of African slaves and the influx of missionaries into a continent where societies were being devastated by colonial conquest and internecine conflict. Although the Church was clearly an arm of the slave-owning economy and racist colonialism, the doctrines of the Christian religion were gradually fashioned by Africans to be absorbed into their worldview. A distinctive Afro-American form of Christianity, 'actually a new religion of an oppressed people', has developed in the United States (Wilmore, 1973), leading to a Black Liberation Theology allied to Black Power (Karenga, 1982). And in South Africa, Black Theology as 'the perception that Jesus belonged historically in a situation of oppression, that he was a member of an oppressed people in an oppressive society, and that he came to set people free' (Stubbs, 1988), is now supporting Black Consciousness in the modern African worldview.

Eastern culture

The traditions of India, China and Western Asia ('Middle East') dominate the cultures that are generally termed 'Eastern', 'Oriental' or 'Asian'. In general, the traditions themselves remained for many centuries located in geographical areas – except for Islam. Although originating in the same area as Judaism and Christianity, Islam had, very early in its career, more contact with other traditions than any other major religion (Nasr, 1980):

> It encountered Christianity and Judaism in its cradle and during its first expansion northward. It met the Iranian religions, both Zoroastrianism and Manichaeism, in the Sassanid Empire. . . . It met Buddhism in north-west Persia, Afghanistan, and Central Asia, and Hinduism in the Sind and later many parts of the Indian subcontinent. There was even contact with Mongolian and Siberian Shamanism on the popular level, mostly through the Turkish tribes who had followed Shamanism before their conversion to Islam. Moreover the Muslims of Sinkiang were in direct contact with the Chinese tradition.

However, it seems appropriate to include the worldview of the Islamic tradition within that of an overall Asian or Eastern tradition. Christianity, too, spread across many continents in the wake of European imperialism and colonisation but it remains mainly a Western tradition. The Judaic tradition, having become largely located in Europe for many centuries and having given rise to (Western) Christianity, is clearly not an Eastern tradition any longer.

Although the East, like Africa and America, has been devastated by Western military might and economic greed, the basics of its cultural traditions have been maintained. Indeed, Islamic tradition appears to be vying with that of the West in terms of political influence, and the philosophies of India and China draw many 'Westerners' seeking an alternative to the materialism of their scientific world. Although their origins are lost in time, they are not 'old' in the sense of being outdated or the opposite of 'modern'; according to Capra (1982), the spiritual tradition of the East is akin to the approach of modern physics. Writing for a Western audience, Graham (1986) states: 'Eastern culture and its institutions are traditionally humanistic in the sense that they are centred around the human potential for transcendence or becoming.' But Eastern culture is not humanistic in the sense of worshipping the human being as being noble and all-powerful – the sort of thinking that forms the basis of Western culture. Religion and psychology are integrated in the traditional philosophies of Hinduism, Buddhism, Zen, Taoism and Islam. In the Eastern tradition, rationality is seen as *maya* – illusory and superficial. Chinese philosophy sees reality, whose ultimate essence is called *tao*, as a process of continual flow and change. Its *yin/yang* terminology represents a systems view – a general systems theory in Western terms. 'Systems theory looks at the world in terms of the interrelatedness and interdependence of all phenomena, and in this framework an integrated whole whose property cannot be reduced to those of its parts is called a system' (Capra, 1982). Graham (1986) writes: 'Eastern culture, in its concern with intangibles rather than "facts", with emotionality rather than rationality, gives pre-eminence to the subjective and experiential.'

Indian psychology is a part of Indian philosophy that has a rich and extensive recorded literature. Safaya (1976) calls it 'the science of consciousness' – not just a personal quality of an individual but a consciousness that pervades the entire universe. He describes fundamental doctrines of Indian philosophy in the *Upanisads* which have a bearing on psychology. These concern the doctrine of ultimate reality (*brahman*), the pure self (*atman*) as the essence of individuality, the identification of *atman* with *brahman*, the individual personality that is bound by the phenomenal world, and the law of karma.

As Upanisads discuss human personality as a whole, there is no separate account of mental functioning. Whatever references there are regarding particular aspect of mental functioning, those are incidentally mentioned with respect to any particular philosophical or theological view-point. Again, it is rather difficult to present an equivalence of Mind (used in Western philosophy) with any of the terms used in Upanisads. (ibid.)

Mind, in Indian psychology, is an organ of action – not just of thinking; it is seen as being material but 'subtle' (as opposed to 'gross'). The physical body is also material but 'gross'. Consciousness is vested in the 'self', not in mind or body. It is the power of consciousness that illuminates the whole person and pervades the cosmos. There are four states of consciousness at a personal level, namely the wakeful state, the dream state, the state of deep sleep and a fourth state in which the mind is non-functioning – a state of 'oneness with Brahman'. The self is perceived as experiencing all these states except the fourth which is a 'superconscious state' beyond experience. According to Safaya, the hierarchy of mental functions are given in the *Upanisads* as: (1) the five sensory organs; (2) *manas* or receiving mind, the coordinating organs of perception; (3) *buddhi* or *vijnana*, the intellect – the higher organ of thought, discrimination, reasoning and intelligence; (4) *ahankara*, the self-sense, the organ of personal ego; and (5) *citta*, the subconscious mind, the storehouse of past impressions. Other systems of Hindu philosophy deviate from the basis established in the *Upanisads* but the triune of soul, body and mind is generally accepted. The concept of the mind that underlies the traditional Indian system of medicine, Ayurveda, derives from the *samkya* system (Obeyesekere, 1977). In this, two primary principles, *purusa* (spirit) and *prakrti* (primordial matter), interact at various levels (Safaya, 1976):

> The existence of the dynamic Universe owes to the interaction of spirit and matter, Purusa and Prakrti. Their mutual association is necessary, as spirit without matter is inactive and matter without spirit is blind. They are like the lame and the blind friends. They appear as consciousness and unconsciousness, subject and object, knower and known. Their relation can be metaphorically explained by fire and iron or crystal and object. Matter is reflected in the spirit, or it becomes charged with the power of spirit, as iron is charged with fire. This also explains that both Matter and Mind are inter-dependent. Neither is Mind derived from Matter, nor Matter from Mind.

The human personality in Hindu psychology is the product of a pure spirit (*purusa*) and matter (*prakrti*); the constituents of Western mind are contained in the latter. It is from their interaction that ego-consciousness, self-consciousness, intelligence and other aspects of Western mind, develop; but these are conceptualised as being at a cosmic or individual level. The mind in the Western sense is subsumed within the subtle body (as distinct from the physical body that perishes at death) which is both conscious and subconscious with 'a repository of innumerable impressions of not only the present life, but of innumerable past lives' (Safaya, 1976). According to Obeyesekere (1977), the functions of mind in classical Ayurveda resemble the ego-functions of psychoanalytic theory, but, unlike in psychoanalytic theory, 'symptoms of psychopathology are due to malfunctioning of the mind, so that Ayurveda would argue that emotional conflicts such as the oedipal one are not the cause but rather a result of mental malfunction'. The ultimate goal of life, according to all Indian philosophy, is liberation and self-realisation: 'Knowledge of psychology must lead to the understanding of the true nature of the Self, and hence the principle of liberation is part of the subject-matter of Indian psychology' (ibid.).

Buddhism developed from a Hindu tradition but, by transcending the boundaries of India, it has drawn on other Asian traditions. The differing emphases on ethical and metaphysical dimensions are responsible for differences between schools of Buddhism in their psychological speculations. Buddha said that there is no *atman* (individual self) but that five *skandhas* are transferred from one birth to the next to constitute a human identity. This identity is dispersed when the force that binds them is finally extinguished in nirvana. Buddhist idealists believe in a series of momentary cognitions but no self. Tibetan Buddhism has a tradition of getting to know mind and consciousness through introspection – awareness and knowledge (Rinbochay and Napper, 1980). But knowledge is not something separate from the knower: 'consciousness, awareness and knower are synonymous; they are the broadest terms among those dealing with mind. Any mind or mental factor is consciousness, is an awareness, is a knower.' Consciousness is divided into various alternative types: 'Dividing awareness and knowers in various ways into seven, three, and two is for the sake of understanding well the presentation of mind. One will recognize these different types of awareness and understand how they are contained within each other' (ibid.).

'The idea of impermanence and of ceaseless change, due to the never-ending chain of causes and effects' (Nanajivako, 1984), is a fundamental tenet of Buddhism as *aniccam*. This, together with the rejection of a 'soul' or 'self, in the concept of *anatta*, gives Buddhism a soulless psychology that emphasises the here and now, a conscious self of the moment that changes all the time. The Buddhist view is that the world has no purpose to accomplish, although individuals may choose their own ends and thus make their lives purposeful (Jayatilleke, 1984); the way to liberation in the attainment of nirvana forms the practical side of the philosophy–psychology–religion that is Buddhism. But Buddhism itself sprang from the Vedic tradition of India. The ultimate reality, according to all Indian philosophical systems, is a consciousness that pervades the entire universe; individual consciousness is related to it as a spark is related to a fire (Safaya, 1976). The eternal law of karma, unattachment as a means of deliverance and the ultimate goal of liberation through self-realisation are basic principles of Indian psychology embedded in its religion and philosophy. The Indian mystical tradition is mainly concerned with ways of liberation and transformation of consciousness. The Hindu looks to various types of yoga; the Buddhist emphasises meditation. In Sufism, the mystical dimension of Islam, the aim is the inner detachment of the individual without, necessarily, a withdrawal from the world (Nasr, 1980). In all these psychologies, the rational and the mystical are blended together.

The goal of all Eastern religions and psychology is enlightenment through individual striving and seeking, with emphases on personal, subjective experience and meditation. In general, the quest for understanding in Western thought is for facts, in the East for feeling. The Westerner seeks knowledge, the Easterner seeks to know. Systems of psychology/religion with a spiritual and mystical tradition have flourished in the East for centuries giving rise to all the major religions that have spread worldwide; and the East continues to produce religious masters or 'gurus'. As Eastern ideas reach the West and are described in Western terms, they seem to become despiritualised and intellectualised – a drawback that may apply to the presentations in this book.

Native American culture

The people of America, before they were 'discovered' by Columbus, had a sophisticated and distinguished culture or set of cultures. The recording of their history is sparse and severely distorted by European ethnocentricism. For example, English descriptions of native religions of North America were extremely biased (Simmons, 1986): 'Typically the English glossed over native concepts, such as *powwows* (or shamans) and guardian spirits, as if they were identical with English witches and devils about which the English had pre-formed and emotional opinions.' Simmons (1986) has elicited some aspects of the 'spirit' of the New England tribes of North America before the suppression of their culture by European colonialists by analysing their folklore. While believing in various deities, the principal god was Hobbamock whose name was related to the words for death, the deceased and the cold north-east wind. The word for 'devil' was also used for a dead man and they conceived themselves transformed into Hobbamock when they died. Dreams played an important part in their lives: 'These gods appeared in visions and dreams and protected those to whom they appeared.'

Capra (1982) believes that in America, before the European invasion, 'life was organised around a highly refined awareness of the environment' – something more than, but certainly including, an ecological awareness of the interrelationships between nature and people. Clearly the cultures that flourished in the Americas were unique and sophisticated, but unfortunately little of these remain as living societies. The real 'inside' knowledge of the cultures that remain is insufficient to draw any general conclusions about a current Native American worldview that is adequate for the purposes of this book, although an impression about the ethos of the culture comes through in some contemporary writings from America.

Anthropological research into Native American cultures by (mainly) white Euro-Americans is of limited value because of racist value judgements inherent in much of their reporting and the distortion that comes from the imposition of Western anthropological constructs that are alien to the culture being observed and reported. An account by someone who seems to avoid these drawbacks and provide an understanding of the religion of one group of Native Americans – the Yaqui Indians of the American south-west – is given in the series of books written by Carlos Castaneda. These describe his experiences in examining the knowledge of a Yaqui Indian sorcerer by himself undergoing (what he calls) an 'apprenticeship' under the guidance of the sorcerer, Don Juan. In his first book *The Teachings of Don Juan: A Yaqui Way of Knowledge* (Castaneda, 1968), after reporting his recollection of his experiences, Castaneda makes a structural analysis from his unique data: The goal of the Yaqui Indian sorcerer's teachings was to become a 'man of knowledge' and seven components characterised this concept:

> to become a man of knowledge was a matter of learning; (2) a man of knowledge had unbending intent; (3) a man of knowledge had clarity of mind; (4) to become a man of knowledge was a matter of strenuous labour; (5) a man of knowledge was a warrior; (6) to become a man of knowledge was an unceasing process; and (7) a man of knowledge had an ally. (ibid.)

Castaneda reckoned that the last component 'was the most important of the seven' because 'having an ally was what made him different
from ordinary men'. In the teachings of the particular sorcerer that
Castaneda studied under, the 'allies' were contained in the *Datura*
plants and the mushroom of the genus *Psilocybe*. An 'ally' was conceptualised as a 'power capable of transporting a man beyond the boundaries of himself' to transcend the realm of ordinary reality; 'an ally was
believed to be an entity existing outside and independent of oneself,
yet in spite of being a separate entity an ally was believed to be
formless'. As a result of his experiences in Yaqui religion, Castaneda
reckons that he was left with 'two units of the conceptual order' [a sort
of self-knowledge]: (1) the idea that there was a separate realm of
reality, another world, which I have called the 'reality of special
consensus'; (2) the idea that the reality of special consensus, or that
other world, was as utilizable as the 'world of everyday life'. It seems
that in Native American culture mysticism is combined with a feel for
ordinary practical living; it is said that Native Americans appreciate
two levels of consciousness – in the way that visionary painters of
the West appreciate an 'alternative reality' as well as 'reality'.

Jamake Highwater (1981) has tried to analyse the traditions, visions
and perceptions common to the indigenous cultures of America,
comparing them to Western equivalents, in order to draw out some
aspects of the Native American worldview. 'Indians do not believe in
a 'uni-verse' but in a 'multi-verse'. Indians do not believe that there is
one fixed and eternal truth; they think there are many different and
equally valid truths. He deduces that the duality of thinking characteristic of Western thought is generally absent among these Americans.
Their 'concept of harmony among all things includes the absolute unity
of spirit and flesh'. And the expressive act of dancing 'is the "breath-
of-life" made visible':

This concept of 'breath-of-life' is discovered everywhere in the unique spiritual
world of [American] Indians; in the ceremonial stem of the sacred pipe, in the
heart line of animals imprinted on pottery, in the rites of inhaling the first light of
day and the conferring of blessing by exhaling into the hands of the devotee. All
these symbolic images and gestures are associated with the wind and with the
breathing of the living cosmos – the visible motion of the power that invests everything in existence.... The breath-of-life and its associations with song, rhythm,
dance and motion are central to [American] Indian culture. It is a theme that runs
elaborately through every [American] Indian tradition, illuminated by ceremonies, the music, and the dances of American Indian tribes. It is also a conceptual metaphor that is the background of the religious viewpoint of Native

Americans despite the fact that there has been great diversity among the tribes and abundant influence from European religious forms after the invasion of 1492. (ibid.)

Although the Native American is closely identified with the tribe and the place (the land) that provides its centre, there is 'a startling form of individualism unknown in the West'. Each individual is known by a personal name given in a tribal ceremony to denote a uniqueness; further, since 'names are sacred designations of being, people also have the ability to be transformed – briefly or permanently – into other human beings and animals'. Thus, a person who would be derided in the West as psychotic or perverted has an acceptable place in the community.

Conclusions

Although the historic past of a people forms the background to their worldview in the present day, a current worldview must incorporate the effect of their recent experiences and their hopes for the future. Just as Western (traditional European) culture retains a worldview which incorporates a sense of power, Asian, African and (Native) American cultures retain the scars of imperial domination and persecution during the era in which genocide, slavery and colonialism flourished, as well as the effects of current economic oppression and indirect political control, i.e. 'neocolonialism'.

The subjugation of Asian people was accompanied by a stifling of their cultures, an assault upon their traditional values and a devaluation of their religions and philosophies. But, since their recorded history was extensive and their subjugation never really complete, much of Asian culture survived the imperial onslaught. The devastation caused in Africa by the advent of Europeans seeking wealth was more complete. African culture and its worldview retain the very deep scars of the holocaust that was slavery and of the colonialism that attacked its traditional values and ways of life. And Africa, and hence everyone identified as being of African descent, continue to suffer from the effects of neocolonialism and racist oppression. Steve Biko (1971), writing about South Africa, states that the culture that emanates from the common experience of oppression is one of 'defiance, self assertion and group pride and solidarity'. This has happened in parts of Asia and is happening in Africa as well as in the African diaspora. Further, the basic spirituality of the African worldview has been revitalised in the diaspora in order to make sense of the 'insanity of slavery' (Richards, 1985). It keeps going by its expression through ritual, music and song, whether in Africa itself or across the water. Now, in spite of the continuing devastation of Africa by the exploitation by multinational companies (the new colonialism), the spirit among black people of African descent is one of angry self-confidence and pride – and this characteristic now forms a part of the African worldview. Although white domination was universally destructive outside Europe, it was in America that the colonialists achieved their supreme prize. There, slavery led to genocide and a racism that destroyed indigenous cultures wholesale; the power of present-day European America is the result; Native American people and their cultures are completely suppressed.

Racist oppression of people and suppression of culture are the common experience of what is now referred to as the 'Third World'. The sum total of the negative effects of oppression at a personal level has been vividly described and psychologically analysed by the black psychiatrist, writer and freedom fighter Frantz Fanon. He begins his book *Black Skin, White Masks* (Fanon, 1952) by quoting Aimé Césaire: 'I am talking of millions of men who have been skilfully injected with fear, inferiority complexes, trepidation, servility, despair, abasement.' He contends that the 'Negro' is sealed into his blackness by European culture that clings to an archetypal image of the black man as 'an expression of the bad instincts, of the darkness inherent in every ego, of the uncivilized savage, the Negro who slumbers in every white man'. Fanon saw the black person as a victim of white culture analogous with the Jew who was seen by Sartre (1948) as being poisoned by the stereotype that other Europeans had of Jews. The positive effects of resisting oppression are seen at a psychological level in the movements of negritude (Senghor, 1965) and more especially in the philosophy of 'Black Consciousness' which 'expresses group pride and the determination by blacks to rise and attain the envisaged self' (Biko, 1972).

Fanon's early writings dwelt on the psychosociology of the African diaspora, but later, having taken up the colonial struggle himself, Fanon (1961) surveyed the predicament of the 'Third World' in general – of black people in Asia, America and Africa. He identified the origin of the so-called 'sensitivity' of the 'native' (i.e. black people) in the colonial situation, in 'the number and depth of the injuries inflicted upon a native during a single day'. In analysing how natives in a colonial state were denied the 'attributes of humanity', being lumped together with the bush, mosquitoes and fever as the 'hostile environment' that had to be 'tamed', Fanon saw the struggle for liberation as a 'cultural phenomenon':

> The struggle for freedom does not give back to the national culture its former value and shapes; this struggle which aims at a fundamentally different set of relations between men cannot leave intact either the form or content of the people's culture. After the conflict there is not only the disappearance of colonialism but also the disappearance of the colonized man. (ibid.)

The emergence, after the last European war, of independent black states in Asia and Africa, the political growth of China as a major power in Asia, the black rights movement of the 1960s in the United States and 'Black Consciousness' in Africa, have combined together to give a new affirmation of black identity 'best reflected in the famous slogan: "Black is Beautiful"' (Tajfel, 1982). Black people all over the world now demand social and economic equality as of right; this, together with a self-confidence, strengthened in rediscovering their ancient heritage, is a part of the worldview of African and Asian people across the globe. Native Americans, Hispanics and other black people too may soon follow.

Although there are many cultural differences within each of the entities designated as Western culture, African culture, Eastern culture and (Native) American culture, it is possible to draw some broad generalisations in terms of overall differences in worldviews between them in order to derive some 'feel' about the meaning of mental health across cultures. However, these must not be taken as guidelines for judging individuals or individual cultures, but merely meant to provide the reader with a feel of the differences that there are in concepts of mental health seen in a global perspective. In the West, health is felt as something that is attained by control and domination, in keeping with a worldview that emphasises aggressive control – of emotion by reason, of nature by people, and of 'them' by 'us'. The Western concept of health is a matter of overcoming illness – destroying 'pathology'. The worldviews of Asia and Africa and, possibly, Native America promote a sense of health arising from *acceptance* – of emotion, of nature, of 'others'. Together with this there is a striving for 'harmony; both within a person and between people and their surroundings in 'nature', the spirits and the cosmos – a way of thinking that is often dismissed in the West as 'superstition'.

The Western worldview, based on control, has within it an assertiveness that has paid off in the achievements by the West of material gain; African and Eastern acceptance has promoted a passivity that allowed the West to dominate and exploit both the people and resources of the earth to the point of destruction. But the Western worldview about health has had always within it guilt and fear, promoting 'ill health', interpreted as depression (often defined in terms of guilt) and anxiety, giving rise to movements such as psychoanalysis. And within the apparent passivity and acceptance of Eastern and African cultures has been always anger and aggression leading to irrational violence, sometimes seen as 'illness' and dealt with culturally by spiritual and religious movements. However, the rational, justifiable anger of African and Asian people and the 'understandable' guilt of the West (both arising from recent history) are entwined respectively with traditional non-Western acceptance and traditional Western aggressiveness in the feelings that determine the concept of mental health in their cultures today.

Distress: idioms of expression

In Western thinking, mental health or ill health is to do – partially or entirely – with emotions felt by people within themselves. These internal episodes of feeling, conceptualised as emotions, are different from sensations such as touch, hearing, etc., which are also 'felt', but felt in a different way. The term 'affect' is used to describe the psychological state underlying an emotion but often used loosely as meaning emotion in general. Although sensations may be bound up with emotions or combinations of emotions (as, for example, in fear associated with pain), they are different: sensations are localisable while emotions are not (Coulter, 1979), being perceived as feelings affecting the whole person. But, since both emotion and sensation are conceptualised as 'felt', they are confounded in both psychology and Western philosophy.

In psychology, the term 'emotion' or 'affect' is usually used to describe such intense states of feeling as anxiety, depression, happiness, contentment (and their opposites), as well as milder 'moods' such as feelings of pleasure, displeasure, anger, fear, shame, jealousy, hunger and sexual urge. Emotions are usually conceptualised as internal, subjective experiences, peculiar to the individual and expressed by verbal or non-verbal behaviour – the latter being seen as social signals of subjective experiences used for communication, or as signs of physiological changes that accompany emotion (Argyle, 1975). The

James–Large theory of emotion, in which affect is deemed to be entirely determined by physiological changes, is not usually acceptable to modern psychology, but the general approach in the West is that affect is determined by various internal events of both psychological and physiological nature. They are seen as complex, psychophysiological reactions composed of cognitive appraisals, 'action impulses' which either inhibit or express emotion and patterned somatic reactions (Lazarus *et al.*, 1970, 1980). A person's emotions are recognised because they are expressed through behaviour, either verbally by the person concerned describing them in language that another person understands, or by means of non-verbal communication – for example 'body language'. Social and cultural influences on the phenomena of affective states and conduct are usually studied in terms of the context in which the affect is felt or expressed. It is also important to note that the very ways in which emotions are conceptualised in other cultures are different from those in the West.

In his classic book *The Expression of the Emotions in Man and Animals*, Charles Darwin (1872) established a way of thinking about emotions that led to a study of behaviour (called ethology) that emphasises the biological evolution of behaviour, including emotional expression. Ethology sees cultural differences in the expression of emotions as a reflection of evolutionary difference, i.e. differences determined by the environmental modification of heredity. Inevitably, this approach succumbs to racism since cultural differences of behaviour (including the expression of the emotions) are perceived hierarchically, those of some cultures being seen as superior to those of others. Konrad Lorenz, an outstanding ethologist, is quoted by Kalikow (1978) as advocating the 'elimination of "invirent types" [of human beings]: those which, in the most dangerous, virulent increase, like the cells of a malignant tumour, threaten to penetrate the body of a *Volk*'. According to Kalikow, Lorenz feared that natural selection may be inoperative in civilised conditions, with the result that 'the increase in the number of existing mutants' might lead to an 'imbalance of the race' – the white race.

Coulter (1979) argues convincingly that sociocultural dimensions are not mere contexts for emotional expression but are primary determinants of affect and integral to their very constitution:

> Not only do emotions characteristically have meaningful objects or situations as their occasions, but such objects or situations *make emotions intelligibly present*. This is not a psychological point, but a logical one. It is not that it is impossible to

experience some feeling previously associated with being ashamed in the absence of the recognition that one is open to criticism of some kind; the only argument being made here is that the *rational* avowal or ascription of shame is conceptually tied to the recognition on the part of the person of some responsibility for the object or situation of the shame, and a susceptibility to personal criticism for it.

It is the failure to acknowledge the importance of sociocultural determinants of emotion that has led to emotions being theoretically 'reduced' to just biological impulses as in ethology. Even if biological determinants are combined with psychological ones, the author believes, with Coulter, that the 'psychological model of the emotions as internal episodes...can never illuminate, only distort, our appreciation of the variegated ways in which emotions figure in the weave of our lives' (ibid.).

When emotions are expressed, they are assumed to reflect underlying feelings. But this approach is too simplistic. Complicated personal, cultural and social meaning complexes may fashion the way in which emotion is expressed through behaviour; and the sociocultural context in which an emotion is felt and expressed may affect the outcome. Not only that, but emotions may be suppressed, distorted or exaggerated for psychological, social or cultural reasons; and some feelings, or the way they are expressed, may be designated as 'illness'. Feelings may be expressed in terms of idioms – complex behaviour patterns including music, poetry, dance, art forms, etc. – that have become imbued with meaning through usage underscored by symbolic associations. Inevitably, such idioms of feeling states are heavily determined by habits and traditions arising from culture as well as contextual factors and personal inclinations. The validity of these idioms stems from their usefulness as forms of expression and/or adaptation for the individual. Thus the sociocultural dimensions of emotional expression are varied and complex.

Just as happiness or life satisfaction is a concomitant of mental health, mental distress of one sort or another is associated with unhappiness or dissatisfaction with life, related in general to a state of mental ill health. In studying the idiomatic expression of psychosocial distress (by which he means 'a range of feelings including vulnerability, apprehension, inadequacy, dissatisfaction, suppressed anger and other anxiety states which might otherwise take the form of an untenable social conflict or rebellion'), Nichter (1981), an anthropologist, believes that the judgement of a particular idiom of distress as normal or abnormal, adaptive or maladaptive should not be made until the following have been considered: 'An individual's socio-cultural constraints against and opportunities for expression, alternative modes of expression, personal and cultural meaning and social ramifications of employing modes, and a person's past experience and familiarity with alternative modes.' Nichter's interpretations of idioms of distress that he observed among Havik Brahmin women in South India may or may not be correct, but indicate their complexity. In Nichter's view, obsessive–compulsive preoccupation with purity of the household by a mother-in-law was an expression of aggression towards her daughters-in-law as competitors for the attention of sons, while similar concern by a middle-aged childless wife or young widow was an expression of low self-worth. Nichter saw ambivalence towards household rituals by women as aggression towards their husbands, and reckoned that the 'illness idiom' was used in various complex ways: for example, 'emphasis on the disruption of routine body cycles, such as the digestive or menstrual cycles' served to impress the Ayurvedic *vaidya* (medical practitioner) with the severity of a problem and 'a general loss of well-being'. However, the *vaidya* followed the pattern of symptoms by asking about essential life processes, 'inviting discussions of general well-being, not just symptoms'. For example, when the symptom of dizziness was presented to the *vaidya*, the latter 'elicited a history wherein dizziness and weakness were interrelated to the patient's weak position in her family in the absence of her husband and feelings of anxiety related to his belated return from a distant contract work project'. Following her discussion with the *vaidya*, 'the patient, who had complained of feeling dizzy during the consultation, once again took up her head-load at its conclusion and walked off with a steady gait'.

Clearly, the question of communication and rapport between patient and physician is fundamental to the idioms used for the expression of distress. The 'symptoms' presented by a patient are a reflection of this interaction as well as a result of biological and/or 'functional' processes in the patient. This applies to all interactions in the field of mental health where there are encounters between professionals and clients, either in a context of treatment/assessment or in a research setting. In situations where both participants in an interaction have similar understanding of the idioms, communication is easy and the idioms of expression that are 'natural' to both can be usefully employed. But if there is a cultural gulf between them, problems arise. Such a gulf can be overcome by knowledge, which can be obtained from the patient (assuming there are no serious language problems), but this may be blocked if the interaction takes place in a context where the physician is influenced, consciously or unconsciously, by racist value judgements of the patient or his/her culture. Thus culture plays a major part in the idiomatic expression of distress, while both race and culture are involved in the recognition of the idioms.

Coping with stress

The concept of coping discussed here is to do with the preservation of health – mental health. Hence, in this sense at least, 'coping' is intimately concerned with the meaning of mental health explored in various ways throughout this chapter. The fundamental question of what coping is for, is related to cultural values; it is to do with such matters as the desirability of control over distress as opposed to its acceptance, and the significance attached to satisfaction, through distress relief, of the individual as opposed to that of the family or group. Thus coping practices or processes cannot be considered in isolation from culture. However, coping is to do primarily with the alleviation of distress and it may be an acceptable generalisation that, when distress is associated with a person's behaviour or experience, coping may be involved – whatever the judgement within the culture (of the behaviour/experience) in terms of normality/ abnormality. This then can be a basis for universal criteria for the need for coping, notwithstanding the lack of universal criteria for mental illness or psychopathology noted earlier. It is not the intention of this section to describe various strategies of coping across the globe and across cultures; such a list would be meaningless without a detailed description of their correlates and contexts. It is proposed to provide a background to the consideration of coping with stress in different cultures and to avoid racist judgements in doing so.

In psychology, coping with stress is usually perceived in behavioural terms or in relation to an ego psychology model of human functioning (Folkman and Lazarus, 1988). The former, being derived from studies of animal behaviour, emphasises learned behaviour contributing to survival in the face of dangers that threaten life; in the latter, coping consists of cognitive processes, such as denial, repression and intellectualisation. In both, coping is viewed as a response to emotion, felt and/or expressed, and a means of reducing tension – at least unwanted, distressing tension. These concepts of coping ignore the fact that coping is influenced by the significance of what is happening in a wide sense, both personally and socially; they ignore the cultural context in which coping occurs and the way coping is perceived and judged in a racist milieu. Folkman and Lazarus (1988) note that 'emotion and coping influence each other in a dynamic, mutually reciprocal relationship'. Culture must play a large part in determining the way in which a particular event of emotional distress is conceptualised in the first place – for example, whether it is seen as 'illness' to be cured or endured, or as a spiritual crisis to be resolved or experienced; the former will call for 'coping' and the latter for understanding. This interrelates with culturally determined concepts of distress, discussed earlier.

A problem that arises in delineating coping mechanisms cross-culturally is the possible confusion of coping strategies with psychopathology. Conditions, such as depression, anxiety, 'hearing voices', guilty preoccupation, passivity feelings, aggression, anger and emotional withdrawal, are usually recognised in psychiatry as symptoms of illness – and all too often assumed to be of universal validity – but may be coping strategies for individuals in particular situations. Knowledge of cultural background may be important in differentiating normal coping from symptoms. In essence, a coping strategy is understandable as a way of relieving distress and, broadly speaking, desirable, in that it is likely to benefit the person involved. The ascription of some desirable and beneficial behaviour or experience as a symptom of illness arises through the inherent confusion in psychiatry itself. For example, depression may well be considered understandable as a way of coping with bereavement but also designated as a symptom of illness treated with antidepressants. Coulter (1979) argues that this sort of confusion may be avoided by ensuring that the designation of 'psychological phenomena' as abnormal depends on the (culturally determined) judgement of intentionality and understandability:

> The public criteria for 'understanding' and 'intending' are circumstantially bound and not restricted to some codified set of associated behaviors or experiences, as if these could be listed as a fixed set of 'conditions'; members of a culture must exercise situated judgements, must analyze contexts for what could count as criteria for proper ascription or for the ratification of an avowal in those specific cases.

Thus if a form of behaviour or a type of experience in a particular setting is neither understandable to others nor intentional on the part of the person concerned, psychopathology, or its equivalent, is diagnosed. Otherwise, the particular behaviour is not (in Western terms) a 'symptom' of illness. A coping strategy, by its very nature of being understandable as one, is 'normal'; it should never be seen as a symptom if the judgement is based on culture-sensitive evaluations free of racism. Racial attitudes may play their part by designating a hierarchy (in effectiveness) of the strategies. 'Hearing voices' may be perceived as a primitive type of coping characteristic of black people and depression as a strategy of advanced white people; the result is that hallucinatory experiences are discounted as undesirable because they are seen as a 'primitive' way of coping and thence slip into being treated as symptoms of illness in spite of being recognised as a coping strategy.

Coping strategies have been delineated by Folkman and Lazarus (1988) as 'problem-focused' and 'emotion-focused'; the former is geared to resolving the problem(s) giving rise to the distressing emotion and the latter directed at reducing distress, irrespective of its underlying cause. Both forms of coping are necessary, but the effectiveness of coping in any given situation depends on the propriety of the choice between the two. In a global, transcultural context, the conceptualisation of 'problem' and the level of 'problem-solving' are crucial matters. The cultural viewpoints on mind and body and the ways in which the individual locates the problem is clearly significant. In both psychology and psychiatry, the depth at which a problem may be located is very limited, even using concepts of the unconscious mind or 'group mind', compared, for example, with the way in which problems may be viewed through 'the cultural prism' (Kakar, 1984) of the Indian tradition; here, problems of an individual encompass 'the constituents of the person, his/her limits and extensions in time, the nature of his connection with the natural environment on the one hand and with the psyche (or soul) on the other, the nature of the body's relationship with the psyche but also with the polis and the cosmos in determining health and illness'. Emotion-focused strategies may be aimed at various levels too. Some cultures may promote coping strategies for the understanding of distressing emotions while others may be primarily concerned with their eradication. In the former case, the emphasis given to strictly personal matters (in Western terms), as opposed to broader issues concerned with, say, spiritual values, is determined by the worldview of the culture, depending on its approach to questions of religious salvation in, for example, the 'hereafter' or the next birth, of economic gain or of immediate gratification.

Summary

There are fundamental differences between concepts of mental health and mental disorder derived from Western culture and those from non-Western cultures in Asia, Africa and (pre-Columbian) America – differences that continue to exist in spite of the so-called 'Westernisation of the world' (Harrison, 1979). The thinking that results from the demarcation of psychology, religion and philosophy as relatively separate subjects does not apply in Asian cultures nor, perhaps, in African and Native American cultures. Western 'scientific' medicine tends to exclude ethical and spiritual considerations, but the indigenous medical traditions of Africa, Asia and America are different. Describing other cultures using Western concepts and ways of thinking has serious limitations; the former are very likely to be distorted by both the racism of Western thinking and the ethnocentricism inherent in its analyses. Furthermore, all non-Western cultures suffer from the effects of the destruction caused by Western imperialism expressed, in its extreme forms, as genocide, slavery and colonialism but, in lesser forms, as the suppression of languages and religions, and the invalidation as inferior of many aspects of (non-Western) cultures.

Western observation of other cultures as exotic led to the definition of 'culture-bound' syndromes. Although the term may be useful to describe forms of behaviour identified by a society as deviant *and* inexplicable and/or incomprehensible without an in-depth knowledge of its culture, it is important to stress that all 'psychiatric illness' is patterned by culture and to note that racism may be implicit when a disease is designated as 'culture-bound'.

In studying cross-cultural differences in the worldviews that underlie concepts of health and illness, some writers have focused on narrow areas of study, such as the concept of the self or the attribution of illness to supernatural causation. But the examination of 'individual' concepts in this way is misleading, primarily because they are defined and analysed in Western terms. It is the total worldview that must be the background and meaning against which questions of mental health and mental illness are considered. However much they are rooted in ancient history and traditional ways of thought, current worldviews in all non-Western cultures are strongly influenced by their recent historical experiences – in particular the attacks on them and their people by Western military might – and by racism. The struggle for freedom from Western domination has left an indelible mark on life in the non-Western world and continues to fashion the worldviews of African, Asian and Native American peoples the world over.

The concept of mind and body being distinctly separate entities is inherent in Western thinking but not evident in other cultures. The West has delineated 'mental illness' as some 'thing' separate from the person suffering it – a way of thinking about 'madness' and misfortune that is probably alien to all non-Western cultures. But, because of the political and economic domination of the West with its racist tradition and the prestige of 'scientific' thinking, Western modes of thought are considered to be superior to those of other cultures – especially those derived from 'black' or 'Third World' countries.

A reliable and unbiased body of information about African culture is not available for historical and political reasons. However, the continuity of culture between Egypt and the rest of Africa has been established and this 'cultural continuity' now includes the 'African diaspora' across the Atlantic. The vitality of religious feelings and the importance given to family and ancestors in African culture comes through as significant (Mbiti, 1969). In African cultures, the spiritual world is varied and complex, being inhabited by spirits of people who died, people who are alive and those about to be born, animals, plants and objects without biological life. The spiritual and physical worlds are not separate entities and mind and body do not exist apart from each other.

The traditions of India, China and Western Asia may be classed together as 'Eastern' or 'Asian'. Unlike those of Africa and America, the basics of Asian cultural patterns are well documented. Ideas of the impermanence of any single life, the unity of mind and body, the ceaseless change and interdependence of all phenomena, and the relative nature of all things physical and spiritual pervade Asian culture.

Cultures native to America, which were all but destroyed by Europeans grabbing wealth and land for the extension of Europe into the 'New World', are recently showing some degree of a revival. A 'refined awareness of the environment' (Capra, 1982), a unique sense of individuality and a strong community identity (Highwater, 1981) characterise the cultures that once thrived in America.

The expression of emotion and the diversity in ways of coping with stress across cultures cannot be adequately dealt with by listing behaviour patterns peculiar to each culture. Questions of rapport and communication are involved in idioms of distress and so they are unlikely to be static, especially in a multicultural society. The concept of coping may be seen in purely behavioural terns or, much more widely, as referring to all attempts to deal with problems at various levels. Coping strategies may be mistaken for 'symptoms' or a reflection of psychopathology at a deeper level, through ignorance of their cultural contexts, the inherent confusion within psychiatry between coping and symptoms, and racist attitudes that invalidate the authenticity of some forms of behaviour or thinking because they are designated as 'primitive'.

3

Culture of Psychiatry

The 'culture' of an institution or professional group refers to the ethos or ways of functioning of that system or group in a particular context (Chapter 1). Many of the basic questions that arise today about the validity and relevance of psychiatry concern the belief systems implicit within it, its ethos, its philosophy and its stance on race. In other words, the questions are about its *culture*. In considering this topic, the context in which psychiatry developed is crucial – referred to in Chapter 2 as (broadly speaking) Western culture.

Western culture derives from Greek roots and many of the ideas in psychiatry of today – and hence Western concepts of mental health – can be traced back to Greek roots (Simon, 1978). Methods of dealing with deviancy evident today were foreshadowed in Greece when, for example, Plato (427–348 BC) proposed in his Laws that atheists, whose lack of faith seemed to arise from ignorance rather than malice, should be placed for five years in a *sophronisterion* ('house of sanity'). The roots of Freudian theories, too, may be seen in ancient thinking. Plato talked of unconscious motivation and the interpretation of dreams, and defined the soul as a part of the brain. In his book *The Republic*, Plato divided the mind into three parts likened to three different kinds of men: the lover of wisdom (*philosophus*) corresponding to the rational, the lover of victory (*philonikos*) to the spirited-affective, and the lover of gain (*philokerdes*) to the appetitive. These ideas led to the concept of mind as being composed of 'higher' and 'lower' parts, the former being 'rational', 'intellectual' and 'aware', the latter being concerned with appetites of the body, somatic sensations and dreaming. Socrates (469–399 BC) saw knowledge as dormant in the soul and talked of unconscious processes. Hippocrates (400 BC) described mania, melancholia and 'phrenitis' (causing mental confusion) with accounts that stand up well when compared to descriptions of diseases recogniscd by prcsent-day psychiatry. It is the Hippocratic tradition that continues as the basis of the present system of Western medicine permeating psychiatry, although Hippocratic explanations for diseases, based on humoral theories that quote an imbalance of forces, have been replaced by aetiological models that attempt to find specific causes for specific diseases.

Psychiatry did not develop in isolation from its social environment – far from it; social and political norms of European society in the nineteenth century strongly influenced the subject from its very beginnings (Castel, 1985). And, since psychiatry developed at a time when racist doctrines were becoming established in Western culture, the ideology of racism became incorporated into the discipline and its ways of working. Furthermore, while psychiatry was attempting to become 'scientific', racism, too, took on a 'pseudo-scientific' guise in the nineteenth century. According to Fryer (1984), 'the pivotal book' in the turn to 'pseudo-scientific racism' in Western culture was *History of Jamaica* in which Long (1774) used the social system of the West Indian plantocracy as a model for a racist ideology for the 'home country' (England), justifying the degradation of blacks by claiming that they were morally and mentally inferior to whites. And Long's arguments were reinforced by reports from biological studies and the writings of anthropologists in Europe and the United States. As European power expanded to dominate Asia, Africa and America, this domination itself reinforced the myth of white superiority – an ethos that still pervades all aspects of European culture and influences thinking in the sciences, medicine and psychiatry.

This chapter will review the history of psychiatry including its racist traditions and then examine some aspects of its diagnostic process. The clash between its philosophical basis and that of non-Western cultures will be analysed by describing some cultural differences in medical systems, approaches to mind and body, and the questionable capacity of psychiatry to understand the 'whole' person.

History

Ideas and methods present in contemporary psychiatry may mirror Greek counterparts (Simon, 1978). But modern European psychiatry, with its hallmarks of an adherence to a biomedical model of illness, the study of the mind as distinct from the body, and the claim to distinguish 'mad' from 'bad', does not derive from the thinking of ancient Greece – at least not directly. The Arabic Empire that stretched from Persia to Spain had, by the eighth century, established a medical tradition that included a type of 'psychiatry'; a standard textbook of medicine by Avicenna, a Persian poet, philosopher and physician, included mental diseases in a chapter on head diseases (Ellenberger, 1974). However, little remains of the medical learning documented in Arabic literature. Zilborg (1941) notes that the medical study of human behaviour emerged (again) in the late sixteenth century when the word *psychologia* began to be used; he states that in 1590 Rudolf Goeckel published his *Psychologia – Hoc Est de Hominis Perfectione* translated as 'Psychology, or the Improvement of Man'. But even earlier, in 1586, *A Treatise of Melancholy* by Timothy Bright had been published in England and, in 1621, Robert Burton's *The Anatomy of Melancholy* was available. Medical psychology or psychological medicine, later called 'psychiatry', developed in West European culture through two movements in thinking that arose after the Renaissance (Bynum, 1981): first, certain behavioural patterns and kinds of mental states were attributed to disease meriting medical interest, rather than to such postulates as possession by demons, a state of sin, or wilful criminality; and secondly there appeared the idea of the mind as an expression of brain activity and the concept of 'mental physiology'.

Ellenberger (1974) states that a medical–institutional approach to the management of 'madness' had occurred in the Islamic Empire and that many mental hospitals, called *moristans*, were established during the thirteenth and fourteenth centuries, including an asylum for the insane in Granada (Spain) founded in the mid-fourteenth century; but very little is known about the way these Islamic mental institutions functioned. The asylums that were founded in Europe during the fifteenth century, including a series in Spain based on the Arabic *moristans*, were largely under religious (Christian), rather than medical, jurisdiction. However, it was in the early nineteenth century that the asylum movement really took off. Scull (1979) argues that 'the advent of a mature capitalistic market economy' resulted in a segregative response to madness leading to the building of large asylums in Britain; and similar movements occurred all over Europe and North America. The building of asylums for lunatics separated off the insane from the wider category of troublesome people and 'insanity was transformed from a vague, culturally defined phenomenon . . . into a condition which could only be authoritatively diagnosed, certified and dealt with by a group of legally recognised experts'; psychiatry was given a base in society and psychiatrists given considerable power over their charges.

Medical psychiatrists, faced with being in charge of asylums housing large numbers of people designated as mad as well as 'ill', were impelled to organise their work and make sense in medical terms of the diverse types of people in their asylums. They developed systems of diagnosis, drawing on whatever information they could get hold of including classical descriptions of illness by Hippocrates (Zilborg, 1941). Each institution tended to develop its own classification. The first English textbook on psychiatry – *A Manual of Psychological Medicine* by John Bucknill and Daniel Hack Tuke – appeared in 1858. In 1885, the Congress of Mental Medicine in Antwerp appointed a committee to develop a uniform classification but without much success in having it accepted generally. Then, in the 1890s, Kraepelin (in Germany) described dementia praecox and manic depression in the sixth edition of his book *Psychiatrie: Lehrbuch fur Studirende und Artze* (Kraepelin, 1899). The former, which was renamed 'schizophrenia' in 1911 by Bleuler (1950), was underpinned by the concept of degeneration popularised by Morel (1852) – a matter described in some detail elsewhere (Fernando *et al.*, 1998). In the 1890s, Janet and Charcot in France popularised 'hysteria' as an illness and in the 1920s, Freud developed the notion of hysteria as linked with anxiety. The concept of melancholia developed into that of depression after Meyer (1905) spoke against the use of the older term; depression was given a new impetus by Freud (1917) when he linked it to guilt, and the diagnosis of depression has soared in popularity ever since the 1950s when antidepressant medication was introduced.

Psychiatry in the United States developed in tandem with its European counterpart but was less hospital centred than it was in Europe, especially England, until the Second World War (Lewis, 1974). The first institution to care for the 'mentally ill' was a hospital, Pennsylvania Hospital in Philadelphia, which started to admit mentally disordered patients in 1752 and kept them in cells in different parts of the hospital. One of the first asylums, i.e. institutions specifically for the mentally disordered, was the Bloomingdale Asylum in New York City that opened in 1821, although this, too, was linked to the New York Hospital. In the early part of the twentieth century, Southard 'developed the psychopathic hospital idea and also brought into the foreground the training of social workers in psychiatry' (Lewis, 1974). The influence of Freud was more strongly felt in psychiatric circles in the United States than it was in Europe, thus promoting the development of psychotherapy in that country and a psychoanalytic approach in psychiatric practice generally.

The medical viewpoint with a one-illness-one-cause approach dominated psychiatry in Europe until the Second World War, since when there has been a slight swing to empiricism – defining each illness in terms of observed phenomena – and away from looking for a single cause into the concept of multifactorial aetiology. In the 1950s, a tendency to think of illness and normality on a continuum model appeared; for example, Eysenck (1952) advocated that disorders should be classified on the basis of points on three dimensions, psychoticism, neuroticism and extraversion–introversion. Psychiatrists holding on to the concept of specific disorders (all-or-nothing approach) then found in-between diagnoses, like 'schizo-affective disorders' and 'borderline syndromes', appearing in their vocabulary. Attempts to preserve the one-diagnosis model when illnesses are not clear-cut have given rise to a hierarchy of 'importance' in classification. Thus, for example, organic disorders, schizophrenia, manic depression, neurotic depression and anxiety states form a hierarchy in which the diagnosis higher up on the list takes precedence over the ones lower down. Psychiatry in the United States was strongly influenced by psychoanalytic theory, but since the 1980s there has been a swing to a more organic approach and diagnoses based on definable phenomena. The present situation is one of some confusion; the latest attempts to bring about uniformity in diagnosis are the classification systems called *ICD-10* (World Health Organisation, 1993) and *DSM-IV* (American Psychiatric Association, 1994). The former maintains the traditional views of psychiatry while the latter tries to limit the wide diagnosis of schizophrenia in the United States and open the way to multiple diagnoses instead of a hierarchy.

Although the asylums established in the nineteenth century were mainly for custodial care, 'treatment' had to be given since the inmates were deemed 'ill'. As with diagnosis, there was little to go on. Concepts of morality vied with those of active illness, usually on the model applied to infectious diseases. Both moral treatment and physical treatment went hand in hand, but the former 'threatened the status and very existence of physicians within asylums: if cures could be affected by nonmedical means, then the administrators of physic were reduced to mere custodians of the insane' (Cooter,

1981). For a time, in England, phrenology was allied to moral therapy, thereby elevating the latter to a scientific status (ibid.). But, as
some agreement on the classification of mental illness began to
emerge among European psychiatrists and organicity (in psychiatry)
was supported by the discovery of organic pathologies for the diseases
'general paralysis of the insane', 'senile psychosis' and 'alcoholic
polyneuritis' (Mora, 1961), moral therapy dropped away as a 'medical'
approach began to dominate the scene towards the end of the nineteenth century. Mental illnesses were delineated and formulated,
the discipline of psychiatry gathered strength and status as a medical
specialty, and psychiatry followed other medical specialties in looking for causes of illnesses. By the turn of the century, psychiatry was
fully accepted as a medical discipline and its medical orientation has
persisted until the present day.

The power of psychiatry as a social force in Western society
developed rapidly in the nineteenth century in spite of rivalries
between various groups of practitioners (Busfield, 1986). And by
the end of nineteenth century, psychiatry was well established as an
integral part of Western culture. In England, the Association of
Medical Officers of Asylums and Hospitals for the Insane was established in 1841, although even earlier, in 1811, the first chair of psychological medicine was established in Leipzig, Germany (Hunter
and MacAlpine, 1963). The American Psychiatric Association – originally called the Association of Medical Superintendents of American
Institutions for the Insane – was established in 1844 (Mora, 1961).
As the power and status of psychiatry were recognised, its practitioners were given legal functions with power attached and psychiatry
became an important part of the structure of Western society. By
the end of the nineteenth century, psychiatrists were the custodians
of those people that society excluded from its mainstream as well as
the 'alienists' who decided who was acceptable and who was alien to
society. But the status of the psychiatric profession was, from the
start, closely connected with the acceptance of psychiatry as a 'medical
science'. Psychiatry is now seen by society as having the final word
on the presence or absence of mental illness, but more importantly,
society still looks to psychiatrists to carry out their traditional 'alienist' function by diagnosing not just 'illness' but forms of behaviour –
and the potential for behaviour – that are unacceptable to society.
Thus psychiatrists are seen as 'experts' in the prediction of dangerous
behaviour, although the validity of doing so is questionable (Steadman, 1983; Estroff and Zimmer, 1994).

The myths and realities of race are described in Chapter 1; the ways in which racism was incorporated into psychology and psychiatry are considered in Chapter 4. The point that needs making here is that racism has been a central feature of psychiatric thinking from its very beginning and continues to permeate current psychiatric theory and practice. The arguments in the mid-nineteenth century that slavery was conducive to the maintenance of the mental health of black Americans, Carl Jung's theory in the early part of the twentieth that perceived white people as being adversely affected psychologically by living in close proximity to blacks, and the claim made in the 1950s by J. C. Carothers that the brain of a black person resembled that of a 'leucotomised' white person, are but examples of explicit racism that prevailed in psychiatric circles in the past. Although more recent psychiatric literature is not so obviously racist, the racist tradition of psychiatry continues in current writings – for example that of Leff. (The writings of Jung, Carothers and Leff are discussed in Chapter 4.) Furthermore, the World Health Organisation spreads Western concepts of mental illness through studies like the International Pilot Study of Schizophrenia (IPSS), thereby undermining indigenous means of conserving mental health in Asian and African societies, because the superiority of Western ways of thought over those of other traditions is assumed on a racist rather than rational basis. (The IPSS is described in Chapter 5.) In analysing the commercial interests that shape scientific power, Robert Young (1987) notes that the London School of Hygiene and Tropical Medicine has set the pattern of health systems and practices throughout the Third World and that the Tavistock Institute of Human Relations has played a leading part in the use of psychodynamic ideas in industry. In both these cases, racist assumptions are accepted without any thought at all; the very existence of worldviews different from those that underlie the organisation of health systems in the West and of psychological theories developed in nineteenth-century Europe are ignored, not because they are not known, but because they are seen as inferior to those developed by white people.

Psychiatry maintains its status today as a medical specialty by claiming to use scientific methods of study and research, objective techniques of observation and assessment of patients, and an open mind about its information base. Its influence in Western societies and other Western social systems stems from its recognition as a 'medical science'. However, the history of psychiatry, summarised

above, shows the discipline to have developed as a social entity
within a particular cultural tradition imbued with the racism characteristic of that tradition.

Diagnosis

The diagnosis of a psychiatric illness represents the analysis by a
practitioner of the problems presented by a 'patient' – but one that
conforms to a particular style and theoretical framework, the 'medical model'. The practical importance of diagnosis for evaluating
emotional disturbance arises from the practitioner's need to be
sufficiently informed in order to prescribe treatment – for it is
assumed, in a medical model, that treatment is geared to diagnosis.
The development, in the 1950s, of powerful drugs affecting behaviour and thinking of human beings led to an increasing popularity of
psychopharmacology and a shift towards a biological approach in
psychiatry. The availability of these (seemingly) specific treatments
resulted in an apparent need for consensus in diagnosis and the
need to demarcate diseases firmly from each other. In attempting to
be 'objective' and 'reliable', psychiatry has turned increasingly to
diagnoses based on the 'descriptive approach' (Tischler, 1987). This
involves the description of people, seen as patients, in terms of
'symptoms' complained of by the 'patient' and 'signs' deduced from
'observed' phenomena which, in turn, are deduced from the so-called
'mental state examination'. In reality, signs and symptoms tend to
overlap and interrelate and a sharp distinction between them does
not exist. But the deductions made via the mental state examination
are structured in terms of ideas about mental functioning present in
Western culture. The 'mind' in psychiatric thinking is a combination
of intellect, thinking, feeling and emotion, with a firm distinction
between cognition (intellect and thinking) and affect (emotion and
feeling). And mental functioning is related to these different 'parts'
of the mind, rather than the person as a whole. The effect of psychiatric treatment is measured and analysed in terms of changes in symptoms or signs, i.e. what the patient complains of or the practitioner
observes – or thinks (s)he observes.

The status of psychiatry as a scientific medical specialty is dependent on its strict adherence to a diagnostic classification based on a
system of 'examination' of the 'mind' and the use of specific forms of

treatment. Signs and symptoms deduced from an interview are assumed to be analogous to physical signs and symptoms obtained by examination of the body; and mental disorders are assumed to be equivalent to disorders of the heart, the lungs or the nervous system. However, this is far from being the case. First, 'findings' in the 'mental state examination' are not valid objective observations but are inferences deduced from behaviour, including speech, during a psychiatric interview. Such an interview is essentially an encounter between two or more people and hence affected by all the tensions, etc. that may exist between the participants; the observations that one person makes about the other is likely to reflect these tensions as well as the attitudes and beliefs of the 'observer'. Secondly, the inferences deduced by the observer are obtained and fashioned by a structure that represents Western thinking about the meanings given to various aspects of the 'person', matters concerning 'illness' and the concept of 'health'. As Fabrega (1989) points out, this structure is well illustrated in an interview schedule that is popular in Anglo-American psychiatry – the present state examination (Wing *et al.*, 1974), commonly known as the PSE. The line of questioning in the PSE pursues key ideas that are important in Western thinking concerned with (say) 'physical health', 'relaxing', 'anxiety', 'control over thinking' and 'feeling depressed'; the detection of so-called symptoms, such as 'thought broadcasting', 'thought insertion' and 'delusions', implies assumptions about beliefs as 'mental' attributes of the self, forces that operate or do not operate in the world, and 'matters involving the control of human action and worldly happenings that are obviously conditioned by European culture and society'.

Just as psychiatry has developed as a historical process, so have its systems of classification and treatment. Ideas and observations from the basic sciences have influenced psychiatry and scientific methods have been used in investigating and analysing the concepts derived, but the process is essentially one that has grown in a particular social, cultural and political climate. And this climate has influenced, and continues to influence, psychiatry. The nosology of psychiatry is permeated by ideologies prevalent in Western society, and most importantly, psychiatry is based on philosophical concepts, such as materialism and the separation of mind and body, that are present in Western culture. Thus, in considering diagnosis, two facts should be borne in mind: first, psychiatry is ethnocentric and carries in it the ideologies of Western culture including racism; secondly, the practice of psychiatry, including its ways of diagnosing, are influ-

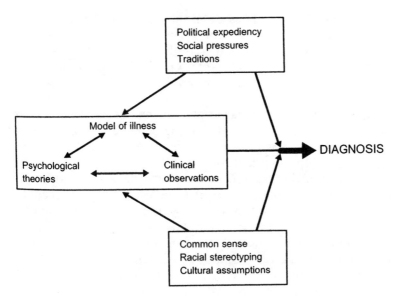

Figure 3.1 Context of diagnosis

enced by the social ethos and the political system in which it lives
and works (Figure 3.1).

Variations in the incidence of diagnosed illness may have a lot to
do with social influences – for example cultural differences (Chapter 2) and racism (Chapter 4) – on the construction of illness. The
main features of psychiatric practice that have questionable usefulness in a global context and across cultural and racial divides include
the conceptualisation of diagnosis in a medical model of (mainly)
biological illness based on the identification of symptoms as objective facts located in individual pathology; the need to justify ways of
helping people as forms of medical treatment; the claim for auton-
omy of 'clinical judgement' as a particular skill in estimating many
forms of human behaviour; the involvement of psychiatry in social
control. However, against this, it is necessary to point to certain traditions in medicine that have rubbed off on to psychiatrists – at least
in the West. The humanitarian tradition of medicine was probably
instrumental in bringing about improvements in the living conditions of 'lunatics' admitted to asylums; and it was the designation of
madness as an illness coupled with the medical tradition to study
'illness' that resulted in serious attempts being made to seek means

of alleviating the problems of the insane. Since medical illness absolves the individual afflicted by 'illness' of responsibility – or partial responsibility – from his/her actions, the intervention of psychiatry has protected countless numbers of people from suffering punishment that may have done no good to anyone (although the 'psychiatrisation' of social behaviour may do more harm than good in the long term). Most importantly, the medical tradition behoves physicians to consider the interests of their patients once disease is diagnosed; and the intervention of psychiatrists has often been crucial in ensuring support for people in trouble of various kinds.

In estimating the social role of psychiatry in Western society and in weighing up its overall effect, it is important to ensure that both positive and negative effects of its practices are respected and that both sides of the balance are used without bias. However, when psychiatry is practised in settings that are alien to the culture in which it has developed and with people who may be disadvantaged by the prejudices inherent in Western culture, a simple balance is insufficient. The culture of psychiatry itself must be analysed first for bias. Then the effect of this bias in its practice must be faced.

Medical belief systems

Cultural differences in medical belief systems (i.e. ideas about illness) can be examined in different ways. It is inevitable that by this very analysis (using concepts based on Western culture), the significance of non-Western ways of conceptualising illness may be missed. In analysing the concept of illness cross-culturally, Kleinman (1978) distinguishes 'disease' from 'illness', the former denoting 'a malfunctioning in, or adaptation of, biological and/or psychological processes' and the latter the '*experience* of disease'. But, as Obeyesekere (1985) argues, cultural meaning or symbolisation being intrinsic to its very nature, 'the *conception* of the disease (i.e. illness) is the disease' (italics in origin) in the case of 'mental illness'. Although Kleinman's illness–disease differentiation is not of much practical help, his emphasis on the importance of culturally determined explanatory models of illness/disease is helpful in a situation where psychiatry is applied in non-Western cultural settings. From a Western standpoint, Western models are generally seen as 'scientific' and others as 'magical'; but as Lewis (1986) notes, 'there is fundamentally a similarity in that both views, ours and theirs, search for some ordering or reason in events'. Another common viewpoint is to see Western explanatory models as being 'natural' and others as largely 'supernatural' in approach. But what is natural or supernatural is determined by the worldview of the culture anyway and is not based on absolute culture-free values. Most cultures blend the natural and the supernatural in determining explanatory models of illness.

Young (1986) distinguishes aetiological explanatory models of illness based on 'externalising' systems of belief from those based on 'internalising' systems, while admitting that 'most belief systems employ both kinds of explanation'. Some internalising systems may use a model of illness as a disturbance: (a) of natural equilibrium, such as the hot–cold balance; (b) of a dynamic relation between parts – in the traditions of European and Chinese medicine; or (c) of internal equilibria that reflect cosmic ones – as in Indian and Taoist tradition – or biochemical –organic equilibria, as in Western medicine. Other internalising systems are models of reduced wholeness of an individual, such as 'soul-loss' in Spanish America, diminished 'life-force' in Africa, and biochemical deficiencies in scientific medicine. Externalising systems perceive pathogenic agencies that are purposive and/or causative and concentrate on discovering what person(s)/event(s) could have brought the sick person to the attention of the pathogenic agency and on identifying the responsible category of pathogen, or even the responsible individual agent. The causes of illness in this model include grudges repaid by witchcraft, ritual lapses punished by ancestral spirits and genetically determined vulnerability. Young's internal–external dichotomy is based on the individual as the reference point in line with the Western biomedical concept of illness; if the starting point is different – for example, if the cultural emphasis is on a social, rather than bio-logical, aetiology for illness as in the African worldview – the division into externalising and internalising belief systems is an inadequate model for analysing aetiological explanatory models of illness.

While particular definitions of illness may vary widely, concern with illness as an area of problematic human experience is universal (White, 1982). And systems of dealing with illness may be referred to as medical systems. At a micro level, they may be seen in terms of health beliefs and practices, explanatory models of illness, roles and status of practitioners, etc. or, at a macro level, as relating to socio-economic conditions, political systems, power relationships between and within organisations, allocation of resources, etc. (Janzen, 1978). Cultural differences and racial discrimination would apply at both levels in somewhat different ways. For example, the value attached to one type of belief or practice in a multicultural and racist society is often determined by its supposed racial connection rather than its cultural relevance or importance; this applies to family and marriage patterns as well as to illness presentations. Thus, the family life of black people in Britain and the United States is often seen as aberrant in terms of sexual behaviour, religion, music styles and eating habits (Brittan and Maynard, 1984). Indigenous beliefs in industrially underdeveloped countries are considered as inferior to those derived from Western sources, irrespective of their usefulness in a particular situation, or of their efficacy in a particular healing model. For example, although it has been shown that a belief in a supernatural cause for 'madness' in Sri Lanka may lessen the negative effects of labelling inherent in the Western view of schizophrenia as a disease (Waxler, 1979), it is the Western view that is usually given credence. At a macro level, racial judgements affect the status of one particular system of medical care in competing with another for resource allocation. The general assumption is that 'scientific' systems are better than 'traditional' ones – and 'scientific' approaches are assumed to come from Western (white) sources. Although the definition of health by the World Health Organisation (WHO) as 'complete physical mental and social wellbeing' is clearly a political statement (Elling, 1978) with implications for a worldwide, non-partisan, cross-cultural approach, the resources of the WHO are allocated to researching mental illness based on an understanding derived from Western philosophy and culture alone. The International Pilot Study of Schizophrenia (IPSS) is a prime example of this; although the definition of the 'illness' schizophrenia used in the IPSS is culture-bound in its derivation within Western culture, it is imposed across the globe by seeing non-Western culture as a sort of contaminant that has to be excluded. This is a matter of racist arrogance resulting in cultural blindness.

Medical systems reflect the culture of the society in which they function. According to McQueen (1978), the healing doctrines underlying current Western medical systems of (European) North America, including 'fringe systems' such as homoeopathy, tend to focus on the individual (as opposed to the society as a whole) and to be concerned with acute care (of crises) rather than longer-term benefit. This applies to European culture generally. But more importantly in the case of mental illness, deviance of the individual from what is seen as the norm of society is designated as 'abnormal' because it is considered dysfunctional for society. And assumptions about 'norms' are influenced by social forces and ideologies, including racism. Healing of mental illness is generally seen in Western culture as a matter of correcting a biological–chemical–physical machine. If a technique from a different culture, such as yoga or meditation, is imported into a Western setting, it may be redefined (i.e. 'adapted') to suit Western ideas of therapy. Alternatively, such a system may fulfil a role as an 'exotic' system that appeals to a small section of the society in the way that some Eastern religions thrive in the West. Similarly, Western techniques may be reinterpreted when they are transported into a non-Western society. These ideas are pursued further in Chapter 7.

Holism, mind and body

Psychology is built upon foundations that incorporate Western ideas about the nature of human beings and their minds. Psychiatry, too, has this same base but also incorporates Western concepts of illness and health. The major difference between Western and older non-Western cultures in their constructions of health in relation to psychology and religion is the emphasis in the latter on a holistic perspective of health. Psychologists, following Descartes, adopted the strict division between *res cogitans* and *res extensa*. Descartes himself suggested that the soul or mind should be studied by introspection and the body by methods of natural science. But clinical psychology in the West developed differently (Capra, 1982): 'The structuralists studied the mind through introspection and tried to analyze consciousness into its basic elements, while behaviourists concentrated exclusively on the study of behaviour and so were led to ignore or deny the existence of mind altogether.' And both 'modelled themselves after classical physics, incorporating the basic concepts of Newtonian mechanics into their theoretical frameworks'. The result is that there is 'confusion [in Western thought] about the role and nature of mind, as distinct from that of brain'. The mind is seen as either a mere function of the brain or, in keeping with the concept of the 'dignity' and individuality of the human being, as an entity independent of the brain but, in some way, related to it. This section considers the meaning of 'holism' and then discusses the mind–body dichotomy which is a fundamental tenet of psychiatry and psychology.

Holism is a term that is used rather loosely at times. The word itself is derived from the Greek *holos* meaning 'whole'; in applying it to the Western medical field, it may be seen as an approach that incorporates the interrelationships between all aspects of bodily functions and mental functions in a sort of multifaceted approach to the human being. Lazlo (1972) identifies two kinds of holism: in a narrow sense, a holistic approach sees the human organism as a living system whose components are interconnected and inter-dependent, while, in a broad sense, 'the holistic view recognises that this system, the human organism, is an integral part of larger systems'; the latter implies that, not only is the individual organism in con-tinual interaction with its physical and social environment and being constantly affected by the environment, but also that it is constantly acting upon the environment and modifying it. But a very different way of applying the concept of 'holism' is totally to avoid recognising the division of the person into different parts in the first place; not to recognise the separation of mind from body or the separation of person from the universe in which (s)he lives. If there is no separation into parts, there is no need to define any connection or interaction between parts. This latter type of holistic approach would see a total functioning person (if used in a narrow sense) or a total functioning entity including a person in his/her environment (if used in a broad sense). The emphasis then is on integrated wholeness where units such as body, mind and environment are seen as semantically convenient but misleading concepts which prevent a true understanding of reality.

Thus holism – or rather the lack of it – may be seen at various levels by looking at the world in terms of divisions on various para-meters. In the field of Western medicine, the division is first into body and mind; then into fragments of the body or mind, depending on objective findings, in the case of the former, and theoretical models, in the case of the latter. The biomedical concept of illness is based on 'the notion of the body as a machine, of disease as the con-sequence of breakdown of the machine, and of the doctors' task as repair of the machine' (Engel, 1977). The approach that is used to understand the working of the body takes the form of concentrating on smaller and smaller parts of the body, i.e. different organs and parts of organs, and identifying functions of each part in greater and greater detail. For example, the brain, heart and liver are studied as separate organs and then particular functions of each of these organs are studied in relative isolation from each other. The aim is to relate the different organs to each other both anatomically (in terms of structure) and physiologically (in terms of function), in order to construct an understanding of the whole person as a combination of its parts. This reductionist method has paid off in terms of the development of knowledge about the workings of the body and the sort of interventions that can correct individual faults in individual organs. But this approach has resulted in medical knowledge losing sight of the whole body functioning as one entity apart from, or in addition to, functioning as a combination of its parts; in other words, it has lost sight of holism in the study of the body, and therefore it is unable to investigate processes that are dependent on the body functioning as a *whole*. Thus the process underlying the healing of wounds is little understood in spite of enormous developments in the understanding of the specific pathology of particular organs; more obviously, the concept of healing of illness in general cannot be conceptualised in reductionist terms and is therefore outside scientific study. When healing occurs without a reason that is identifiable in a reductionist idiom, it is discounted as 'placebo effect' or 'spontaneous remission' (Capra, 1982).

The limitations inherent in Western medicine through the loss of a holistic viewpoint of the person apply much more strongly to those conditions identified as psychological or mental illness, not least because the concept of 'illness' itself carries added problems for psychological medicine (psychiatry). The reductionist approach that breaks up the 'psyche' into smaller and smaller fragments added to the artificial, but very fundamental, conceptual separation of 'psyche' from 'soma' in Western thinking, has led to a situation where psychiatry often appears to be dealing in practice with artefacts described (in medical terms) as objective phenomena, within a framework of a 'scientific method' that feels – at least at case conferences about real people – like an exercise in semantics. For example, psychiatrists, differentiating 'withdrawal' from 'retardation', both psychiatric 'signs' of possible illness, in one case of schizophrenia and in the other of depression, often seem to be more concerned with completing a crossword puzzle by fitting the various words they use into an acceptable pattern, than in building up a meaningful understanding of a person.

The separation of the mind from the body in medical thinking has given rise to the field of 'psychosomatics' searching for ways of overcoming this problem. Capra (1982) contrasts this situation with that in Eastern systems of thought:

> The rich traditions of Indian philosophy have generated a spectrum of philosophical schools, from extreme materialism to extreme idealism, from absolute monism

through dualism to complete pluralism. Accordingly, these schools have developed numerous and often conflicting theories about human behaviour, the nature of consciousness, and the relation between mind and matter.

He adds to this the spiritual traditions 'grounded in mystical experiences that have led to elaborate and extremely refined models of consciousness that cannot be understood within the Cartesian framework but are in surprising agreement with recent scientific developments'. In Buddhism, 'mind is not conceived to be merely a general reservoir of information or just the brain mechanism, but to be individual moments of knowing, the continuum of which makes up our sense of knowing' (Rinbochay and Napper, 1980). Although mind and body are seen as separate, they are inextricably combined in various ways:

> How does the mind abide in the body? There are many different positions on this. Some say that mind's main place of abiding is the brain, whereas others say that it abides at the heart. Some say that it pervades the entire body; some that it does not abide anywhere but is only generated adventitiously upon the contact of an object and a sense of power. They say that if it did abide in the body, it would have to abide throughout it, and this would entail the fault that if one cut off a hand, one would be cutting off the continuum of the body consciousness.

The worldviews of non-Western cultures are discussed in Chapter 2. It is inevitable, however, that discussions about questions concerning mind and body are influenced by the thinking and framework that underlie the language used – namely, Western conceptualisations. Therefore, it is difficult, if not impossible, to do justice to the thinking in other cultures in a discussion written in a Western idiom.

The mind–body dualism in Western thinking is strongly embedded in its culture. However, recent advances in theoretical physics, having superseded strongly held Newtonian concepts in physics, may eventually permeate into the culture to change Western thinking on mind and body. In analysing the present thinking in the West (about mind and body), Torda (1980) considers three models: first, that of materialistic monism; secondly, that of dualism; and finally, holistic monism. Clearly, the first and second are within the Cartesian framework, but the third is a 'holistic' approach in line with quantum mechanics. Materialistic monism sees the mind as a 'wired-in-information propensity of the brain (a machine)'. This model is widely supported (with variations) by pure scientists in psychology, neurology and the neurosciences. According to the dualists, the mind is an independent entity 'with properties that elude all our empirical constraints'. The mind is seen as using the brain to execute its functions (Popper and Eccles, 1977) but also creating consciousness, thinking and all psychological functions. This is the model that fashions the thinking of clinical psychologists and psychiatrists in their day-to-day work; and it underlies the assumptions of much common sense in Western culture, derived from Cartesian concepts of a mind–body dualism. Holistic monism is based on post-Einstein physics as developed by David Bohm (1980). Torda (1980) writes:

> According to Bohm the universe is an unbroken and undivided totality of spatial energy. The entire universe is formed by one energy structure that is enfolded in each of its parts. Bohm first proved that many-body systems cannot be properly analyzed into independently existing parts. The dynamic relationships of the parts depend in an irreducible way on the state of the whole system. The quantum state of the whole system (implicit order) affects the relationship between any two particles (e.g. the explicit order) within the system. The relative independence of a function is only a special case of general and inseparable dependency. The inseparable quantum interconnectedness of the whole universe is the fundamental reality and the relatively independently behaving parts are merely particular and contingent forms within the whole.

Holistic monism postulates that the human brain can only become aware of the explicate form of the enfolded implicate order. Although mind and consciousness are rooted in the implicit order, 'we become aware of them only in their explicit form'. Human beings perceive the communication systems for which they have tunable receptors. The genetic coding of human DNA predisposes the construction of concepts about the environment that are perceived as external.

It is possible that an awareness of modern physics may have a salutary effect on psychology because of the similarity of its knowledge to mystical traditions. Indeed, the holistic monism derived from advanced Western science seems to be very similar to, if not identical with, the spiritual holism of Eastern philosophy and possibly the thinking that underlies many non-Western cultures. Thus the problems for the understanding of mental health that have arisen from the mind–body dichotomy in Western thinking may be resolved if the insights of modern science are taken on by Western psychology and psychiatry, or, these disciplines come round to accepting the validity and relevance of thinking that does not recognise such a dichotomy by absorbing into their theories and practices the spiritual dimension of human beings.

Fritjof Capra (1982) states: 'The extension of the bio-medical model to the treatment of mental disorders has been, on the whole, very unfortunate. Although the biological approach has been useful for the treatment of some disorders with a clear organic origin, it is quite inappropriate for many others to which psychological models are of fundamental significance.' In clinical psychology, too, the psyche is seen in reductionist terms: cognitions are seen as separate from emotions, motivation from drive, etc.; Freudians talk of the ego and the superego as separate entities and see 'the unconscious' and 'the conscious' as occupying different compartments in the mind. Jungians identify different strata of the mind in the way that anatomists see layers in the brain, although it must be admitted that many of Jung's concepts, drawn from Chinese philosophy, seem to transcend the mechanistic models of traditional psychology. However, most importantly, the interest of psychologists and the parameters of psychological research are to do with the *mind* as distinct from the body (except when the body is seen as interacting with the mind), as if the mind and body exist separately from each other. Although many psychologists do not adhere too closely, if at all, to the medical model of illness, and so do not look for 'symptoms' and 'pathology' in the way that their psychiatric colleagues do, their treatment is aimed at the attainment of 'mental health' on the basis of concepts and norms set up by Western culture. In this culture, 'the criteria used to define mental health – sense of identity, image, recognition of time and space, perception of the environment, and so on – require that a person's perceptions and views be compatible with the Cartesian–Newtonian framework. The Cartesian world view is not merely the principal frame of reference but is regarded as the only accurate description of reality' (Capra, 1982). The norms that are assumed within the conceptual framework are themselves culturally loaded and often racially biased.

The terms used in psychiatry to diagnose illnesses have been realigned over the years and officially updated from time to time: the latest version of the 'international' classification is *ICD-10* (World Health Organisation, 1993) and the current American classification is *DSM-IV* (American Psychiatric Association, 1994). However much these systems may try to adapt to changing needs, they remain inevitably geared to the philosophical basis of Western culture alone and reflect the ethos of Western ideologies. But it must be recognised that the nosology of psychiatry could be opened up to new ideas, although its basic ethos, its philosophical base, is unlikely to change. While psychiatry and its nosology cannot shift fundamentally towards holism in the broad sense of the term, they could be made to adapt at a less fundamental level. Capra (1982) believes it can go the whole way if the thinking in modern science is allowed to take over, for modern science offers a 'holistic and eco-logical conception of the world which sees the universe not as a machine but rather as a living system':

> It would seem that the systems view of living organisms can provide the ideal basis for a new approach to health and health care that is fully consistent with the new paradigm and is rooted in our cultural heritage. The systems view of health is pro-foundly ecological and thus in harmony with the Hippocratic tradition which lies at the roots of Western medicine. It is a view based on scientific notions and expressed in terms of concepts and symbols which are part of our everyday lan-guage. At the same time the new framework naturally takes into account the spir-itual dimension of health and is thus in harmony with the views of many spiritual traditions. (ibid.)

Thus the way forward is seen by Capra as being through the insights of modern science reviving within a Western cultural trad-ition the spiritual dimensions of human existence and holistic ways of thinking lost to Western culture. Other systems of medicine which have maintained the spiritual dimension and not taken over biomedical models of illness may not need to follow the same path. Non-Western systems, by being unhampered by an underlying philosophy that sees a clear separation of mind and body, may be able to develop into truly holistic models for considering mental health if, and when, the pressures to take on Western concepts ease. Although these pressures are economic and political, they are under-pinned by racism derived from the cultural traditions of Western culture.

Conclusions

The majority of patients who suffer from mental health problems throughout the world are treated by so-called folk healers or other indigenous practitioners. These people are 'guided by traditional wisdom that sees illness as a disorder of the whole person, involving not only the patient's body but his mind; his self-image, his depend-ence on the physical and social environment, as well as his relation to the cosmos and the deities' (Capra, 1982). The main difference between these non-Western healers and psychiatrists is that the former do not restrict themselves to thinking in terms of purely physical phenomena, as the biomedical model does. Rituals and ceremonies are used to stimulate the natural healing powers that all living organisms possess but, at the same time, such healing ceremonies usually involve an intense relationship between healer and patient. But the approach to healing in non-Western cultures must be seen in the context of worldviews in those cultures – a subject pursued in Chapter 2. Some of these approaches as well as the approaches inherent in the Asian medical system of Ayurveda are discussed in Chapter 6.

This chapter carries the message that the thinking in psychiatry is at variance with that in other cultures across the world. Having developed from a philosophical basis that sees a clear distinction between mind and body, adhering to a secular principle that rejects the spiritual dimension of human beings, and failing to exclude racist ideologies, the culture of psychiatry prevents it from ever becoming universally useful as a practical proposition. That is unless psychiatry is able to change its culture radically, either by looking to a much wider basis (than just Western traditions) from which to draw and/or (as Capra suggests) by opening itself to the insights of modern science (which may be akin to those of non-Western cultural traditions). Either way, psychiatry would need to give up its outdated model of the individualised person, rewrite its diagnostic systems in line with a holistic understanding that addresses the connectedness between people, the environment and the cosmos, and build up systems within it to counteract its racist traditions. But if such changes occur it may be difficult to recognise the result as 'psychiatry' anyway.

4

Racism in Psychiatry and Psychology

Psychology and psychiatry complement each other, the former as the study of the 'normal' human mind and the latter as a medical specialism concerned with the 'disordered' human mind. Thus both disciplines are concerned with identification of normality and pathology – *psychopathology* – interpreted as 'symptoms' and/or dysfunction in mental processes, recognised on the basis of theoretical conceptions of, and about, the (human) 'mind'. When 'mental health' is identified under the influence of these disciplines it is seen inevitably as dependent on the lack of a significant degree of psychopathology denoting 'mental illness'. Psychology and psychiatry developed within European culture (including its extension across the Atlantic). Thus the ideologies represented in theories of mind and in concepts of illness and health represent worldviews prevalent in European society; and European thinking about race and culture has been naturally incorporated into psychology and psychiatry (see Chapter 1). Psychiatrists and psychologists, like others around them, had very definite ideas on which races were civilised and which were not. A paper published in the mid-nineteenth century, in the *Journal of Mental Science*, by a former physician superintendent of Norfolk County Asylum who was working in Turkey, referred to that land as 'a country which forms the link between civilization and barbarism' (Foote, 1858); in the same journal, another British psychiatrist, Daniel H. Tuke (1858), denoted Eskimos, Chinese, Egyptians and American blacks as 'uncivilised' people, contrasting them with Europeans and American whites referred to as 'civilised' people, but with a grudging reference to China as 'in some respects decidedly civilized'. The description of Africans as 'child-like savages' by Arrah B. Evarts (1913), a physician at the Government Hospital

91

for the Insane in Washington, DC, was typical of American opinion of his time – views that persisted in that country until recently.

The history of racism in psychology and psychiatry is as old as the disciplines themselves. Both disciplines developed together in relation to each other and, from the very start the disciplines took on the then prevalent racist ideologies in European thinking. In the nineteenth century Darwin's theory of evolution was used as a model for theories of psychological and social development: races were held to exist at different stages of development on a bio-logical ladder of human evolution. An important proponent of this phylogenetic concept of race, or 'evolutionary racism', Herbert Spencer saw 'primitive' races as having minds like those of the chil-dren of 'civilized' races (Fryer, 1984) and social practices, such as monogamy, as characteristic of 'higher races' (Thomas and Sillen, 1972). Nineteenth-century anthropologists were strongly influ-enced by this type of thinking (Harris, 1968); and sociologists saw European civilisation associated with white skin as 'the culmina-tion of the evolutionary process' (Fryer, 1984). Francis Galton (1869), a cousin of Charles Darwin and the founder of eugenics, claimed that the 'Negro race' included a large number 'of those whom we should call half-witted' (1869: 339). The main thrust of the pseudo-science of eugenics was to identify 'inferior' races; and eminent people, such as Karl Pearson (1901), saw the extermina-tion of such races as an inevitable part of the evolutionary process. The view that black people had inferior brains and/or defective personalities were commonplace in the nineteenth century and early part of the twentieth; and these ideas were taken by psychia-try and psychology. Although overt racism has been less obvious since the Second World War, racism persists into the present in the common sense of traditional European thinking. Thus in British society today, pairs of words such as 'culture' and 'race', 'primitive' and 'underdeveloped', 'advanced' and 'Western', 'alien' and 'inferior', 'immigrant' and 'black', etc. are often confounded or used purpose-fully to obscure racist contentions. Further, racial images are raised in references to 'muggers', 'inner-city decay', 'alien cultures', etc.

Mind and mental illness

Three distinct views about the mind of non-Western peoples, usually identified in racial terms, were discernible during the development of psychiatry. In the mid-eighteenth century, Rousseau's concept of the 'Noble Savage' proposed the view that 'savages' who lacked the civilising influence of Western culture were free of mental disorder; later, in the late eighteenth and nineteenth centuries, Daniel Tuke (1858) and Maudsley (1867, 1879) in England, Esquirol (cited by Jarvis, 1852) in France and Rush (cited by Rosen, 1968) in the United States voiced similar views, expressed most firmly by J. C. Prichard (1835) in his *Treatise on Insanity*: 'In savage countries, I mean among such tribes as the negroes of Africa and the native Americans, insanity is stated by all . . . to be extremely rare.' But Aubrey Lewis (1965) has pointed out that a second, somewhat different, stance was also evident in Europe about that time, namely, the view that non-Europeans were mentally degenerate because they lacked Western culture. A third viewpoint was voiced in the United States by psychiatrists arguing for the retention of slavery: epidemiological studies based on the Sixth US Census of 1840 (Anon, 1851) were used to justify a claim that the black person was relatively free of madness in a state of slavery, 'but becomes prey to mental disturbance when he is set free' (Thomas and Sillen, 1972). The underlying supposition was that inherent mental inferiority of the African justified slavery. However, Benjamin Rush, the father of American psychiatry, refuted such arguments and maintained that the mental capacity of black people could not be evaluated while they were slaves because of the effect on the mind of the condition of slavery (Plummer, 1970).

Although the 'Noble Savage' viewpoint idealised non-European culture in some ways and the 'degenerate primitive' attitude vilified it, both approaches sprang from the same source – a racist perception of culture which supposed that European culture alone, associated with white races, was 'civilised'; the culture of black people being 'primitive', rendered them either free of mental disorder or inherently degenerate. American views determined by a warped perception of the lives of black Americans – or more correctly, determined by a need to justify slavery – had no room for cultural considerations at all; in fact an assumption that black Americans lacked a culture was implicit in the way these ideas developed. Almost into the twentieth century, Babcock (1895), a psychiatrist from South Carolina, was to use pro-slavery arguments to develop the theme that Africans were inherently incapable of coping with civilised life. In a paper, 'The Colored Insane', Babcock juxtaposed the idea that mental disease was 'almost unknown among savage tribes of Africa' with the alleged observations in the United States on the 'increase of insanity [among African Americans] since emancipation'; he quoted such causes for this increase as the deleterious effect of freedom on 'sluggish and uncultivated brains' and 'the removal [during emancipation] of all healthy restraints', and forecast 'a constant accumulation of [black] lunatics' in the years to come.

The underlying theoretical question that was being addressed in the discussions about 'civilisation' and mental disorder (noted above) was akin to the current discussion about the universality of schizophrenia – reviewed by Richard Warner (1985) and Fuller Torrey (1987). As then, the matter is currently confused by racism. It is less easy to discern the racism inherent in the methodology of studies than it is to appreciate the racist influences in the way they are perceived and interpreted. Most cross-cultural studies in the first 40 years of this century designated or perceived – and reported – non-Western cultures as 'primitive' cultures. Demerath (1942), reviewing a spate of such studies, observed that some of the non-Western societies that had been studied 'were not truly primitive, but on the contrary were either traditionally literate, or had been exposed to Euro-American culture', i.e. suggesting that not *all* non-Europeans were 'primitive' since some had languages of their own or had become civilised by contact with Europeans! An important review by Benedict and Jacks (1954) of studies on Maoris of New Zealand, indigenous Fijians, Hawaiians of the United States and people of so-called 'Negro Africa', was entitled *Mental Illness in Primitive Societies* – a review which, according to Torrey (1973), was largely responsible for the acceptance by mainstream psychiatry of the universality of 'schizophrenia' as an illness.

One of the earliest observations reported by a psychiatrist about mental illness among Asian people was the claim by the German psychiatrist, Kraepelin (1913), that people of Java, now a part of Indonesia, seldom became depressed and that when they were depressed they rarely felt sinful. Kraepelin (1920) perceived the differences in terms of genetic and physical influences rather than cultural ones – a reflection, not only of the biological orientation in German psychiatry at the time, but also of the acceptance of racial explanations for cultural difference. In fact, Kraepelin (1921) saw the Javanese as 'a psychically underdeveloped population' akin to 'immature European youth', and looked to ways of racial–cultural comparison as a method of scientific study. Sashidharan (1986) believes that Kraepelin's notion 'became detached from main-stream psychiatry over the next few decades and gradually reorientated itself around emerging ideas from anthropology and psychoanalysis'. Since both these disciplines also carried racist ideas about culture, the 'transcultural psychiatry' that arose continued a racist tradition. Theories have emerged in modern psychiatry about culturally determined brain function, emotional differentiation, personality defects, family life, etc., all of which harbour racist doctrines (Fernando, 1988).

From the mid-nineteenth century onwards, racist ideas were evident in many scientific theories. For example, in the seminal paper describing the syndrome that became known as 'Mongolism', John Langdon Down (1866) proposed that many so-called idiots and imbeciles were racial throwbacks to 'the great divisions of the human family', namely races. He claimed that physical characteristics of Ethiopian, Malay, American and Mongolian racial types were present among patients in asylums housing 'idiots and imbeciles', and estimated that more than 10 per cent of all patients were 'typical Mongols' – a condition that he postulated as 'an instance of degeneracy arising from tuberculosis in the parents'.

Psychological and intellectual differences

The nineteenth-century anthropological and medical tradition that the brains of black people were inferior to those of white people was supported by dubious research. For example, even as late as early in the twentieth century Robert Bean (1906) claimed that in 103 brains from American Negroes and 49 white Americans he found that: '[The] Negro is more objective and the Caucasian more subjective. The Negro has lower mental faculties (smell, sight, handcraftmanship, body-sense, melody) well developed, the Caucasian the higher (self-control, will-power, ethical and aesthetic senses and reason)' (1906: 412). Significantly, reports that did not support the ethos of white superiority, such as the report that brains of Eskimos were larger than those of the average white person (Connolly, 1950), were ignored.

A racist ideology was evident very early in the development of modern psychology. Nineteenth-century study of facial expression and the emotions attached great importance to blushing as a particularly human characteristic; in his classic *The Expression of the Emotions in Man and Animals*, Charles Darwin (1872) devoted a whole chapter to it. Blushing and conscience were thought to be related; the debate that ensued about the capacity of Negroes to blush was 'not so much a physiological one, as one about moral development' (Skultans, 1979: 63). Francis Galton (1865) claimed that European 'civilised races' alone possessed the 'instinct of continuous steady labour' while non-European 'savages' showed an innate 'wild untameable restlessness' (1865: 157). A classic text on adolescence written by Stanley Hall, the founder of the *American Journal of Psychology*, was published in 1904; in a chapter on 'Adolescent Races' Indians, Africans and North American 'Aborigines' were likened to immature children who 'live a life of feeling, emotion and impulse' (Hall, 1904: 80). The author of a standard textbook on social psychology, McDougall (1921), formulated the concept that different races produced different 'group minds', Nordics showing a propensity for scientific work, Mediterraneans for architecture and oratory and Negroes an 'instinct for submission' (1921: 119).

Carl Jung fancied himself as a specialist on black people since he had actually visited Asia and Africa. Following his travels in India, he observed a 'very characteristic defect in the Indian character', i.e. 'deception' (Jung, 1939a). British psychologist Dalal (1988) sees this theory as 'the Jungian version of "original sin"', in that deception is seen as a 'defect' as well as a 'natural' characteristic of the Indian mind. On visiting the United States, Jung (1930) felt dissatisfied at being unable to 'size them up' – referring to the white population; he could not, at first, understand 'how the Americans descending from European stock have arrived at their striking peculiarities' (1930: 195). He focused on 'the Negro' as the cause. In postulating a psychological danger to white people of living in close proximity to blacks, Jung (1930) deduced the theory of 'racial infection' as 'a very serious mental and moral problem wherever a primitive race outnumbers the white man' (1930: 196):

> Now what is more contagious than to live side by side with a rather primitive people? Go to Africa and see what happens. When the effect is so very obvious that you stumble over it, then you call it 'going black'. . . . The inferior man exercises a tremendous pull upon civilized beings who are forced to live with him, because he fascinates the inferior layers of our psyche, which has lived through untold ages of similar conditions.

Although Jung clearly attributed the 'peculiarities' that he saw in the behaviour of (white) Americans to this 'racial infection', it was not clear from his writings whether the 'infection' spread via socio-psychological influences or through genetic means. But, either way, the infection was seen by Jung as detrimental to white society and white individuals.

Jung's model for the mind of the infant was very similar in many ways to that of 'primitive' humans: both were not conscious of self as opposed to 'other', had no sense of individuality, related to the world as a collective, confused the objective with the subjective and had no will or volition (Dalal, 1988). Jung (1921), quoting an observation that the experience of a 'savage' during a dream was just as real to him as what he saw when he was awake, stated: 'What I have seen of the psychology of the negro completely endorses these findings.' Clearly, Jung identified the modern African as 'primitive' in every sense of the word; according to Dalal (1988), Jung then went on to see all non-Europeans – the (politically) black – in similar terms, as people who cannot separate out as individuals, in whose minds object and subject were not differentiated and whose feelings were concreistic, i.e. 'the antithesis of abstraction' (Jung, 1921). In developing his theories of the mind, Jung saw the mechanism of 'projection' as being different for the 'primitive' when compared to the European. In describing 'primitive projection' of the Buddhist person, Jung (1939b) stated: 'To the oriental, therefore, the world must appear different to the occidental who animates it with his empathy.' In analysing Jung's writings, Dalal (1988) concludes that Jung equated the white unconscious with the black conscious, and then assumed that what he could discern of his own unconscious life represented the symbolism used by black people: 'It is certain that Jung feared the black man. . . . His error was in assuming that because the blacks symbolised the primitive to himself, therefore they were primitive.' Such an explanation for the racism of Jung sees it as an abnormal event due to a personal quirk or psychopathology. A more realistic approach is to accept that racism is inevitable and normal in any theory within a framework of Western thinking – and psychology is very much so – that addresses any aspect of culture or race unless specific efforts are made to exclude racism from it. Jung is one of the very few psychologists who attempted to devise theories incorporating race and culture – and clearly did not recognise the extent to which his thinking was fashioned by racist notions. Freud, on the other hand, did not venture into theorising about race and culture. However, when he did, racist notions were not far from the surface.

Freud (1913) saw similarities between 'the mental lives of savages and [European] neurotics' in his *Totem and Taboo*; and Devereux

(1939), an anthropologist, viewed non-Western healers (generally referred to as 'shamans') as neurotics or psychotics. Freud (1930) envisaged the development of civilisation being dependent on suppressing instinctual behaviour under the guidance of the superego, elaborated into a 'cultural superego'; it was natural for him that the 'leadership of the human species' should be taken up by 'white nations' (Freud, 1915, 1930), and that 'primitives' have a lower form of culture. According to Hodge and Struckmann (1975), Freud's primitives included Melanesian, Polynesian and Malayan peoples, the native people of Australia, indigenous people ('Indians') of North and South America and 'the negro races of Africa'.

The study of intelligence is another field in which racism has a long history. Army data on cognitive test results gathered during the 1914–18 war led to a discussion of the reasons for racial differences in scores on intelligence tests (IQs) done in the United States; a 'racist IQ movement' that envisaged genetic inferiority of blacks in comparison to whites (Thomas and Sillen, 1972) developed, but died down after the horrors perpetrated by the Nazis in the name of race. But Arthur Jensen (1969), professor of educational psychology at the University of California, revived the argument with a paper in the *Harvard Educational Review*. Jensen proposed that differences between blacks and whites on scores on IQ tests were genetically determined. Further, he postulated two categories of mental ability – abstract reasoning ability characteristic of white people and rote learning among blacks. Eysenck (1971, 1973) supported Jensen's views while he was professor of psychology at the Institute of Psychiatry, but other psychologists (Kamin, 1974; Stott, 1983) opposed them as scientifically invalid. The racist tradition in studies of intelligence carried into the 1990s in books such as *The Bell Curve* (Herrnstein and Murray, 1994) and numerous publications by Rushton quoted by Richards (1997).

Post-war psychiatry and psychology

A British colonial psychiatrist who achieved the distinction of producing a monograph for the World Health Organisation (WHO), *The African Mind in Health and Disease*, was J. C. Carothers (1953). His first paper (Carothers, 1947) was an analysis of Africans admitted to a mental hospital in Kenya between 1939 and 1943. He proposed several explanations for the 'peculiarities' he observed: first, he deduced that 'the rarity of insanity in primitive life is due to the absence of problems in the social, sexual and economic spheres', while contending that the 'African may be less heavily loaded with deleterious genes than the European' because 'natural selection might be expected to eliminate the genes concerned more rapidly in a primitive community'. After commenting upon the lack of pressure on Africans because they (allegedly) had no long-term 'aims' in life, he commented on the apparent lack of depression among Africans: 'Perhaps the most striking difference between the European and African cultures is that the former demands self-reliance, personal responsibility, and initiative, whereas there is no place in the latter for such an attitude.' Carothers did suggest that the differences were cultural, because of the 'primitive' nature of African society, rather than intrinsically 'racial', but clearly he had a racist view of African culture as inferior in terms of its influence on mental health.

Four years later, Carothers (1951) took his 'studies' much further. On following up 'a request by the Kenya Director of Laboratory Services for tests of character which would help him to select *reliable* Africans for work in the Laboratory', Carothers apparently noted a 'striking resemblance between African thinking and that of leucotomized Europeans'. After analysing his clinical experience with patients and the experiences of colonial European employers dealing with 'domestic servants, mental hospital attendants, laboratory employees and various other persons', apparently 'without bias and selection' (!), Carothers (1951) concluded:

> The African attitude implies that, apart from certain swift and almost automatic responses and inhibitions, he can do what he likes from moment to moment and feels little need to think of the future or indeed of any other than the immediately presenting aspect of the situation. So he feels free to exercise his most egotistic and emotional impulses (within well defined limits) and such mental organisation as he evinces is imposed from without and not self-developed. He is hardly in fact an individual in our sense of the word, but a series of reactions.

It is hardly surprising that Carothers 'found' what he suspected: 'Except in so far as the African's ritual training mitigates some of the more socially flagrant symptoms (e.g. rudeness and tactlessness), and except that the African shows no lack of verbal ability or of phantasy, the resemblance of the leucotomized European patient to the primitive African is, in many cases, *complete*.'

In his monograph for the World Health Organisation, Carothers (1953) reiterated the racist views propounded earlier and quoted, with approval, claims that the brains of African and American blacks were inferior to those of Europeans. This monograph was presented and widely quoted as an authoritative treatise on the psychology of Africans. It was, in effect, a compendium of racist stereotypes of black people, referring to their (alleged) failure in psychological development after puberty with a 'total absorption ... in the pleasures of sex', impulsiveness of behaviour, inability to sustain personal relationships, lack of 'personal integration' as an adult, etc. Although Carothers referred frequently to 'culture' as the basis of all their (alleged) peculiarities, the discussion and presentation in his treatise, with references to blacks in both Africa and America as equivalent, clearly indicates the racial nature of his assumptions.

Apart from the publications by Carothers, overt expression of racism has been rare in post-war psychiatric and psychological literature. In fact, a contemporary psychiatrist and researcher, Torrey (1973), has referred to Carothers' work as being 'more appropriate as classroom works on racism'. However, there is little doubt that racism continues to manifest itself in the writings of eminent researchers in subtle ways which are no less damaging to black people.

A theory that has been propagated over several years and now even in psychiatric textbooks is concerned with the 'differentiation of emotions'. The original study (Leff, 1973) reported the alleged emotional expression of subjects in various countries obtained from data collected for the International Pilot Study of Schizophrenia (IPSS); Leff equated 'emotional expression' (based on deductions from measures of anxiety and depression made by psychiatrists) with the ability of the subjects actually to experience emotions, and then added on supplementary data from the US–UK study (Cooper *et al.*, 1972) on black Americans and white Americans. The conclusion arrived at was that people from 'developed countries showed a greater differentiation of emotions' than did people from 'developing' countries, with American blacks resembling the latter in this respect. The racial undertones in Leff's initial presentations of the studies become less subtle when the theory is presented later (Leff, 1977) as representing an 'evolutionary process', whereby the state of being industrially underdeveloped or being an American black is seen as culturally inferior to being industrially developed or being an American white. The racial nature of the theory and the racism in its conclusions are obvious; and, as with the writings of Jung and Carothers several years earlier, the theories represent the racist ethos of psychiatry and psychology.

The basic fallacies of Leff's theory, when viewed in a global, multicultural context, are described by, among others, Lutz (1985) and O'Nell (1989): Leff derives his data from ethnocentric methods of assessment, mainly the psychiatric tool devised in Britain called the 'present state examination' (Wing *et al.*, 1974); he uses culturally constructed concepts of emotional expression *cross-culturally*; and he takes a 'paternalistic and judgemental view of non-Western idioms for emotional distress' (O'Nell, 1989: 54). A similar way of thinking to that of Leff is shown by Bebbington (1978), also from the British Institute of Psychiatry, in a review of depression: Bebbington uses the term 'primitive cultures' as meaning non-Western cultures and, more significantly, argues for 'a provisional syndromal definition of depression as used by a consensus of Western psychiatrists against which cross-cultural anomalies can be tested'. In other words, the 'depression' of non-Western peoples is hailed as an 'anomaly' and the paper indicates that these so-called anomalies are found among black Americans, Africans, Asians and 'American Indians'. It is not necessarily the racial prejudices of individual research workers, but the pervasive influence of a racist ideology within which they carry out their work, that is expressed in these theories and ideas.

Diagnosis

The identification of mental illness in terms of diagnosis is a sine qua non of psychiatry; and diagnosis is based on a medical model of illness that has developed in Europe over the past 300 years. But this has not occurred in a vacuum or as an objective process uninfluenced by social milieu. 'On the one hand, it [psychiatry] deals with mental phenomena (actions, beliefs, motives, feelings) which look very much like the sort of things that societies regulate; on the other hand, its roots in objective, physical knowledge of how the brain works are extremely shallow' (Ingleby, 1982). The social construction of mental illness is shown up dramatically in the political abuses of psychiatry in the Soviet Union (Bloch and Reddaway, 1984) and the decision of the American Psychiatric Association in 1973 that homosexuality should cease to be an 'illness' (Bayer, 1981). In both instances, political forces determine the nature of what constitutes illness. Similarly, racist considerations are evident in the construction of two diagnostic categories reported in the United States at the time of slavery and described by Cartwright (1851) as peculiar to black people.

Dysaesthesia Aethiopis was described as a disease affecting both mind and body, with 'insensibility' of the skin and 'hebetude' of mind, commoner 'among free slaves living in clusters by themselves than among slaves in our plantations, and attacks only such slaves as live like free negroes in regard to diet, drinks, exercise, etc.' Cartwright claimed that nearly all 'free negroes' were afflicted by this condition 'if they had not got some white person to direct and take care of them'. Consequently, he saw the 'disease' as 'the natural offspring of negro liberty – the liberty to be idle, to wallow in filth, and to indulge in improper food and drinks'. Stating his lack of interest in treating the 'disease' among 'free negroes', he described the symptoms that he observed among slaves:

> they break, waste, and destroy everything they handle – abuse horses and cattle, – tear, burn, or rend their clothing, and paying no attention to the rights of property, they steal from others to replace what they have destroyed.... They raise disturbances with their overseers and fellow servants without cause or motive, and seem to be insensible to pain when subject to punishment.

He argued against the alleged view of overseers that this was 'rascality' and suggested a regime of 'treatment' consisting of hard work in the open air with rest periods and 'good wholesome food'. The second disease described by Cartwright was more straightforward – '*Drapetomania* or the disease causing slaves to run away'. After attributing the condition to 'treating them as equal' or frightening them by cruelty, Cartwright advocated a mixture of 'care, kindness, attention and humanity', with punishment 'if any one or more of them, at any time, are inclined to raise their heads to a level with their master or overseer ... until they fall into that submissive state which was intended for them to occupy'. Daniel Tuke (1858), referring to Cartwright's accounts of these diseases, approved of *Dysaesthesia Aethiopis* but even he ridiculed the attribution of a diagnosis to the propensity of slaves to run away: 'In our judgement, the absence of such a propensity would be a melancholy proof of imbecility or incipient dementia.'

The influence of ideological and political forces in determining diagnosis, and sometimes treatment, is not usually as obvious as it is in the four examples given above, namely, the illness contained in dissenting politically in the Soviet Union, the demedicalisation of homosexuality in the United States, the illness induced by freedom given to black slaves, and the disease of running away that affected black slaves. The ways in which the racist ideology inherent in Western culture permeates the construction of illness categories must take note of the diagnostic process itself. Ingleby (1982) makes three observations about the diagnosis of mental illness: first, although it is not usually made on the basis of observed pathology, the existence of such pathology is implied when a diagnosis is made; secondly, criteria for mental illness refer to intelligibility of feelings and behaviour which in turn refer usually to common sense and clinical experience; finally, some types of irrationality are designated as illness for various pragmatic and traditional reasons. The influence of racism in the social construction of commonly diagnosed categories of mental disorder is not always easy to discern. Political, social and ideological pressures current in society always impinge on the diagnostic process by influencing questions of intelligibility, common sense, clinical opinion, pragmatism and tradition. And racism acts through these pressures. It is in this light that observations about racial differences in 'rates' of 'mental illness' and diagnostic patterns, especially those of 'schizophrenia', should be seen – a matter explored in Chapter 6.

Psychiatric diagnoses carry their own special images which may connect up with other images derived from (say) common sense. Thus, alienness is linked to schizophrenia (as a diagnosis) and to racial inferiority (as a human type). The result may be an overdiagnosis of schizophrenia among black people who are seen as both 'alien' and 'inferior'. Similarly, if psychiatry is called upon to 'diagnose' dangerousness, common-sense images of dangerous people are taken on – and black people seen as excessively dangerous. In some situations, pragmatic considerations may promote the denial of illness if political influences encourage some types of behaviour to be ignored or punished. Racist images of the 'lazy black' may lead to the ignoring of self-neglect as indicative of illness among black people; the idea that blacks should not smoke cannabis, but do so, enters into the construction of the disease of 'cannabis psychosis' – a British diagnosis that is given almost exclusively to blacks (McGovern and Cope, 1987). In a context in Britain where public images, fostered by the media and police, associate race with drug abuse and attribute the anger of black youth to their use of cannabis, value judgements attached to drug abuse and the need to 'pathologise' the anger of black people seem to come together in this diagnosis. Also, perhaps a pragmatic need to avoid the diagnosis of schizophrenia because of public criticism of its overuse among blacks may play a part. Diagnoses specific to groups of people identified racially may carry racism within them, when they are derived in a racist context. Thus, many of the so-called 'culture-bound' syndromes are seen as conditions that are alien to mainstream psychiatry and so diagnosed among people considered to have 'alien' cultures – a matter usually seen in racial terms. (Culture-bound syndromes are discussed in some detail in Chapter 2.)

Depression is a diagnosis of increasing popularity; Brown and Harris (1978) refer to it as an illness with a 'pivotal position in the explanation of what is wrong with our society'. The history of its diagnosis may reflect wider issues. The following comment by the clinical director of Georgia State Sanatorium (Green, 1914) about the apparent rarity of depression among blacks in the American South in the early part of the twentieth century is typical of the general views among psychiatrists at the time:

> It appears that the negro mind does not dwell upon unpleasant subjects; he is irresponsible, unthinking, easily aroused to happiness, and his unhappiness is transitory, disappearing as a child's when other interests attract his attention.... Depression is rarely encountered even under circumstances in which a white person would be overwhelmed by it.

Carothers (1953) (referred to above) is among many white psychiatrists who have claimed that depression is rare among black Africans, attributing his alleged observation to 'the absence of a sense of responsibility' among blacks. In reviewing the reports on depression from Africa, Raymond Prince (1968) notes that, although this condition was reported as uncommon among Africans well into the 1950s, since 1957 – the year of Ghana's independence – papers have appeared reporting that depression is not rare but common among Africans. Prince refers to 'the climate of opinion' about Africans having determined observations made by psychiatrists; another form of words would designate racism. It seems likely that depression is found to be rare among Africans when they are seen as lacking a sense of responsibility, rather than vice versa. Since that particular racist stereotype has lessened in popularity, the syndrome of depression is now as recognisable in Africa as it is in Europe. (The questionable validity of designating the syndrome of 'depression' as an illness in the African cultural context is referred to elsewhere.)

In addition to the (racist) pressures arising from the context in which diagnoses are made, the diagnostic process is affected by racism at various points – during the recognition and evaluation of symptoms or psychopathology, in their assessment for the purpose of illness recognition, and in making the decision on the propriety of designating illness. For example, the failure to acknowledge racism as a real threat to black people may result in the designation of anger and fear as 'paranoia'; the dismissal of culturally determined ways of emotional expression by a black person as an 'inferior' mode of expression may negate the value of 'symptoms' that are identified. Also, racism may play a role in diagnosis by its effect on the context in which the diagnostic interview itself takes place. For example, in transactions between a black patient and a white professional, the former may be unwilling to divulge information because of the racist misperceptions (held by the latter) of his/her family life and culture, while the white professional may have very little knowledge of, or 'feeling' for, black lifestyles and attitudes. Indeed, the rapport between the participants of an interracial psychiatric interview may be totally disjointed in a racist context. What happens after diagnosis – the 'management' of the patient – is also affected by racism. American stereotypes of the patient who is perceived as 'non-Western', usually on the basis of colour, are described by Sabshin *et al.* (1970): 'Hostile and not motivated for treatment, having primitive character structure, not psychologically minded, and impulse-ridden.' Similar myths prevail in Britain, with additional stereotypes (for example, the passive Asian) derived from Britain's colonial past. The images of black people as lacking the capacity for insight or 'somatising' their psychological feelings (reinforced perhaps by their reluctance to divulge these very easily to white therapists), may influence the decision of psychotherapists to accept them for treatment and/or the referral of blacks for behaviour modification therapy. The emphasis on the perceived dangerousness of black people may lead to the excessive use of seclusion or high levels of medication.

Thus, it is in diverse ways, often peculiar to the particular society or situation concerned, that racism affects the way that mental disorder is conceptualised and so-called mentally disordered people managed. The extent of its influence is not just determined by tradition and history but also by current political and economic forces that promote the ethos of white supremacy.

Post-war social and cultural studies

Although sociology had shown little interest in issues around racism in the early part of the twentieth century, social science studies after the Second World War appeared to recognise the importance of doing so. A renowned study that focused on the effects of discrimination and social conditions on the personalities of black people was the book *The Mark of Oppression* by Kardiner and Ovesey (1951). The book is based on a psychodynamic assessment of 25 case records of black people considered against a background of the history of African-Americans in American society. The authors argued that the original (African) culture of black people in America had been 'smashed, be it by design or accident' (1951: 39); African-Americans were seen as people living in a sort of cultural vacuum, their family life as disorganised and the dominance of African-American women as disturbing family cohesion. The authors concluded that racial discrimination had resulted in a low self-esteem and self-hatred within the black personality, partly dealt with by being 'projected' as aggression and anxiety. 'There is not one personality trait of the Negro the source of which cannot be traced to his difficult living conditions. There are no exceptions to this rule.... The final result is a wretched internal life' (1951: 81).

Later studies of black families and culture were gathered together in a report by Moynihan (1965) which informed American social policy and also influenced the thinking of psychologists and sociologists. Moynihan argued that the experience and deprivations of slavery had resulted in a matriarchal structure in African-American families that is out of keeping with 'American society'. Although the book by Kardiner and Ovesey and Moynihan's report highlight racial discrimination as the main problem, their lines of argument were often flawed, and the conclusions drawn on black family life, and indeed on personalities of black people, were generally as racist as earlier views focusing on (alleged) inferiority of black brains. The arguments themselves were based on a naive view of human development where negative experiences were assumed to lead to personality defects. Judgements about family cohesion, the role of women, etc. were deductions made from a white perspective assuming that white families and white people were the norm. A major failure was not to recognise that oppression might uplift as well as depress self-worth and may promote as well as destroy communal cohesion. A sociological approach that transfers the focus of emphasis from the oppression – racist oppression in this case – to the oppressed, inevitably has the effect of pathologising and stigmatising the oppressed.

American ideas about black families were taken as fact in crossing the Atlantic to become evident in British research; negative images developed about African-Caribbean and Asian families. According to Lawrence (1982) the former were seen as having a family life that was weak and unstable, with a lack of a sense of paternal responsibility towards children; and Asian families were seen as strong 'but the very strength of Asian culture ... [was seen as] ... a source of both actual and potential weaknesses' (1982: 118). The American 'Moynihan Report' (Moynihan, 1965) called the black American family 'a tangle of pathology'; in the UK, a Select Committee on Race Relations (1977) reported a connection between the problems of African-Caribbean British families and family life in the Caribbean which was seen as unsuited to British society.

Fortunately, the decade beginning in the 1980s saw a shift away from the racist notions of the earlier years. This change resulted not from academic studies using scientific (*sic*) methods but from black people themselves striving for equality by political action – for example in challenging police brutality and psychiatric racism – supplemented by writings of black and Asian authors on both sides of the Atlantic – such as (to mention a few) Toni Morrison (1987), Paul Gilroy (1993), homi bhabha (1994), Edward Said (1994), bell hooks (1994) and Cornel West (1994). A review of their work and other relevant literature is beyond the scope of this section. The main lessons for the mental health field that come through are about the positive results of the struggles of black people during the many years of slavery; about the richness and variety of black and Asian cultures that have developed in the UK and USA; about the interaction and melding together of cultures; about the changing nature of racism; about the forging of new identities and ethnicities; and about the struggles against racism. Unfortunately mainstream psychiatry and psychology have so far failed on the whole to take on board the insights available in the progressive thinking that has flooded the British and American scene at the end of the twentieth century.

Conclusions

Although it is important to recognise and oppose racism in psychiatric and psychological literature and in the literature that is likely to inform these disciplines, it is the racism of everyday psychiatry and psychology that is really dangerous, not just to the future of the disciplines but to the social fabric of Western society as a whole. And, of course it is this grass-roots racism that creates problems for people who come into contact with mental health services. The (racist) attribution of primitiveness to non-Europeans, i.e. peoples seen as originating in Africa, Asia and the Americas, and their cultures is an ideology that continues to inform much psychiatric and psychological practice. The racist IQ movement within clinical psychology remains strong. The universalist psychiatric/psychological doctrine, i.e. that Western concepts of the mind, of illness models and of treatment have global relevance, subsumes within it a distinct racist judgement of cultures and peoples – often only partially concealed. And psychiatric diagnoses continue to carry racist undertones. Current practitioners tend to ignore the racist dimension of their disciplines and therefore little, if any, action is usually taken to counteract the effects of racism in practice. Consequently, not only are racist traditions perpetuated, but also, racism in Western culture continues to permeate the disciplines of psychology and psychiatry in research, theory and practice.

Black professionals in the USA have come together to devise a strategy known as 'black psychology'. According to Watson (1973), who, incidentally, regrets the need for a 'black psychology', this movement addresses three areas of concern: first, black psychologists provide a picture of black family life that is different from that presented by conventional white wisdom, emphasising the strengths within it and its ways of making out in the world that blacks live in. Secondly, in highlighting the excessive numbers of black people being diagnosed as mentally ill, the movement tends to concentrate on white racism as the cause for black mental illness. Watson believes that 'Blacks have chosen this because in so doing they have been able to caricature white racism itself as a sickness.' Thirdly, in questioning the validity for black people of established IQ tests, black psychologists have devised new tests geared to the black experience. 'These tests ... can be seen as a response to what was viewed as a growing racism not just in society at large but in the psychology profession itself.' In the field of psychiatry too, black professionals have formed an association – the Black Psychiatrists of America (Pierce, 1973). Attempts by black and Asian psychologists and psychiatrists to oppose racism within their professional practices have been few and far between. In practice, any individual who does this becomes marginalised within his or her respective profession and there is little in the way of supportive organisations among these professional groups that they can have recourse to. Similarly, the situation in the UK is that, although white service users have formed bodies to press their case – mainly one of 'anti-psychiatry' – black users of psychiatric services have yet to get together in an effective way.

Although there is some concern in Britain about racism in psychiatry, this has not led to the adoption of any particular strategies to counteract it – although the author suggested some in a book (Fernando, 1988) published over 12 years ago. The Transcultural Psychiatry Society (UK) changed its constitution in 1985 to specify its opposition to racism as a primary object (Transcultural Psychiatry Society, 1985). In 1987, the Royal College of Psychiatrists established a committee to consider 'problems of discrimination against trainees, other doctors in psychiatry and patients on the grounds of race' (Royal College of Psychiatrists, 1989); but the report of the committee was ignored by the governing body. Successive biennial reports of the Mental Health Act Commission, a sort of inspectorate established by the British government, have identified the needs of black and ethnic minorities as a priority, quoting the disadvantages that are being suffered by black people in Britain because of racism (Mental Health Act Commission, 1991, 1993, 1995). And in 1993, a report of a inquiry into three deaths of young black men in Broadmoor Hospital (SHSA, 1993) found that 'subtle racism' (akin to 'institutional racism') was a significant problem that should be addressed as a matter of urgency; but the (then) governing authorities of the hospital rejected this contention and took no action on it.

Thus purely from the point of view of an insider within the psychiatric system, the future looks bleak. However, the challenges to both psychiatry and psychology are increasing, particularly from users of psychiatric services and from voluntary (not-for-profit) organisations run by black and Asian people (see Fernando, 1995). The struggle against racism in the British scene is particularly hopeful in the aftermath of an inquiry into police practices following the racist murder of a black teenager (Home Department, 1999); although the report of the inquiry highlighted institutional racism within the police, the reaction of the government has been to intensify examination of institutional racism in all public bodies, including its own Department of Health, and in services such as the mental health services. A further reason for optimism is the increasing willingness of black and Asian people, including professionals and academics working within mental health services, to speak out about racism within mental health services and develop alternative, culturally sensitive approaches in the voluntary sector which may demonstrate ways forward. In such a context, it is inconceivable that mainstream psychiatry and psychology could carry on much longer without undergoing radical changes and survive as disciplines that address human problems – mental health problems.

PART II

Practice and Innovation

5

Psychiatry Applied Universally

The application of psychiatry in communities whose main cultural background may be described as 'non-Western' raises several issues. At a fundamental level, there is the question of the validity of employing Western ways of thinking about 'psychological' processes and about 'illness', irrespective of culture – and the corollaries that spread from doing so. Then there are the biases and misconceptions within psychiatry that arise from racism and the damage that results. Finally, there are the problems and injustices that arise from the actual practice of psychiatry, because of the way it handles – or colludes in handling – people deemed to be 'mentally ill'. This chapter considers the effects of all this: of the use of psychiatry in multiracial and multicultural societies in the West; of the spread – or imposition – of psychiatry on indigenous methods of dealing with emotional problems and on the management of 'madness' across the non-Western world; of the viability of psychiatric diagnoses and treatments cross-culturally, leading to questions about the meaning and usefulness of the descriptive diagnoses of psychiatry which tend to be adopted as being of universal relevance – as allegedly valid indicators of illness to be treated by the 'treatments' attached to them by psychiatry; and finally, of the overall effect on human society of the descriptive models of psychiatric illness currently being refined and spread across the globe with all the power of the West behind it.

This chapter will cover some questions of national and international importance thrown up by examining racial and cultural issues in the practice of psychiatry. Issues of practical importance to ethnic minorities in the West, particularly those perceived as 'black' (in a political sense) in Britain and the United States, must be seen in the context of the current struggle for equality by black people; they are concerned

113

with the way that psychiatry functions in racist societies, its lack of objectivity in the making of diagnoses and the provision of treatment, and its involvement in social control. Do psychiatric diagnoses and treatments carry the racial bias against black people that Western culture carries? If so, how is this bias manifested? Does black anger or protest against white domination get presented as high rates of diagnosed 'illnesses', such as schizophrenia, that carry anger within them and does this anger, coupled with the need by the state to suppress it, lead to disproportionate numbers of young blacks being admitted compulsorily to forensic psychiatric institutes in Western societies?

Wider issues about psychiatry in a global context concern the effects of promoting Western systems of categorisation, treatment and research that go hand in hand with the adoption of Western styles of 'management' of the insane – based, until recently, on institutional-isation, now giving way to 'community care'. A critical survey of a well-known series of ongoing international studies will be used to explore this topic. And finally, the dangers of a colour-blind and culture-blind approach to mental health, in both national and inter-national perspectives, will be discussed and conclusions drawn.

Racial bias

The importance of racial bias in the practice of psychiatry in multi-racial settings is often ignored except when it is very obvious – as it was in the case of South Africa in the days of apartheid (WHO, 1977; Jewkes, 1984). However, the question of racial bias must be seen in the context of racism inherent in Western culture, of psychiatry being a part of that culture, and of the fact that cultural differ-ences are present in many societies in the West (as well as elsewhere). Issues of race and culture are often confounded and thereby obscured in many settings – in politics, in literature, and in both psychology and psychiatry. Two points are fundamental: first, racism in psychiatry is not an aberration – it is the normal condition; and secondly, it is not the recognition of cultural differences that is racist, but the attribution of values to these differences. In practice, racist bias may be overt and deliberately planned, or covert but accepted as a part of institu-tional processes, often ignored and sometimes not even noticed.

With the overthrow of apartheid in South Africa, it could be said that overt, unashamed racism, acknowledged and pursued officially by the state, is not found anywhere today. But there is little doubt about its persistence in most, if not all Western societies (as argued in Chapter 1). In Britain, racist practice is not publicly or openly encouraged by local or central government, but there is little doubt that it exists – usually as institutionalised racism (Brown, 1984; Home Department, 1999). In general today, both within nations like Britain and the United States and in the international arena, racism in psychiatry is not usually a matter of prejudiced behaviour by individual practitioners or of an organised movement to deprive black people of their rightful access to services aimed at mental health care. Racism within psychiatry derives from the traditions of the discipline, its history, its ways of assessing and diagnosing, the criteria it uses for designating treatment, its organisation, its involvement with the powers of the state and with Western power internationally (and the racist dimension to the exercise of power), and its struggle to be accepted as a scientific discipline. Racism in the provision of (psychiatric) services derives from the manner in which institutions are constructed and fashioned and the failure by most organisations to confront the fact of inherent and historically determined racism.

Clinical evaluation

The practice of psychiatry at an individual level depends, in the final analysis, on the process of 'clinical' evaluation – a concept with a wider remit than a diagnosis. This is primarily based on a patient's history, basic personality and current 'mental state', obtained by interviewing the 'patient' in a standard manner. The history is often regarded as being composed of objective facts but, in reality, it is a highly selected account of whatever information has been acquired from the 'patient' and others – the crucial sorting out being done by the psychiatrist. The psychiatrist influences the content of what is obtained as 'history' in two interrelated ways within the overall, variable limitations of communication. First, the type and extent of information given by the patient and others are fashioned by the perceptions of the psychiatrist about the people providing the information and vice versa; for example, a black Asian patient, aware of the negative value attached to Asian marriage customs, is unlikely to tell a white doctor or social worker much about his/her marriage. This may be interpreted usually as secretiveness or deviousness, of the patient, not as a quality of the doctor or social worker. Secondly, the picking and choosing that occurs during history-taking – the emphasis given to one item of information as opposed to another or the meaning attached to an incident – is dependent on the beliefs, value judgements, understanding and knowledge of the psychiatrist; for example, a psychiatrist, who is a part of an establishment that does not appreciate the extent of racial discrimination in employment, is likely to take down a history of persistent unemployment of a black person without qualification, i.e. as having the same significance for both black and white patients. Since white psychiatrists lack personal experience of predominantly black areas, such as Harlem (New York), Tower Hamlets (London) or St Paul's (Bristol, England), they are likely to be unaware of the pressures impinging on black people who live there and so to misinterpret their lifestyles and behaviour – misinterpretations which often reinforce their racist prejudices.

The mental state examination is of utmost importance in determining the diagnosis given to a patient – probably the major determinant (Gauron and Dickinson, 1966). Here, the patient's reports of experiences are construed as depicting an inner state of mind – 'the mental state'. The validity of such a deduction is suspect (Grounds, 1987) at the best of times, i.e. when there is absolute rapport and full understanding between the participants at the interview, but, in a multicultural setting, and especially when barriers arising from racist preconceptions are rife, the possibility of making valid deductions from questions asked at an interview is highly questionable. The meanings attached to experiences and perceptions, the concept of illness, and the overall significance of the interview situation (during which 'the mental state' is deduced) are but some of the parameters along which variation must occur when cultural differences are present between the participants of an interaction. And racism adds to this problem in ways best illustrated by quoting, in summary form, a case given in detail elsewhere (Fernando, 1988: 112–13):

> A black person on remand in prison presented to me as suffering from a chronic schizophrenic illness with an acute exacerbation. He was said to have 'mainly negative symptoms' of withdrawal, social deterioration, and emotional blunting, and to lack 'insight', to be unwilling to have treatment informally and to be 'near-mute'. When I met him in prison he welcomed me with a smile (for I had known him earlier) and told me his story. Soon after I left, it seems, he relapsed into the earlier state. Clearly, his schizophrenia came and went but I declined to accept him as requiring compulsory admission.

It was argued earlier (Chapter 3) that deductions made from an 'examination' of 'the mental state' cannot be viewed as being equivalent to a medical description of the state of a bodily organ since these are described in terms that have objective validity – or at least some degree of such validity. What a doctor 'finds' in a 'mental state' is as much a reflection of the observer as the so-called patient. It is the result of an interaction rather than a one-sided observation. The mental state of the patient referred to above was accurately described in the tradition of psychiatry and the diagnosis was reasonably reliable, since it was just on the one occasion that he behaved in a way different from that of a 'schizophrenic' patient. *In psychiatric terms he had schizophrenia.* It is the application of a medical model to that man's particular situation that was at fault; it was the meaning given to his 'schizophrenia' that was misleading. And the whole process added up to a racist system.

Issues in diagnosis

The psychiatric diagnostic process, critically described in Chapter 3, allows the discipline of psychiatry to function in such a way that racist ideology is absorbed and applied in a scientific guise. Since objectivity is the supposed aim of a psychiatry that tries hard to be 'scientific', practitioners of the discipline do not recognise the fact that the evaluations they make are far from objective. Hence, they fail to allow for the biases that come into such assessments – biases endemic in the culture in which psychiatry has grown and in which psychiatry functions. This is an ideal setting for racism to flourish in; the way it has done so in the diagnosis of psychosis and schizophrenia in the United States and Britain is strikingly similar although the historical backgrounds of the two countries in relation to racism are somewhat different.

Early reports of a relatively high rate of black in-patients being diagnosed as 'psychotic' in the United States during the latter part of the nineteenth century and the first half of the twentieth (e.g. Babcock, 1895; Wilson and Lantz, 1957) were criticised by Pasamanick (1963) on methodological grounds; he concluded from studies in Baltimore that, while the non-white rates for 'psychosis' were higher than those for whites in state hospitals, the white rates were higher in Veterans Administration hospitals and private institutions. Moreover, he calculated that, for non-institutional patients, the white rate for 'psychosis' was higher than the non-white rate. Also Pasamanick observed that, between 1920 and 1955, there was a change in the style of diagnosis of black people in the United States; the diagnosis of schizophrenia increased while that of manic depression decreased. Indeed, American studies in the 1950s and 1960s (e.g. Jaco, 1960; Simon, 1965) reported a lower 'rate' of affect-ive illness among blacks compared to whites and, corresponding to this, reports published in the 1970s claimed that a higher rate of schizophrenia was being diagnosed among blacks (compared to whites) – for example, nearly double in the case of male admissions to state and county hospitals in 1969 (National Institute of Mental Health, 1971) and 60 per cent higher among referrals to a private psychiatric in-patient service of a university hospital in Brooklyn (Steinberg *et al.*, 1977). Further, when a distinction was established in diagnosis between 'process schizophrenia' and 'reactive schizo-phrenia' (the former seen as having a relatively high 'genetic' compon-ent), blacks, particularly black males, were disproportionately given the diagnosis of process schizophrenia, irrespective of socio-economic status (Allon, 1971). At the same time, American psy-chiatrists noted difficulties encountered by white psychiatrists in comprehending, and therefore evaluating properly, the feelings and behaviour of black people because of mutual mistrust and hostility between racial groups (St Clair, 1951) leading to 'diagnostic problems' (Simon, 1965).

The 'overdiagnosis' of schizophrenia in the United States may not be confined to African-Americans but may well apply also to Native ('Indian') and Hispanic Americans. A hospital survey of in-patients reports a diagnosis of schizophrenia being given at a significantly higher rate to patients from 'Indian reserves' compared to 'non-Indian' patients in Saskatchewan (Roy *et al.*, 1970) and a community survey reports a relatively high 'prevalence rate' of all major psychoses among Eskimos in the Canadian Eastern Arctic (Sampath, 1974). Hispanic Americans seem to be underrepresented as patients attending both public and private psychiatric services (Karno, 1966) and are thought to suffer mainly from major psychiatric disorders (Adams *et al.*, 1984). A study of outpatients of an inner-city municipal hospital in New York and diagnosed as suffering from bipolar illness (manic depression) found that previous 'misdiagnosis' as 'schizophrenic' was significantly greater for both Hispanics and blacks when compared to whites (Mukherjee *et al.*, 1983).

Several studies of British in-patients in the 1960s and 1970s (Bagley, 1971; Cochrane, 1977) revealed that the diagnosis of schizo-phrenia was given more frequently to people from many immigrant groups when compared to native-born people, especially people originating in Africa, Asia and the Caribbean (Carpenter and Brockington, 1980; Dean *et al.*, 1981) – all 'black' in racial terms. A more recent survey of in-patients compulsorily detained in a hospital in Birmingham (England) shows that about two-thirds of (black) West Indian patients, as opposed to one-third of the whites, are diagnosed as 'schizophrenic' (McGovern and Cope, 1987); and studies in Nottingham (Harrison *et al.*, 1988, 1997) and London (King *et al.*, 1994; Bhugra *et al.*, 1997) confirm that black people are being diagnosed as 'schizophrenic' or 'psychotic' to a disproportionately excessive extent – 12–13 times more often than expected in one study.

Researchers in New York (Simon *et al.*, 1973) comparing diagnoses given by hospital psychiatrists and research psychiatrists using a structured interview, conclude that the excessive diagnosis of schizophrenia among black people by the former is a reflection of US hospital psychiatrists' 'diagnostic habits'. But others (e.g. Adebimpe *et al.*, 1982) claim that symptom profiles for 'schizophrenia' differ across racial groups for cultural reasons. Another American team (Bromberg and Simon, 1968) suggests that African-Americans may present with (what they call) 'protest psychosis' – essentially an expression of anger with repudiation of white people and their social structures. And a British study (Littlewood and Lipsedge, 1981) suggested that atypical syndromes among black patients may be 'misdiagnosed' as schizophrenia.

Some British researchers who have found relatively high rates of schizophrenia being diagnosed among black people (Harrison *et al.*, 1988; King *et al.*, 1994) argue that, by using the present state examination (Wing *et al.*, 1974) 'misdiagnosis' is avoided. But what they and others often fail to address is the influence of race – or more specifically racism – in distorting the 'objectivity' of the *diagnostic process* itself – a field that is poorly researched and often ignored. However, Loring and Powell (1988) did investigate this very issue in a carefully controlled study of the diagnostic approaches of 290 American psychiatrists. When the psychiatrists were asked certain questions after written case histories, using exactly similar information about clients except for details of gender and race, were circulated to them, black clients, compared to white clients, were given a diagnosis of schizophrenia more frequently by both black and white clinicians – although this was done to a lesser extent by the former; the clinicians ascribed feelings of violence, suspiciousness and dangerousness to black clients even though the case studies (apart from racial designation) were the same as those for the white clients. It has been noted in Britain too that black people in psychiatric hospitals are being seen as 'dangerous' without adequate objective reasons for doing so (Harrison *et al.*, 1984) and that black patients are overrepresented among compulsorily detained patients in hospital (Ineichen *et al.*, 1984; McGovern and Cope, 1987; Owens *et al.*, 1991). Loring and Powell (1988) draw the conclusion that whites and blacks are 'seen differentially even if they exhibit the same behaviour', and point out that 'these differences will be reflected and legitimized in official statistics on psychopathology'. And so through the power of myths, self-fulfilling prophecies and genuine but inappropriate diagnoses, the racist tendency to designate black people as schizophrenic is perpetuated.

Treatment

Psychiatric treatment falls into two main groups – psychological treatment and physical treatment. The former includes 'psychotherapy' which is generally regarded as a highly specialised form of treatment suitable for selected people only, the criteria for selection being concerned with their 'understanding of problems in psychological terms', motivation for 'insight', 'capacity to form relationships' etc. (Brown and Pedder, 1979). However, physical treatment, mainly the use of electroconvulsive therapy (ECT) and psychotropic medication, can be given to most people even, under certain circumstances, without their consent. The medical model of psychiatry separates diagnosis (and assessment) from treatment, although in practice the two processes blend together and influence each other. Also, treatment cannot easily be separated from 'management' or 'care', although the latter is generally seen as the context in which treatment is given; for example, the ward environment (of in-patients) may be seen as 'care' but also, perhaps more appropriately, as 'treatment'. Similarly, methods of control or discipline including the use of 'seclusion' (a form of solitary confinement) may be seen as treatment. The objectivity of the (psychiatric) diagnostic process is always very limited but, in the case of cross-cultural situations where the practitioner is uncertain of his/her role, the kind of treatment (including management/care) that seems, on general (or 'common-sense') grounds, to be necessary often influences the diagnosis. For example, if a patient in hospital is judged to be in need of control because the reasons for his/her anger cannot be understood, a repressive or controlling treatment such as seclusion or tranquillisers at a high dosage may be perceived as being required, while, on the other hand, if the anger is recognised as emanating from psychological or social problems, psychotherapy or 'sociotherapy' (ways of influencing behaviour by manipulating the environment) may be seen as the patient's need. If the cause of a person's depression is appreciated by the psychiatrist, psychological treatment may be used, while if it is not, ECT or antidepressant medication may be considered. And, in all such instances, the diagnosis that is given will often be geared to the need (in terms of 'treatment') as perceived by the professional.

A high 'drop-out' rate from psychotherapy was reported many years ago in the case of black patients in the United States – for example by Rosenthal and Frank (1958). A major study of nearly 600 outpatients attending a (public) state hospital in California found significant differences in the treatment of ethnic minorities (mainly African and Hispanic Americans) when compared to that of white Americans (Yamamoto *et al.*, 1968): the former were less often taken on for psychotherapy, more often given minimal support or drug therapy, and much more likely to end treatment, either by self-discharge or discharge by therapist. In a complementary study (Yamamoto *et al.*, 1967), the researchers showed clearly that the differences were largely related to what they called 'ethnocentricity' of the therapist, which may be described more aptly as racism. A similar situation probably exists in Britain, too (Campling, 1989), although it is inadequately researched. Littlewood and Cross (1980) found in Hackney, London that 'stereotyped attitudes' led to 'assumptions that (a) ECT is suitable for non-depressive reactions in black patients, (b) black patients require more ECT and (c) intramuscular medication is more efficacious in black patients'. Also, Shaikh (1985) observed in Leicester 'an excess of electroconvulsive therapy use among Asians who received the diagnosis of schizophrenia as compared to indigenous patients with this diagnosis'. A study in Newham, east London, strongly suggested that black men born in the West Indies, compared to British-born white men, were more likely to be given long-acting ('depot') injections of tranquillisers (Glover and Malcolm, 1988).

A retrospective study of over 100 male patients diagnosed as 'schizophrenic' admitted to a teaching hospital unit in Illinois, USA revealed that, although black patients were similar to white patients on illness ratings, chronicity, marital status, employment level and age, the former spent less time in hospital, obtained less privileges while there, were given more emergency ('prn') medication, were less likely to receive recreation therapy and occupational therapy, and more likely to have been placed in seclusion (Flaherty and Meagher, 1980). The authors postulated that 'the stereotype of the black male' led to a situation in which the staff felt and acted as if blacks were excessively dangerous, needing restrictive measures and fewer privileges. In a different study (Lawson *et al.*, 1984), researchers in California found that, although ward physicians and nursing staff believed that their black patients, compared to white patients, were more violent, when a graduated behaviour count of violent behaviour was carried out, blacks were significantly *less* violent. In fact, there is no doubt that seclusion is overused for black patients because of racist stereotyping: a detailed study of seclusion in a university hospital in Pittsburgh found just three factors, all independent of each other, to be associated with the increased use of seclusion, namely, chronicity of illness, legal status (of being 'committed'), and the fact of being black (Soloff and Turner, 1981). British studies on racial aspects of repressive types of psychiatric treatment are few and far between. Bolton (1984) found that in a south London hospital, of patients recognised as uncooperative but not aggressive, West Indians, Indians and Africans (i.e. black people) were more likely to be sent to locked wards when compared to white English patients, irrespective of diagnosis. Many anecdotal reports and the author's own observations indicate that in Britain, as in the United States, hospitalised black patients, compared to white patients, are more likely to be 'treated' with seclusion or other repressive conditions of 'care' – and the racist stereotype of 'black violence' is the basic reason for this.

Although racism resulting in the differential use of specific forms of therapy (such as psychotherapy) and repressive forms of treatment (such as seclusion) causes most concern, racial bias in treatment goes much further. Indeed, the perception of the ward atmosphere as a whole, which should be 'therapeutic', is often very different for black people, compared to whites, in most British and American hospitals – where most of the senior staff are white – because they have a racist 'feel' about them. This situation is difficult to pinpoint or research, but a study of the perceptions of in-patients in a Veterans Administration Hospital in Illinois shows that blacks, compared to whites, have a significantly negative perception of ward environment as restricting their spontaneity and exercise of responsibility (Flaherty *et al.*, 1981). The high black 'drop-out' rates from treatment reported in the United States and the frequently reported tendency for black people to 'abscond' from psychiatric facilities in Britain (personal communications from various people) are very likely to represent the effects of racism institutionalised in psychiatry.

Conclusions

The status of psychiatry as a medical discipline and the power of people working in its institutions provide a 'cover' for racism to operate unchallenged. Although direct and overt racism is sometimes seen, a common manoeuvre by which psychiatry conceals, defends and maintains racism is that of 'culturising' it; this is a trap that transcultural psychiatrists, among others, fall into easily in a society that is reluctant to face up to its racism. Injustices and disadvantages suffered by black and ethnic minorities are attributed to *their* culture which causes *them* to distort patterns of illness (for example, by somatising psychological symptoms), to make unreasonable demands (for instance, by exaggerating symptoms or not expressing them – by being too 'demanding' or too 'passive'), or, to not benefit from treatment (by not speaking a European language, by communicating in ways that psychiatry sees as 'primitive', etc.). By culturising the problem of racism, both the power structure within psychiatry and the power of white over black is maintained because the explanations for 'ethnic problems' are looked for in the 'alien cultures' and the blame for the problems is attached to *them* – the 'cultural aliens'. The result is that the service providers look for ways of teaching *them* how to use services, rather than examining the content of the services; black people are encouraged to present illnesses in the 'right' way as white people present them and not in 'primitive' ways brought over from 'underdeveloped' countries.

The situation in the United States is somewhat different from that in Britain for there appears to be some recognition of the importance for psychiatry and psychology to be aware of the cultural diversity of its people: for example, books such as *Counselling across Cultures* (Pedersen *et al.*, 1981) and *Cultural Conceptions of Mental Health and Therapy* (Marsella and White, 1982), contain many articles about 'cultural' psychiatry and psychology by American writers. Also, 'cultural psychiatry' is a well-recognised branch of psychiatry.

However, there is no doubt that racism plays an important part in the practice of psychiatry in American multicultural settings; the position of African and Native Americans – and possibly also Hispanics – vis-à-vis American psychiatry seems to be similar to that of Afro-Caribbeans, Asians and other people of Britain's black 'ethnic minorities' in relation to British psychiatry. A striking feature of American articles (in the books referred to), as well as many other 'cultural' publications, is that they focus on Asian, especially Chinese and Japanese culture, with very little interest in the cultures of African, Hispanic and Native Americans. The failure by American psychiatry to appreciate the culture of these (American) people and to acknowledge the importance to psychiatry of the vast differences that exist between their current life experiences and that of white Americans, is indicative of ongoing American racism.

The global scene: psychiatric imperialism

As Western influence spreads across the world and Western ideas, technology and politics are imposed upon, or taken on by, Asian and African countries, psychiatry follows suit for several reasons. First, psychiatry, as a part of a medical system, accompanies Western medicine. And Western medicine, through the wonders of medical technology, its drug treatment, its surgery and its techniques for the treatment of specific illnesses, has clearly outshone other systems of medicine across the globe. The fact that psychiatry itself has not been shown to be applicable cross-culturally or to be free of both racial and cultural bias becomes obscured by its overt attachment to medicine – the prestige of the latter rubbing off on to psychiatry. Secondly, psychiatry, being presented and accepted as a part of scientific medicine, is assumed to be a scientific discipline with objective diagnoses and treatments that are free of cultural bias. As such, psychiatry is seen as being applicable to all people in all conditions, irrespective of culture, race and social system – although this is clearly not so. Thirdly, psychiatry, like all things Western, is perceived as superior to non-Western ways of conceptualising and dealing with 'mental illness'. Its content is not questioned; it is taken 'on trust'. Finally, psychiatry is pushed on to non-Western societies by economic and political forces allied to Western power. The promotion of drugs manufactured in the West goes hand in hand with psychiatry; centres of 'excellence' usually based in the West, or their copies in Asia and Africa, maintain their dominance as the fonts of all knowledge. And the type of psychiatry that is promoted, with drug therapies, psychotherapies, sociotherapies, etc. that are suited to Western political systems – and sometimes not even that – are imposed globally. One of the practical consequences of psychiatric imperialism is the underdevelopment and suppression of approaches to mental health and 'mental illness' indigenous to Asian and African cultural traditions – a matter dealt with in Chapter 6.

In colonial times, European culture and languages, such as English and French, were imposed on colonial countries thereby suppressing indigenous cultures and languages; in the same way, the global imposition of psychiatry, both as a system of dealing with human problems by diagnosing illnesses and as a means of inter- vening in social and personal situations (whether with drugs or psychotherapy, with institutionalisation or community care), results in the suppression of indigenous ways of dealing with human suffer- ing, family problems and social disturbance. The direct imposition of psychiatry across the globe is seen in the development of mental health services in many countries. The mental hospitals in countries which were occupied and colonised by Britain and France are little different from those in Europe; the institutional approach to the control of 'mad' people, taken over from the West with no regard to the social consequences of doing so, continues virtually unaltered, although such an approach was, and is, alien to the traditions of most non-Western cultures. (In fact the asylum movement in the West was a result of political conditions peculiar to Western devel- opment, although it stayed to fashion much of the thinking in the West about 'insanity'.) The mental hospitals in the ex-colonial coun- tries continue to be staffed by professionals trained in Western methods of psychiatry alone; for this and other reasons, changes in ways of working that should come from a sensitivity to indigenous cultures are not occurring. The main resistances to such change may arise from political pressures: the indirect imposition of psychiatry now takes place through subsidised training, advice by Western 'experts' and the promotion of drug therapy by Western drug firms – sometimes subsumed under the aegis of 'aid'; and bolstering all this there are the research projects which promote psychiatry. Thus, by using models and systems devised in politically powerful Western centres of 'excellence' and backed by the prestige and finance of powerful organisations, Western expertise, Western 'aid' and Western research combine in stifling indigenous systems of psychology, philosophy and medical care in the name of imposing modernisation, development and uniformity.

Scientific research is a powerful force in the promotion of psychiatry across the globe. The biggest and best-known international research project that claims to be 'cross-cultural' is the International Pilot Study of Schizophrenia (WHO, 1973, 1979), commonly called the IPSS. The aim of the study was defined as 'to tackle certain methodological problems and to answer questions about the nature and distribution of schizophrenia' (WHO, 1979). Other expressed aims were to establish differences in 'form and content' of schizophrenia which could be 'cultural' in origin and to compare the course and outcome of the 'disease'. Nine centres were chosen for the study to 'represent several of the major cultures of the world' (WHO, 1973) and three basic instruments were selected for use – the present state examination (PSE), the psychiatric history schedule (PH) and the social description schedule (SD). The PSE (Wing *et al.*, 1974), a structured interview schedule, was adjusted and abbreviated from an earlier version and the collaborating psychiatrists were trained in its use. Each patient was given a 'centre diagnosis' and a reference classification based on a computer program using the 'symptoms' elicited by the interviewing psychiatrist.

Since, in the initial part of the IPSS, the centre diagnosis and the reference diagnosis were highly concordant, the researchers drew the conclusion that the IPSS was successful in identifying groups of 'schizophrenics', i.e. patients judged to be showing similar psychopathologies, in nine countries, and that this justified the instruments they used. The circular nature of this argument was apparently unnoticed at the time. However, in admitting that the study did not deal with questions of validity, the initial report (WHO, 1975) actually admitted that 'whether a diagnosis concordant with the reference system . . . can help a clinician to be useful to his patient is quite another matter'. That report envisaged that 'it should become easier to investigate validity in the future than it has been in the past and studies of etiology, treatment, management, and prognosis should all become more comparable'. In the follow-up evaluations made two years later (WHO, 1979), the course and outcome of the 'illness' (as identified earlier) were analysed. The outcome of patients from (industrially) developing countries was significantly better than that of patients from (industrially) developed countries. For example, 'in Ibadan (Nigeria), 36 per cent of the followed-up schizophrenics had an episode of inclusion (as suffering from 'schizophrenia') which lasted less than one month, followed by full remission throughout the follow-up period, and 46 per cent had an episode of inclusion that lasted less than three months and was followed by full remission lasting throughout the follow-up period. The corresponding percentages for Agra were 27 and 40 per cent, while at the other extreme, the corresponding figures for Aarhus (Denmark) were 2 and 6 per cent, and for Moscow (USSR) 1 and 4 per cent' (ibid.).

The basic assumptions underlying the IPSS are concerned with the meaning of 'schizophrenia': it is assumed to be an objective entity rather than a 'hypothesis' or a mere diagnostic formulation, and, moreover, an entity that is 'present' in objective form all over the world with a universally similar, if not identical, meaning irrespective of culture. The validity of schizophrenia as a universally applicable concept or illness is not questioned and not researched. The tentative attempts to examine predictive and content validity are unconvincing; in the case of the former, there seems to be a lack of validity. The main, perhaps only, aim of the IPSS may have been to establish a reliable method of diagnosing schizophrenia in terms already established in the West, but the WHO researchers do not question the usefulness, and certainly do not appear to appreciate the dangers, of doing so. The centres used for the IPSS were centres of 'excellence' in applying Western models of diagnosis and treatment; but the distortion introduced by limiting centres in this way is a matter ignored by the WHO researchers in discussing the sampling procedures. The instruments used for assessment of patients were never validated for cross-cultural use; instead, the researchers assumed that concepts of illness embodied in the PSE were universally applicable, irrespective of culture. The design of the research method used in the IPSS specifically excludes cultural variables from its protocol (Favazza, 1985). The fact that all centres picked out similar groups of people for designating as 'schizophrenic' was clearly a reflection of the training given to the researchers – a classical self-fulfilling prophecy.

Kleinman (1977) identifies the fundamental fault of the IPSS as the decision to impose categories derived in the West on to the study of mental disorder in other cultures. He calls this a 'category fallacy':

> Its strength comes from reifying a narrowly defined syndrome affecting patients in nine separate cultural locations, but that is also its weakness. It is unable to systematically examine the impact of cultural factors on schizophrenia, since its methodology has ruled out the chief cultural determinants.

A striking feature of the IPSS is the notion implicit throughout the study that 'schizophrenia' exists as a biomedical illness that is, by implication, both culture-free and biologically based, if not actually determined genetically. The illness is diagnosed by 'clinical assessment' using Western models of 'functional illness' and a diagnostic method, the PSE, described by one of its inventors, John Wing (1978), as 'a special technique of interviewing patients...which is simply a standardised form of psychiatric diagnostic interview ordinarily used in Western Europe, based on a detailed glossary of differential definitions of symptoms'. It has been likened by Wing (1985) to a telescope – 'within its specifications it can be used by trained people to look for a limited range of phenomena'. If Wing's analogy is accepted, it is a telescope in which the lenses are preset by the makers to pick out selected phenomena expressed in specific ways without any power to discriminate their meanings; the view through the telescope imposes a structure, an artificial structure, on what is observed – you see what the makers of the telescope want you to see, and that is all. The IPSS was largely successful in publicising the PSE as a tool for identifying (Western) schizophrenia. And it is because of its prestige that the PSE has been used outside Western culture – for example, in Africa (Orley and Wing, 1979), Egypt (Okasha and Ashour, 1981) and South Africa (Swartz *et al.*, 1985). Although never validated properly anywhere in the world, the PSE seems to be regarded as 'scientific' and 'objective'; and it is being spread around the globe through training provided – at a fee – by prestigious institutes in London. Its use keeps London as the centre from which all knowledge flows and the base from which 'experts' go out to give advice. It is integrated into the exercise of imperial power across the globe.

Like the IPSS, later studies conducted by the WHO – the Collaborative Study on the Assessment and Reduction of Psychiatric Disability (Jablensky *et al.*, 1980) and the Determinants of Outcome of Severe Mental Disorders (Sartorius *et al.*, 1986; WHO, 1986) – take as their starting points assumptions about the universal validity of Western diagnostic formulations. The latter (the most recent of the WHO studies) aims to study schizophrenia 'in greater depth' addressing, among other issues, the influence of culture on 'content and expressive style', mechanisms in psychosis and the effectiveness of treatment (Katz *et al.*, 1988). The samples of 'schizophrenics' used in this study are drawn from people making contact with both Western-type psychiatric facilities as well as indigenous healers, religious shrines, etc. (Sartorius *et al.*, 1986), thereby gathering under an umbrella of 'personal illness' with a biological basis a variety of experiences that may be related to social functioning, spiritual life or whatever. The justification for so doing, when the universal validity – or the usefulness – of such an illness model for 'schizophrenia' has not been shown, is questionable; the only reason is one that derives from the tradition of Western imperialism. All through the series of WHO studies reported so far, there is an assumption that, if a system that is developed in Europe and seemingly suitable for Western cultures can be reliably applied, it is good enough for other cultures. This is a position of cultural arrogance, bordering on racism.

The usefulness of applying a particular concept of illness, rather than a whole system of medicine, can be examined by investigating whether such an application leads to treatment that is valuable – in other words, by examining the predictive validity of the diagnosis (Kendell, 1975). For example, the diagnosis of epilepsy or diabetes (using the Western system of medicine) is clearly useful cross-culturally because the treatment of these conditions by the methods developed in the West are beneficial to patients wherever they may be and whatever their culture or racial category. Fortunately, the follow-up studies of the IPSS enable the effectiveness of treatment to be examined vis-à-vis (the diagnosis of) schizophrenia. In evaluating the cohorts of patients who had been identified as 'schizophrenic', the IPSS found that those living in industrially underdeveloped countries had a better outcome in terms of 'recovery' from the diagnosed 'disease' and in terms of social functioning, when compared to those in Western countries (WHO, 1979), although the latter had more thorough psychiatric treatment, after-care, etc. than their counterparts in underdeveloped areas of the world. Thus, diagnosing schizophrenia in order to provide treatment that has been found to be efficacious for this 'illness' in Western society does not appear to be justified. Either, the 'schizophrenia' diagnosed in different cultures is not an illness which is equivalent (as an illness) cross-culturally and/or diagnosing 'schizophrenia' as an illness has no predictive validity in terms of outcome associated with established treatment. In any case, there is no demonstrable advantage for non-Western countries in using the psychiatric system – at least as far as the diagnosis of schizophrenia is concerned. It is extremely doubtful whether other psychiatric diagnostic models, for example that of 'depression' and 'personality disorder', are any more useful for application cross-culturally in their present Western form.

The concept of depression as an illness arose from that of 'melancholia' which has a history in Western culture going back, at least, to the times of Hippocrates (Jones, 1823). But the validity of the current understanding of depression as an illness in other cultures is very dubious. Reviews of cross-cultural research based on the imposition of a Western model of depression (as an illness), such as that by Singer (1975), produce the inevitable conclusion that a 'core illness' of depression is universally recognisable. But it is not just this 'core' illness that is diagnosed as depression; and Marsella (1978) suggests that since the 'clinical picture' of the condition varies so much cross-culturally, depression as understood in psychiatric circles should be regarded as a disorder of the Western world alone. Taking the alleged reports that 'depression' in non-European cultures is characterised by somatic symptoms rather than 'psychic' ones, he argues that, if depression is essentially an experience, a psychologically experienced 'depression' is different from one associated with somatic experience.

While acknowledging that 'a painful series of affects pertaining to sorrow' may be universally identifiable, Gananath Obeyesekere (1985), an anthropologist, believes that it is illogical to assume that a constellation of symptoms reflecting this situation is a universal illness just because it has been designated as such in Western culture. He argues that if a constellation identified in Asian cultures, such as weight loss, sexual fantasies, night emissions and urine discoloration (designated in parts of Asia as the illness of 'semen loss') is identifiable in other cultures, a contention that it is therefore a universal illness would be 'laughed out of court'. He sees the fault in the methods of psychiatric epidemiology where 'symptoms are treated in isolation from their cultural context. While it is true that the disarticulation of symptoms from context will facilitate measurement, it is also likely that the entities being measured are empty of meaning' (ibid.). The wider fault is in the context in which research is generally carried out with Western backing: although the fact that different cultures devise illnesses differently is often accepted, the ethos of white superiority ensures that illness models derived from Western experience are paramount and supersede others whenever possible. It is in this spirit that a recent reviewer of depression, Bebbington (1978), refers to non-Western presentations of the 'illness' as 'anomalies'.

The World Health Organisation (WHO) colludes in – or actively promotes – the imposition of depression as illness across the world by the way it goes about researching 'depression': 'One of the major

aims of the WHO at the outset of the series of clinical, epidemiological and therapeutic investigations on depression which will continue in the 1980s was to develop a "common language" for the
assessment of depressive states and for the communication of findings
in a cross-cultural context' (Sartorius *et al.*, 1980). The 'language'
which was imposed by the WHO through its research was that of
psychiatry. As in the studies on 'schizophrenia', the validity and usefulness of defining certain social situations and/or personal distress
as the illness of 'depression' were not questioned because they have
been accepted in the West. The fact that each culture deals with
disturbing affects in ways which are congruent with the rest of that
culture was ignored. As Obeyesekere (1985) points out, the affects
that are designated as the 'illness' of depression in the West are seen
in Buddhist culture and in West Africa as arising out of life conditions and inseparable 'from their involvement in an existential issue
(such as the nature of life)'. In these cultures (and possibly many
others), they are 'anchored to an ideology' and dealt with culturally without recourse to an illness model. Redesignating these
affects as 'illness' does not benefit the people concerned but does
benefit imperial purposes – the provision of markets for Western
products, such as antidepressants and 'experts', the dependency on
the West of Asian and African nations for advances in knowledge
and promotion of research, and the overall domination by the West of
the 'Third World'.

The deleterious effects of imposing Western illness models across
the globe is not just applicable to the use of specific diagnoses, such
as schizophrenia and depression, cross-culturally; a general change
that is occurring with the spread of psychiatry into the non-Western
– especially the vulnerable 'Third' – World is that personal distress,
normally dealt with in religious modes or as problems within family
and social systems, is being forced into illness modes to be treated
by manufactured drugs or psychotherapies developed in an alien
culture. This is the imperialism of psychiatry – an imperialism that is
less obvious than the military domination by Europeans in the
nineteenth century and its economic counterpart of the twentieth,
but no less powerful and as destructive to the vast majority of people
in the world. In the past, it has resulted in the imposition of the
'lunatic asylum' as a way of dealing with 'madness'; in the future, it
will no doubt result in the imposition of other, equally alien, systems
of 'care' derived in the West for 'psychiatric cases' – defined on
Western terms. That is, unless something is done about the relentless

'Westernisation of the world' (Harrison, 1979) currently taking place, carrying psychiatry with it.

Colour-blind, culture-blind psychiatry

The tendency to deny the importance of race and culture in psychiatric practice may be termed the colour-blind, culture-blind approach in psychiatry. The defects of a colour-blind approach are twofold. First, the observer's own racial bias is likely to be denied or ignored and therefore not taken into account. And, even if the observer has allowed for this bias, the effects of racism in society at large are often ignored. Secondly, the person being observed is invalidated by being seen as a person without a colour – and colour represents race, an important determinant of self-perception as well as of social opportunities open to people, their rights and their life experiences in a racist society. A colour-blind approach is therefore a denial, both of individual perceptions in a racist society, and, more importantly, the fact that race matters because of the way most – or all – societies function. The effect of a culture-blind observation, i.e. seeing an individual without perceiving his/her culture, is somewhat different but also twofold. First, the person is out of context; (s)he is not a part of a society or a group, with, for example, allegiances and hostilities towards other people, influenced by other people and dependent on a wide circle of people for what (s)he is. Secondly, any difference (from other people) that the person may show is likely to be perceived as an individual difference to be judged in terms of its deviance from a generalised 'norm', rather than one determined by upbringing or experience reflecting a cultural norm. Thus the colour-blind, culture-blind approach in psychiatric practice falls into a trap of denying social realities of race and culture.

Culture-blindness interacts with colour-blindness, when, for example, a 'symptom', such as retardation (slowness), is being considered in an Asian person. The 'observation' fails to note that the person concerned may consider a passive demeanour to be a correct posture in an interaction with a professional; alternatively, the person may be intimidated by the racism in society that gives black people an inferior position in comparison to whites. The possibility that the apparent 'retardation' is 'cultural' rather than pathological will be distorted by the racist belief that Asian behaviour is 'primitive'; the corollary is the belief that the Asian should not be retarded, and the push is towards diagnosing the retardation as pathological. Similarly, identification of excitement, disinhibition, paranoia, aggressiveness and 'hearing voices' as 'symptoms' would be carried out in a context where cultural and racial stereotypes are allowed to exert their influence by a psychiatry that is blind to the influence of culture and race in the process of diagnosis. It is through these influences that British African-Caribbeans are excessively diagnosed as disinhibited and/or aggressive, leading to relatively high numbers being compulsorily detained in hospital, and that black Americans are denied psychotherapy or excessively diagnosed as schizophrenic.

Conclusions arrived at in a culture-blind and colour-blind way are reinforced by being acceptable to the general common sense of society, often fitting into political and social 'norms' which may include the need for minority groups to be exploited, integrated or rejected. Two illustrations are given, one drawn from American cross-cultural clinical research and the other from British clinical experience of the author.

A study of refugees from Laos settling in Minnesota (USA) is reported by Westermeyer (1989) as confirming that 'the prevalence and incidence of paranoid disorders among refugees are high compared to other groups'. The Hmong people who were selected for this study were given both self-ratings and psychiatrist ratings for 'paranoid symptoms', as well as scores on a 'Hmong culture scale' and an 'American acculturation scale'. The researchers found 'considerable stability' over time in the level of 'paranoid symptoms' on the self-rating scale but a low correlation between this and the psychiatrist rating of paranoia. In line with usual psychiatric practice, the latter were seen as 'objective' ratings, implying that these are correct, while the self-perception of the Hmong, their 'subjective ratings', were given a lower status. The researcher reported that Hmong people 'with more subjective (but not objective) paranoid symptoms retained more traditional affiliations and behaviour'; and that low acculturation (to American ways of life) correlated positively with two of the three 'objective' measures of paranoia that were used. The culture-blind, race-blind approach is shown by the following facts: the items selected for identifying paranoid tendencies/symptoms were 'imposed' on the Hmong, disregarding their origins in Western questionnaires and the different meanings they may carry in the Hmong cultural context; the meaning of paranoia in a setting where an influx of Asians may have aroused hostility (because of racism) was ignored; the attitudes of psychiatrists towards the Hmong and racial stereotyping (racism) inherent in the process employed by them in making their ratings, were not considered; finally, the feelings engendered in the Hmong people by being interviewed was largely disregarded. It is not surprising that the conclusions of the research were political, rather than psychiatric, reflecting American expectations and cultural arrogance.

> These data suggest that efforts aimed at enhancing acculturation might reduce paranoid symptoms among refugees in settings that would expose them to mainstream United States society. On the contrary, welfare dependence may contribute to paranoid symptoms by facilitating unemployment with its subsequent isolation from United States society and intensification of contacts back into the expatriate refugee community. (ibid.)

The illustration from British experience is a case study of a man of West Indian origin who was seen by the author in the Accident and Emergency Department of a general hospital near London:

> An Afro-Caribbean man in his late twenties was brought to hospital by four policemen under section 136 of the Mental Health Act (Her Majesty's Stationery Office, 1983) which entitles the police to apprehend a person in a public place who may be suffering from mental illness. The police alleged that he was dangerous and that he had a history of psychiatric illness. They insisted on staying with him in the Accident and Emergency Department. The staff, including doctors and nurses, reckoned that he was in need of further observation in hospital but too dangerous to be kept in a general hospital. Their assessment was based on three bits of psychiatric information obtained in the usual professional manner. First, there was the police report that he had talked to strangers in the street in an abusive manner; secondly, it was observed that he would not speak to anyone in the Accident and Emergency Department, that his reactions – and hence his 'affect' – was not in keeping with the situation and that his behaviour and speech indicated 'grandiose delusions'; and finally, 'everyone' agreed that he 'looked' dangerous. When the consultant, a black doctor, was called, he decided to interview the man on his own. The staff expressed alarm at this and stayed nearby. It turned out that he was an artist who could not get a job; he had been looking for a friend, but not knowing the exact address was looking at houses along a street trying to recognise the friend's house. He had tried to talk to people but was brushed off and became angry. He remained angry, claiming that he had often been tricked into hospitalisation in this way.

This man had a 'history' of 'psychiatric illness', namely admissions to hospital. He was dealt with impartially in the best traditions of psychiatry; the consultant who was called was not even told that he was 'black'. His level of dangerousness was assessed objectively on the basis of information and the likelihood of mental illness based on his history and an examination of his 'mental state'. His race and culture (in this case of artistic eccentricity) seemed not to cloud the psychiatric assessment; but clearly the 'assessment' that he was dangerous – and a lot more besides – was determined by racial stereotypes of black people. His inability to gain employment and his general low status in society, probably determined by racism, was rationalised into an illness because his race and culture were ignored.

The culture-blind and colour-blind approach – particularly the latter – in psychiatric practice is sometimes claimed as a liberal stance because the person being judged – the 'patient' – seems to be considered as an individual irrespective of cultural and racial background. This is a serious fallacy arising from the notion that being 'blind' to something nullifies its effects or significance. Justice cannot be done in any judgement – and psychiatric observations and diagnoses are judgements – unless a person is seen in context. And the context includes his/her culture and, more importantly, the racism that is prevalent both at individual and institutional levels in British society. To ignore culture in psychiatric practice is a mistake; to ignore race is racist.

Conclusions

In its confrontation with people traditionally seen as inferior in the Western cultural tradition, whether they live as majorities outside Europe and North America or as ethnic/racial minorities within the European world, psychiatry fails to recognise the validity of cultural experiences outside the Western culture (in which psychiatry has developed) and the practical realities of racism. In the context of multiracial and multicultural populations of Britain and the United States, a major problem for people who are designated 'black' is the 'overdiagnosis' of schizophrenia that they are subjected to. In an effort to counteract this problem, which is potentially as dangerous in its implications as the genetic explanations for IQ differences between races, propagated by Jensen (1969) and Eysenck (1971, 1973), the British Transcultural Psychiatry Society agreed the following statement quoted in a letter to the *Psychiatric Bulletin*:

1. Schizophrenia as a concept used in medical circles to denote an illness is as much socially constructed as it is biologically determined. In the present state of social and medical knowledge, the diagnosis of schizophrenia tells us as

much about the biases in our society and in the person making the diagnosis, as it does about the 'patient'.

2. The effects of research published in scientific journals must take into account the prevailing political context. It is naive to assume that research on issues involving race are value free when conducted in a racist society, within a discipline, such as psychiatry, with a powerful racist tradition.

3. While accepting that schizophrenia is diagnosed to a relatively disproportionate extent among black people in the United Kingdom, we deplore the impression that may have been given in some recent publications that this fact reflects a biological inferiority of Blacks in comparison to Whites. In particular, we are concerned to hear that these reports may lead to studies which concentrate on genetics of black people to the exclusion of other issues and/or the investigation of possible virus infections being carried by Blacks. We believe that such studies will have seriously damaging political implications for black people in this country in the present political context of racism while any conclusions drawn from such research are likely to be, at best, of very limited use, and, at worst, extremely misleading, given the present state of knowledge in psychiatry. (Fernando, 1989a: 251)

The introduction of psychiatry into societies where cultural traditions are very different from those in the West results in the suppression of indigenous, culturally consonant, ways of dealing with emotional problems and 'madness'. Further, current psychiatry is failing to meet the challenges of a changing world, where many societies are increasingly multiracial in composition and self-conscious about being multicultural. As a discipline and an institution concerned with the promotion of mental health, psychiatry is, at best, an irrelevance in a global sense, and, at worst, a part of an imperialist system in alliance with other forms of Western imperialism, participating in the furthering of Western interests in the 'Third World' and in the control of racial groups trapped in colonial situations – for example, in South African townships, American ghettos and British inner cities. Clearly, psychiatry should not be applied indiscriminately in the style that it is formulated and practised at present; neither its form nor content is suitable for global application and its role in multiracial populations in the West is highly suspect.

It is possible that 'bits' of psychiatry may be useful if they are integrated into indigenous systems of therapy for 'mental health problems' and 'mental illness' identified as such in other cultures and vice versa. But if psychiatry is to participate fully in the promotion of mental health, it must break out of its ethnocentricism, free itself of racism and reach out into the world it has so far ignored. In doing so it must recognise certain social realities concerned with power: the economic and military domination of the world by power blocks which identify with white superiority and with values that are largely to do with Western materialism – values that are promoted as being 'modern' and superior to those of so-called traditional societies; the blending of power with racism, both within nations and internationally; and the involvement of psychiatry with the exercise of power – state power working through psychiatry and personal power of professionals over patients. Then, perhaps by examining its knowledge base and techniques in the wider context of a multicultural world and by incorporating anti-racism into its ways of functioning, psychiatry may be able to apply its techniques – or at least some of its techniques – with cultural sensitivity and freedom from racial bias so that it could form alliances with other humane forces in the world that are concerned with the promotion of mental health across the globe.

6

Asian and African 'Therapy' for 'Mental Health Problems'

In all societies religious healing tends to exist side by side with naturalistic treatment of ailments with medicines, surgery and physical manipulations, but its sphere of influence tends to shrink in the face of secularisation and scientific medicine (Frank, 1963). Scientific medicine is clearly distinct from, and has largely replaced, religious healing in Western countries. But it is different elsewhere. However, it should be noted that it is increasingly the case that, in spite of its basis in Western culture and adherence to a philosophy that is at variance with those of other cultures, psychiatry is being imposed all over the world to the detriment of what may well be more valuable and culturally appropriate measures for alleviating mental health problems – even those diagnosable in Western terms as 'mental illness'. This regrettable political situation – referred to in Chapter 5 as psychiatric imperialism – arises from a combination of factors: first, although a product of a specific cultural ethos incorporating social and political norms of nineteenth-century Europe, psychiatry has managed to clothe itself in the garb of scientific medicine, thereby gaining prestige and status; as a result, so-called knowledge within psychiatry and the practices derived from it, are perceived and promoted as 'scientific' knowledge and scientific therapies on a par with corresponding nominal equivalents that underpin the high standards of medical care and therapy. Second, travelling on the back of what goes as health care, psychiatry is accepted – and often grasped – by Asian and African governments eager to improve the health of their people. Third, and most importantly, Asian and African professionals trained directly or indirectly in Western ways of thinking about mental health – seemingly 'scientific' ways at that – not only fail to question the validity of this knowledge but, even more seriously, slide into backing these Western approaches against (often) their intuitive judgements derived from personal experience

138

and background – either for financial and economic reasons and/or because they find it easier to do so. Thus psychiatric imperialism has become politically institutionalised and actively promoted to such an extent that an ironic situation is discernible in many African and Asian countries where extreme forms of Western biological psychiatry are promoted to the detriment of indigenous systems of care based on and therapy for people with mental health problems.

It is the experience of many people, including traditional healers in (for example) India and Sri Lanka, that there is no clear distinction between religious healing and medical treatment, be it that based on traditional systems indigenous to its culture or on Western, scientific medicine. When an average Indian or Sri Lankan person consults a Western doctor or an Ayurvedic physician – or indeed seeks the services of a religious or semi-religious practitioner – he or she may choose one or other for pragmatic reasons of effectiveness, custom or convenience. Similarly, people in Africa patronise doctors trained in Western medicine and healers practising indigenous systems of medicine simultaneously (Ademuwagun *et al.*, 1979) and, as Ayoade (1979) observes about the Yoruba of West Africa, they make no distinction between 'magic' and medicine as therapy for illness.

The professional healer who has not trained in Western 'scientific' medicine is usually known in Western literature by various names carrying derogatory connotations, such as 'native-healer', 'witch doctor', 'medicine-man' or 'sorcerer'. A name that has been popularised by anthropologists as a generic term for non-Western healers is 'shaman', after practitioners in north-east Asia (Siberia) where, it is traditionally believed (by anthropologists), esoteric healing practices originated before spreading to South Asia, the Americas and Africa (Prince, 1980). Although the term 'shaman' has some respectability in Western literature, the image of a shaman, too, is tarnished by racist thinking since the name is only applied to healers who practise in cultures that are seen as 'primitive' and therefore objects of study by anthropologists. (European, 'advanced' cultures are generally studied by sociologists.) But there is some recognition among anthropologists that the functions of shamans can be understood in social terms: Lévi-Strauss (1963) points out the equivalence of shamans and psychoanalysts, and Leighton and Hughes (1961) write that shamanic behaviour is a 'time honoured ritual through which practitioners heal sick people'.

Shamans have been regarded by some anthropologists as suffering from various types of neurosis, personality disorder or psychosis but, according to Jilek (1971), their image in Western thinking is changing and they are being seen as traditional healers – psychotherapists, in Western terms. He attributes this change to the 'breakdown of positivistic ideologies and their substitution by more comprehensive theories of human behaviour' and 'the abandonment of a eurocentric world view and the relinquishing of Western superiority claims in favour of a postulated human equality' – in other words, the erosion of racism. Unfortunately, this 'change' in thinking has not yet affected the psychiatric tradition of the West; usually, all non-Western healing is subsumed under 'shamanism' and written off by both psychiatrists and anthropologists as 'supernaturally orientated healing', clearly distinct from medical and sociologically orientated healing of Western psychiatric practice (Tseng and McDermott, 1981).

It is clear from earlier chapters of this book that psychiatry as a body of knowledge has been fashioned by ideologies and world-views inherent in what is generally called Western culture. If the practices within psychiatry that are geared towards control are ignored, the practices derived from this understanding – psychiatric therapies – aim to alleviate emotional distress and restore what is conceptualised (within the aforesaid) culturally determined knowledge as mental health. In considering equivalent knowledge and practices indigenous to Asia and Africa, both 'religious' and 'medical' in type, two constraints must be recognised. First, there is an inevitable loss of meaning and significance resulting from the fact that the presentation in this book is in a Western idiom and Western language for predominantly Western-thinking people. Secondly, the literature available on the topics considered is largely based on writings of Westerners observing from the outside, as it were, and from a standpoint of preconceptions that inevitably are ethnocentric and racist. The categorisations of modes of thinking presumed to underlie non-Western conceptualisations of illness are fashioned on Western thinking, as exemplified by the following statement made by Gelfand (1964) when he was professor of medicine at the University College of Rhodesia (now Zimbabwe), in generalising about Africans: 'It is obvious that the traditional African believes firstly that disease is caused by a spirit or supernatural agency, and secondly that many illnesses can be alleviated or even cured by the administration of one of many remedies found in nature.' Many of the assumptions made by Western researchers about the ideologies and practices of medical/religious treatment in Africa and Asia are based on observations of anthropologists who accept, implicitly or explicitly, the sort of racist theories about 'primitive mentality' devised by Professor Levy-Bruhl (1923) to describe the thinking of people who are not 'white, adult and civilised': 'Their mental activity is too little differentiated for it to be able to regard the ideas or images of objects by themselves, apart from the sentiments, emotions, and passions which evoke them, or are evoked by them.'

The documentation of insanity in (Indian) Ayurvedic literature has been studied by Haldipur (1984) and Obeyesekere (1977). The former believes that the division of insanity into two broad causal categories of 'humoral' and that caused by 'spirit possession' may be analogous to divisions of illness into those having 'constitutional' and 'accidental' causation, as in Western medicine generally, or, into being 'endogenous' and 'exogenous' in type – as in psychiatry. But it would be misleading to present the terminology of one or other system in, as it were, 'alien garb' by emphasising similarities between them; the basic approach in Ayurveda is very different from that in Western definitions of what constitutes 'mental disorder'. Obeyesekere notes that humoral disequilibrium is referred to in classical Sanskrit as 'anger' or 'excitement'; the aim of Ayurvedic treatment is the calming of this disturbance and a restoration of a balance of the humoral state. Chinese medicine and Western medicine are very different in logical structure: the former does not deal with causation of illness but analyses the physiological and psychological state of a person in order to identify a pattern of disharmony that describes a situation of imbalance in the individual (Kaptchuk, 1983); in the latter, the ostensible aim of treatment is to counteract or eliminate the cause(s) of illness, although much of what passes for psychiatric treatment is geared to the suppression or control of symptoms and/or behaviour.

The influence of Ayurveda entered Tibet along with Buddhism around AD 650 and entered Indonesia, Cambodia, Burma and Sri Lanka in the first millennium AD (Jaggi, 1981). Tibetan medicine developed into a comprehensive holistic system by about the eighth century AD and continues to be practised widely in Tibet, Nepal and, more recently, in India. In her book *Tibetan Buddhist Medicine and Psychiatry*, Terry Clifford (1984) writes: 'Tibetan Buddhist medicine is a fascinating and complex interweaving of religion, mysticism, psychology, and rational medicine.... Three basic categories of mental illness defined by the Tibetans are expressed in terms of their psychological characteristics. These are 1) fear and paranoia, 2) aggression, and 3) depression and withdrawal.' Unlike classical

Ayurveda, Clifford claims that Tibetan medicine developed a distinct form of (what Clifford refers to as) 'psychiatry'. The treatment programme for a 'psychiatric' case in the Tibetan tradition includes ritual exorcism, mantras and other religious practices, change of diet and environment, acupuncture and, most especially, herbal medicines.

In describing the diverse methods of healing concerned with the restoration of mental health and the variety of practitioners using these methods in contemporary India, Kakar (1984) writes that in addition to medical healers such as the *vaids* of Hindu Ayurveda and Siddha systems and the *hakim* of the Islamic *unani* tradition:

> there are palmists, horoscope specialists, herbalists, diviners, sorcerers and a variety of shamans, whose therapeutic efforts combine elements from classical Indian astrology, medicine, alchemy and magic, with beliefs and practices from the folk and popular traditions. And then, of course, we have the ubiquitous *sadhus*, swamis, maharajs, babas, matas and bhagwans, who trace their lineage, in some fashion or other, to mystical–spiritual traditions of Indian antiquity and claim to specialize (whatever else they might also do) in what in the West in a more religious age used to be called 'soul health' – the restoration of moral and spiritual well-being.

In Sri Lanka too there is a diversity of indigenous approaches to dealing with (what in Western terms may be called) mental health problems and mental illness. The author has much anecdotal information about these, having been born and brought up in that country.

Although colonialists, missionaries and anthropologists have described healing practices in Africa – usually doing so in negative terms such as paganism, fetishism, voodoo and black magic – there is, at present, a lack of a proper understanding of the holistic totality of the African system of medical belief and practice within which individual observations may be located. Most African healing systems have not been set down in writing and the reports and observations of Westerners are often biased or distorted. However, forms of therapy for 'mental illness' may have flourished in ancient Egypt as a part of religious healing (Nasser, 1987) and there was a cultural continuity between Egypt and the rest of Africa (Asante, 1985). The remnants of this tradition that have survived the European onslaught surely continue; in their exploration and understanding lie a gold mine of knowledge.

The greatest problem in drawing any firm conclusions from the available descriptions of religious and medical healing currently practised in Africa, and culturally indigenous to that continent, is that the descriptions are often distorted by condescension and insensitivity reflected, for example, in the name usually ascribed to all types of indigenous healers, i.e. 'witch doctors' (Gelfand, 1964) – a nosology that implies, erroneously, a similarity between them and the stereotype of malevolent European witches of the Middle Ages. But even when these descriptions are sympathetic and sensitive, they are generally based on observations from outside the culture; they pick out particular aspects of healing that fit into a conception of African culture as exotic and/or primitive; and, most importantly, they are made from a standpoint of racist value judgements. But a collection of papers about African healing published together in the book *African Therapeutic Systems* (Ademuwagun *et al.*, 1979) has tried to dispel some of the racist myths about African healing, and the present chapter draws considerably on this book.

There is a dearth of documentation for Western readers concerning the variety of healers practising in African societies today. However, some indication is given by, for example, Edgerton (1980), who, writing about treatment resources available to the Yoruba of West Africa, notes that 'in addition to secretive specialists who utilize sorcery and witchcraft to cure mental illness, there are the public specialists – *babalawo* (divine priest), *onisegun* (herbalist), *aladura* (prophet of the apostolic church) and *oloogun* (herbalist sorcerer)'. But the duties of a medicine man in an African village is varied and his role is not limited to that of healing individual episodes of illness (Mbiti, 1969): 'Every village in Africa has a medicine-man within reach, and he is the friend of the community. He is accessible to everybody and at almost all times, and comes into the picture at many points in individual and community life.' Mbiti gives two examples: among the Ndebele, the medicine man may provide medicated pegs for the gates of a new homestead, combat witchcraft and magic by preventing their action and performs the ceremony of 'striking the grave', if the person concerned had died of witchcraft. Among the Azande, the medicine man cures the sick, warns the community of impending danger and tries to protect hunting and farming from failure. The magic of medicine men is good magic; 'it causes no one an injury and protects many from harm'.

The cultures of Asia are not uniform in terms of their healing systems. Although the medical traditions of Japanese and Chinese cultures are well documented, the author decided to limit the exploration of Asian approaches to 'mental and psychological' matters to those derived from the medical tradition of the Indian and Sri Lanka Ayurvedic system and South Asian healing based on working with and on the spiritual dimension of human beings. Although the cultures of Africa, like those of Europe or Asia, are varied, this chapter will consider Africa as a single cultural entity for the purpose of extracting, from its medical traditions, an 'African approach'. Native Americans come from a cultural heritage as varied and as rich as that of Asia or Africa. Unfortunately, there is insufficient literature on American medicine for this chapter even to begin delineating an approach to matters dealt within (Western) psychiatry derived from the cultures of America that predate the European occupation of that country with the consequent suppression of its cultures and the genocide of its people. In view of the drawbacks (referred to earlier) of using Western descriptions of Asian and African cultures and people, much of the discussion in this chapter avoids literature that may be biased or racist, concentrating on descriptions of personal knowledge of people experiencing and observing non-Western approaches to alleviation of mental distress and 'mental illness' from the inside or of observers whose credentials are not too suspect in a cross-cultural sense. In doing so, the emphasis is on examining the interface between psychiatry and systems indigenous to Asian and African cultures that may be equivalent to 'psychiatry'. Finally, this chapter will examine the question of collaboration between Western and non-Western systems of alleviating mental distress and curing 'mental illness', describing some attempts (at such collaboration) that have been documented.

Asian approaches

Aspects of diagnosis and treatment (in Western terms) that may be applicable to Asian cultures are varied and complex. However, certain basic principles are evident: first, medical illness is not separate from religious problems and practices; secondly, psychology, philosophy and religion are closely interconnected if not integrated – a fact that is particularly evident in the case of Buddhism, which, in Western terms, is more of a psychology than a religion. Finally, a sense of holism underpins all thinking about the person – and it is a 'holism' that includes the individual, the spiritual world, the physical environment and the cosmos, to a greater or lesser extent. These principles pervade the various practices indigenous to Eastern cultures, although the practices themselves may appear very different from each other, and identified (in Western terms) as religious, psychological, mystical or medical – or a combination of one or more of these. The traditional medical system of Ayurveda is discussed in this section as a system comparable to the medical approach of the West. Then, some comments are made about therapeutic approaches to mental health problems that seem to address the spiritual dimension of human existence. Finally, 'Tibetan psychiatry', as described by Clifford (1984), is described since it is the nearest practical system outside the West to psychiatry in the Western idiom.

Ayurveda

Concepts of illness and treatment, as well as those of health, that pervade most of Asia are based on traditional Ayurveda derived largely from the writings of Susruta and Caraka – collected in the *Susruta Samhita* and the *Caraka Samhita*, partially translated into English (Susruta, 1963; Caraka, 1983). But ideas derived from Ayurveda are mingled with those of Indian philosophy/psychology, ritual and religion – in what Obeyesekere (1977) calls 'a meta-medical extension of medical concepts'. In other words, the medical approach does not exclude the religious and philosophical dimensions of human existence and experience, although contradictions may be apparent in some aspects. Further, Ayurveda is as much about 'dissertations on correct behaviour' as about medical treatment and prophylaxis; and, from the psychological angle, Ayurveda is a 'repository' of Indian cultural thinking about the human body and the concept of the person (Kakar, 1984):

> The Ayurvedic notion of the constituents of the person, his limits and extensions in time, the nature of his connection with the natural environment on the one hand and with the psyche (and soul) on the other, the nature of the body's relationship with the psyche but also with the polis and the cosmos in determining health and illness, may not always be at a conscious level.

Ayurveda centres its interest on the person rather than the disease – the person being conceptualised as a totality including physical, psychological, social and metaphysical aspects. And the person is a microcosm of the cosmos. As in Indian philosophy, it is the individual 'self' that is all important in Ayurveda. The Ayurvedic notion of a healthy person is pervaded by ideals of moderation, control and responsibility. The maintenance of good health is inseparable from deliverance from disease. The treatment in Ayurveda for 'mental' disorders is not differentiated from that for bodily illness; and there is no systematic theory of 'mind' and 'mental' processes as there is in Western thought, although some forms of therapy for 'restraining the mind' derive from the various schools of yoga. In addition, 'purification' by, for example, purges and enemas, and 'pacification' by decoctions that tranquillise, counteract depression and strengthen the nerves may be used (Kakar, 1984). Western psychotherapy, rooted in the Western tradition of introspection aimed at knowing oneself and characterised by scrutinising 'events' and 'adventures' of one's own life (Simon and Weiner, 1966), is very different from the Indian tradition of examining one's *self*, characterised by meditative procedures of self-realisation. The 'self' of Indian thinking is 'uncontaminated by time and space' (Kakar, 1984) while the Western 'self', explored by introspection, is made up of deeds and emotions set in history.

Diagnosis

The *Caraka Samhita* lists three methods for diagnosing illness, divided by Jaggi (1981) into 'judgement of the inspired', 'observation' of the patient's body, and 'inference'; these are analogous to the processes in Western psychiatric practice of history-taking, examination and evaluation. Judgement by the specialist is based on history obtained in a comprehensive manner, and inference is concerned with deducing conclusions from the association of the illness with particular events in the patient's life history, diet, character and general conduct. Susruta adds another 'method' for diagnosis called 'interrogation' – a process of direct questioning about the patient's background, etc. One of the main tools of observation is the monitoring of the *nadi*, which means both pulse and nerves. 'With the proper spiritual imagination, developed through the use of an inner ascetic vision rather than relying on the ordinary eye vision (*netra-chaksu*) alone, the adept can "see" the state of a person's five *bhutas*, three humors and the three mental qualities through the examination of a single *nadi*' (Kakar, 1984). But 'diagnosis' in Indian medicine does not mean only identifying the disease (Jaggi, 1981):

To begin with diagnosis is made of the causes (*nidana*), premonitory indications (*purvarupa*), symptoms (*rupa*), and full extent of the disease (*samprapti*). Then the diagnosis is made of the presence of *dhatu-vaisamya*, that is the increase or decrease of some of the *dhatus* as well as those of the *dosas* and *malas*. Then the diagnosis is made of the stage of *dhatu-vaisamya*. As we know, a disease passes through five stages: *chaya*, *prakopa*, *prasara*, *purva-rupa* and *rupa*. Each stage has its own signs and symptoms. To know the stage of the disease is important from the therapeutic point of view, because the same medicine is not useful or may even prove harmful when administered at a wrong stage of the disease. Furthermore, *dosas* rarely get excited or deranged singly, and different *dosas* may be excited or deranged at different stages in different patients having the same disease. All this has to be properly recognised and assessed.

A part of an Ayurvedic diagnosis is the deduction of the patient's personality type; this is perceived in relation to the qualities that are traditionally expected, and (as in psychiatry) social desirability is equated, more or less, with health. In an Ayurvedic assessment, the patient's constitution includes his/her mental state (or state of mind), judged against a norm that rests within Indian philosophy and religion. 'Normal mind (*satva*) consists in memory, veneration, wisdom, valour, purity, and devotion to useful work' (Jaggi, 1981). Dreams of patients are analysed in assessing mental state in order to determine both diagnosis and prognosis. According to Kakar (1984), Ayurveda describes various categories of dreams: some dreams gratify desires that are taboo in the waking state and others depict individual fantasies in dramatised fashion; dreams may foretell the future; and finally, dreams may reflect the disturbance of a particular body humour. *Vaids* maintain that dreaming is the predominant psychic activity even during the waking state, the waking state itself being regarded as delusionary. And Ayurveda has a clear perception of the connections between dreams and bodily processes. Although 'Ayurvedic insights into the working of man's psyche and the causation of mental illness are remarkable achievements' (Kakar, 1984), the insistence of Ayurveda on maintaining *wholeness* (body–mind–cosmos) appears to dilute its 'clinical thrust' and dissipate the force of its psychological insights; consequently, 'mental illness is the province of many kinds of healers apart from Ayurvedic physicians – exorcists, mystics and astrologers.

Madness or insanity (*unmada*) is diagnosed on the basis of certain 'premonitory symptoms' followed by distinctive features (Caraka, 1983). The former include 'emptiness of the head', anorexia, 'fatigue, unconsciousness and anxiety in improper situations', various aches and pains and frequent appearance of certain types of dreams; the latter include 'incoherent speech', laughter and dancing in inappropriate situations, emaciation, excitement, 'observance of silence' and aversion to cleanliness. The particular combination of distinctive features denotes the type of insanity but the basic characteristics of insanity are described as follows:

> Due to the perversion of mind, the patient does not think of such things which are worth thinking; on the other hand, he thinks of such things as ought not to be thought of. Due to perversion of intellect, he understands eternal things as ephemeral and useful things as harmful. Due to the perversion (loss) of consciousness, the patient is unable to have perception of burns caused by fire etc. Due to the perversion of memory, the patient either does not remember anything or remembers things incorrectly. Due to perversion of desire, disinclination develops for things desired previously. Due to perversion of manners, the patient, who is otherwise normal, gets enraged. Due to perversion of behaviour, the patient indulges in undesirable activities. Due to perversion of conduct, the patient resorts to such activities as are against the rules prescribed in religious works.

According to Caraka, *unmada* (insanity) is divided into five types, four caused by vitiation of *dosas* (humours) and one by 'exogenous agents'. The latter includes madness caused by possession, described by Wise (1845) as being a separate kind of *unmada*, namely 'devil-madness', which is composed of *bhutonmada* (possession by bad spirits) and *devonmada* (possession by good spirits). Obeyesekere (1977) quotes Susruta as describing another cause of *unmada*, namely sorrow and shock (*sokaya*) apparently caused by 'violent action of the passions' (Wise, 1845). Three points should be noted: first, there is no mention of the cardinal symptoms of Western schizophrenia. Secondly, *unmada* is accepted as an illness as well as a spiritual possession – the latter initiated by elders, ancestors or such beings as *ghandaras* who affect the patient by touch, *yaksas* by seizure, and *raksasas* by smell. And, finally, epilepsy is described as a separate disease (Caraka, 1983).

Treatment

Ayurvedic treatment is essentially based on drugs and diet, carefully matched by the physician to the temperament of the patient and geared to an assessment of the manner in which the *dosas* (humours) are affected. If the patient requires care, the attendant (or nurse) must be carefully chosen and the patient too must play an active part in the treatment process. Jaggi (1981) quotes an Ayurvedic text, the

Kusyapa samhita, as describing 'four pillars of treatment', namely, physician, medicine, patient and attendant. The patient should possess 'strength of mind, physical vigour, intellect ... and should have full faith in God, Brahmins, teachers, physicians and friends'. The attendant should be 'one whose passions have been extinguished and possessed of good health and strength ... not suffer from duplicity ... and be tolerant'. Drugs are administered through the mouth as well as by enema through the rectum or by inhalations through the nose. The treatment of mental disorders is not separate from that of physical disorders; once an illness is identified, the aim is to purify, pacify and remove the cause (Kakar, 1984). Obeyesekere (1977) quotes the following general approach advised by Susruta: 'In all forms of insanity the restoration of serenity of mind should be first attempted. Mild and gentle forms of these remedies should be resorted to in the case of *mada* (preliminary stage of insanity).' Wise (1845) states that Indian medicine teaches that the 'patient should be treated kindly' but Obeyesekere (1977) states that 'classic texts have harsh measures to control intractable and extreme cases of *unmada*, such as threatening patients with flogging, piercing the patient with pointed instruments, or putting the patient in a dry well with a cover over it'.

In one part of the *Caraka Samhita* (Caraka, 1983) therapies are divided into three general types: 'Spiritual therapy, therapy based on reasoning (physical propriety) and psychic therapy'. The first and last are clearly 'psychological' in the Western idiom. Spiritual therapy includes incantation of *mantras*, wearing of talismans and gems, auspicious offerings, as well as what may be called religious activity such as the 'observance of scriptural rules, atonement, fasts, chanting of auspicious hymns, obeisance to gods, going on pilgrimage, etc.'; psychic therapy is described as the 'withdrawal of mind from harmful objects'. All three types of therapy are recommended for most diseases. But classical Ayurvedic treatment is basically physical; but then the 'mental' and 'physical' are not considered as two separate 'things' or structures, as they are in Western medicine.

Spiritual healing

Although the medical systems, such as Ayurveda, are the best known, there are several other healing traditions in India and Sri Lanka that have given rise to practices that have existed for generations. In general and viewed from outside the culture, these systems appear to aim at counteracting sorcery and/or 'exorcising' malevolent spirits, but clearly they have a much deeper significance to people brought up within its cultural traditions than represented by the superficial one that relates it to 'spirits' or exorcism (of spirits). Although the practices are not necessarily linked to any particular organised (institutional) religion or medical system, such as Ayurveda, they are not 'secular' – meaning, according to *The Oxford English Reference Dictionary* (Pearsall and Trumble, 1995) 'concerned with the affairs of this world' (1995: 1309). On the whole, they appear to address the spiritual aspect of human beings. ('Spirituality' is discussed in Chapter 8.)

Some of the non-medical healing traditions of India have been described by Kakar (1984) in his book *Shamans, Mystics and Doctors*. Although Kakar believes that these Indian practices are analogous to Western psychotherapy/counselling, he contends that they are based on a fundamentally different tradition from that of (Western) psychotherapy and counselling: the latter, underpinned by a tradition of introspection aimed at knowing oneself and characterised by scrutinising 'events' and 'adventures' of one's own life, differs from the Indian tradition of examining one's self by meditative procedures of self-realisation; and the 'self' of Indian thinking is 'uncontaminated by time and space' while the Western 'self', explored by introspection, is made up of deeds and emotions set in history. Kakar's book provides a Western audience with some idea of the complexity of the theoretical bases of Indian (spiritual) healing and their analogies with Western psychological approaches.

So-called exorcism rituals in the Indian tradition predate Ayurveda. These and other ways of dealing with *unmada* (madness) due to spirit possession 'stand out as an uneasy meeting between medical and priestly concerns' (Kakar, 1984) – as they do in the West. The difference is that, in practical terms, they are not in conflict; one merges into the other. Neither Ayurveda nor, for example, Tantric healing, another possible equivalent of Western psychotherapy, is secular in the way that psychiatry is secular. Neither recognises an absolute distinction between mind and body nor sees an individual as distinct from the total environment – the cosmos.

Some types of spiritual healing practised in Sri Lanka may centre on the work of astrologers, who, when they are consulted about 'problems' of various sorts, tend to indulge in prolonged explorations of their clients' lives. Their work as 'healers' has not been investigated or expounded at all. What has been described in the English literature about healing practices in Sri Lanka is mainly concerned with what early colonisers designated as 'devil dancing' and latterly as 'exorcism'. Some descriptions of these practices are contained in *Ceremonial Dances of the Sinhalese* by Otaker Pertold (1930), in *Exorcism and the Art of Healing in Ceylon* by Paul Wirz (1954), in *Medusa's Hair* by Gananath Obeyesekere (1981) and in *A Celebration of Demons* by Bruce Kapferer (1991). However, none of these books address the therapeutic dimension of the practices that they describe and so they are of little value for extracting any lessons about 'therapy' for mental health problems. The ceremonies themselves usually involve dancing where masked actors depict demonic figures (probably representing emotional states) supervised by a specialist called a *kattadiya*, translated as an 'expeller of devils' (Clough, 1999: 13). In general, one would expect people designated (in Western terms) as 'psychotic' to be exposed to these types of healing, while 'neurotic' disorders (in Western terms) may well be dealt with within one or other medical system, if at all.

In addition to specific spiritual healing practices, spiritual healing may be said to occur in the context of worship at shrines and temples that appear to specialise in dealing with people who are seen as 'mad'. It is well known that there are many temples and mosques in South Asia that have the reputation for therapeutic qualities in relation to mental health problems – usually for alleviating or curing insanity. The author has visited one such place – a mosque – near Trivandrum in Kerala (South India) and has heard of many others in South Asia. However, there is a sparsity of English literature on this topic. Such a centre, the Abbasai temple in Phaltan, a small town in Maharashtra, was studied by anthropologist Skultans (1980) and written up in the anthropology journal *Man*. Although interesting and informative, this report, like others, does not provide details of the process of healing in terms of the nature of the 'therapies' (as 'therapy' is understood in psychiatry and psychology).

'Tibetan psychiatry'

It is probably a fair generalisation that the approach to 'psychological' problems within traditional Ayurveda, while being holistic in recognising the oneness of mind and body and the validity of a metaphysical dimension to the human person, is essentially somato-psychic in practice if looked at in Western terms. But medical systems are supplemented in most of South Asia by spiritual healing. Psychiatry from an Asian cultural perspective may well appear as a combination of these approaches – the medical and the spiritual, although secularised to an extraordinary extent. Interestingly, Terry Clifford (1984) has described a system of alleviating mental distress within Tibetan medicine that appears to be akin to the (Western) system of psychiatry. She claims that this 'Tibetan psychiatry' interweaves together the Ayurvedic system of medicine derived from India, treatment by Tantric and yogic practices associated with theories of possession by evil spirits, and Buddhist dharma (religion). The similarity to psychiatry is that this is a distinctive amalgamation of what would be seen in Western terms as religious practice, metaphysical ideas about mental illness and drug therapy. But there are important differences between this and psychiatry. In the West, a medical system took over and secularised human matters concerned with morality, beliefs, thinking and feeling; 'Tibetan psychiatry' never did aspire to be a secular discipline. (Western) psychiatry derived its power by taking political control over lunatics, while the importance of 'Tibetan psychiatry' depended on its roots in Tibetan culture including its religious tradition.

According to Clifford (1984) the discipline akin to psychiatry that developed in Tibet has within it three approaches – religious, organic and psychological. Practices of both orthodox Buddhism and the elaboration of these in Tibetan Buddhism are combined with herbal therapy and diet, derived from Ayurveda, to form a system of treatment for mental and emotional problems, including madness. The approach to psychopathology is grounded in humoral theory – disease being seen as a reflection of humoral imbalance – but 'mental defilements', such as ignorance, unawareness, aversion and craving, are seen as causing changes in humoral balance. This relationship between the humours and human shortcomings, derived from Buddhist teaching, is indicative of the basic theory of psychosomatic relationships in 'Tibetan psychiatry'. Different treatments and medicines are applied to influence the mind through the body, while the (Buddhist) dharma is not only the basis for judging mental functioning but also the basis for maintaining mental health. For example, by practising the dharma, intense suffering can be turned into 'compassion and wisdom' rather than 'self pity and insanity' (Clifford, 1984).

There are no *general* treatments in 'Tibetan psychiatry' – the treatment depends on the patient's humoral type as well as the specific cause of the illness for the individual. The causes of disease in Tibetan medicine are conceptualised in terms of innumerable subtle interwoven factors, but, according to Rinpoche and Kunzang (1973), they are of two general types – long term and immediate: the former stems from ignorance giving rise to anger, desire and 'mental darkness', the three 'poisons' of the mind, which are related to changes in the three humours namely, bile, air and phlegm. The latter arise from environmental changes or various other causes such as the overuse of sense organs, unhealthy diet and bad medicine. Each disease is caused by the imbalance of the humours, sinful actions in one's previous lives or a mixture of both. The diagnostic procedure determines the kind of disease, the cause of the disease in the particular individual and the constitution of the individual developing the disease. How the Tibetan doctor-psychiatrist sets about making a diagnosis has been described by Clifford (1984):

> First he will determine if it is a hot or cold psychiatric disease and then which humor is prevalent, if it is caused by toxins or if there is a demon involved. Even though the patient's mental state is confused or altered in some serious way, the doctor still asks questions about emotional and environmental factors in the patient's life and can tell a lot from the way the patient is 'acting out'.

The 'Tibetan psychiatrist' reckons that mental illness results from 'leading a life that runs counter to one's inherent disposition'. But 'poisons and air disturbances that cause insanity demand different medicines.... In the case of "ghosts" and invisible forces, a main cause of mental illness according to the Tibetan system, religious practices and tantric medicines have to be used in conjunction with herbal medicines and other somatic treatments' (ibid.). 'Tibetan psychiatry' has a complex system of classification of demons that cause mental illness – equivalent to different types of psychoses (ibid.): 'To the Tibetans, "demon" is a symbolic term representing a wide range of forces and emotions which are normally beyond conscious control and all of which prevent wellbeing and spiritual development.' All the special tantric procedures for expelling demons (ritualised in exorcism) are 'in essence different expressions of the ultimate medicines: compassion and emptiness. These are the two great powers, the two great meditations, that subdue all diseases and evil spirits.'

African approaches

In a critical review, Professor Lambo (1969), a psychiatrist from West
Africa who was trained in England, regrets the lack of an unbiased
and comprehensive documentation of the various medical systems
of Africa: 'The material evidence we have today is but an insignificant
portion of the entire corpus of African traditional medicine which is
inextricably set in a matrix of the institution of tribal culture.' While
criticising outmoded anthropological theories about 'primitive mentality' such as that by Levy-Bruhl (1923) which denies the capacity of
Africans to comprehend the concept of causality and generality,
Lambo makes the following generalisation about differences between
the ideologies underlying Western and African medical traditions:

> Reality in the western world has gone the way of attempting to master things;
> reality for the African traditional culture is found in the region of the soul – not in
> the mastery of self or outer things, but in the acceptance of a life of acquiescence
> with beings and essences on a spiritual scale. In this fashion only is the traditional
> culture mystic. Not because of any prelogical function of mind but merely because
> the African is the possessor of a type of knowledge that teaches that reality con-
> sists in the relation not of men with things, but of *men with other men, and of all*
> *men with spirits.*

The ideology of the system of medicine practised among the Yoruba
of West Africa has been described by Ayoade (1979). It is fundamentally underpinned by the belief in a 'vital force' or 'inner essence'
that is present in everything both inanimate and animate – a force
that can be harnessed by its 'distillation' by the specialist through
'contagion' or 'incantation'. The former involves the use of objects
that have been in contact with the person or thing possessing the
'essence', and the latter involves pronouncing certain words in
certain ways.

According to Lambo (1969), African traditions attribute the causation of illness to both natural and supernatural or spiritual factors,
the balance between them varying across tribes: 'The idea of natural
causation reaches its highest peak among the Masai of East Africa
who seldom attribute disease to spiritual agency and only very rarely
to human intervention.' The treatment of an illness is determined
by its cause; non-supernatural illnesses are treated with 'rational'
treatment using medicaments, but the treatment of supernatural
ailments requires a combination of 'rational' and 'preter-rational'
treatment. It is the latter that is often referred to as magic but eluci-

dated by Ayoade as indicative of the significance of a 'higher mind' and the use in treatment of forces outside the mere rational.

The Yoruba 'medicine man' as a psychiatrist is described by Ayoade (1979) as a 'soul doctor'. His treatment includes medication but 'particularly in the case of afflictions which are believed to be due to spirit infusions through an enemy's spells or breach of taboos the corresponding cure takes the form of an exorcism designed to dispel fear and restore confidence'. Incantations and medications go together. The aim of the 'soul doctor' is 'to restore a balance between the body and the mind'. The Yoruba tradition of medicine addresses the 'whole person', physical and spiritual, recognises confession of sin – whether real or imaginary – as vital to the resolution of illness and involves the extended family in therapy (Obembe, 1983). In writing about his observations of treatment by indigenous doctors for problems that may be termed 'mental' among the Yoruba, American psychiatrist, Raymond Prince (1964), states:

> The therapy of Yoruba healers is often effective. The relative importance of the magical (or other psychotherapeutic) factors and the physiological factors in healing is difficult to determine because in almost all the cases I studied the two elements were intertwined. I did follow the management of one severe neurotic who received no physiologically active agents, however. The illness was of four years duration and had been treated by several practitioners, both indigenous and Western, with no more than temporary relief. After commencement of treatment by a competent *babalawo*, the symptoms cleared and the patient remained well for the period I studied him – some thirteen months. His treatment included several expensive sacrifices, a good deal of magical ritual, and initiation into the Ifa divination cult. Here is some evidence that nonphysiological factors may be of considerable importance.

After discussing the elements within Yoruba medicine that may be interpreted in terms of Western concepts such as 'suggestion', abreaction, group therapy and ego-strengthening, Prince concludes: 'Western psychiatric techniques are not in my opinion demonstrably superior to many indigenous Yoruba practices. I feel confident that investigation of the indigenous psychiatry of other [African] groups will lead to the same conclusion.'

Janzen (1979) has described the healing culture called *ksi-nsi* practised in south Zaire (the Congo), central Africa – a system that has survived in spite of the severe suppression of indigenous cultural practices during colonial times. Illnesses are perceived as being caused by witchcraft, magic or God, but more recently, a 'demystification' in the perception of illness has occurred: 'The mystical cause of witchcraft is substituted in diagnosis by an analysis of social relations either within the kin set or beyond it.' The sudden transformation in 1960 of the political and administrative power structure in the Congo and subsequent political changes have led to further changes in the status of indigenous therapy, resulting in a 'medical pluralism' where the techniques of the traditional healer (*nganga*), kinship therapy, purification and initiation, and Western medicine are practised side by side in contemporary Zaire. In this setting, the illness of an individual is usually 'managed' by a group of relatives who 'rally for the purpose of sifting information, lending moral support, making decisions, and arranging details of therapeutic consultation'.

Jahoda (1961) reports a study carried out in Ghana, West Africa, exploring the functions of traditional, transitional and modern agencies dealing with mental illness during 1954 and 1955. He observes that traditional healers 'almost always know, or make it their business to find out, a great deal about the background of their clients; and their way of dealing with a case is guided by this knowledge'. Although the healer may advise the patient on changes in lifestyle, the illness itself is usually attributed to a supernatural cause – or at least that is how it appears to Jahoda, an outsider to the culture: 'The traditional cosmology has no room for a purely naturalistic notion of disease, because there is no clearcut conceptual separation of the natural and physical world on the one hand, and the supernatural, magic, or witchcraft, on the other.' While acknowledging that traditional healers are widely patronised by both literate and illiterate people in Ghana, Jahoda seems to believe that their role is limited to providing support and reassurance that 'often prevents the occurrence of serious breakdown'. The pressures impinging on traditional healers in Africa are indicated by Jahoda's observation that some of the modern healers in Ghana adopt the 'external trappings of the Western medical man', and when questioned by a European person, they seem to reject traditional ideas as 'primitive'. And the patronising derision of Western observers is indicated by his contention that these healers 'are probably less likely to be of real help to their clients than traditional healers steeped in "primitive" superstition'. A feature of modern Ghana noted by Jahoda is that healing churches deal with a range of personal problems that overlap those for which traditional healers cater. Although perceived by Westerners as different from the native 'primitive superstition', they use traditional methods of healing mixed with Christian doctrine.

Even though a specific system of knowledge or therapy analogous to that within psychiatry cannot be extracted out of the African traditions of medicine, philosophy and religion that have been documented, it is clear that African ways of thinking about mental and psychological matters (in Western terms) are very different from those in the West. In that sense, an African system is there to be discovered and developed. The main characteristics of such a system should include a sense of unity of the spiritual and material worlds, perhaps akin to a feeling alluded to in contemporary literature as 'magic realism' (*New Internationalist*, 1989), the unity of animate and inanimate objects within a 'vital force' that pervades all and an individual's sense of belonging to a group.

Cross-cultural collaboration

Since different cultural traditions have developed different approaches to ways in which people deemed 'mentally ill' or suffering from problems designated as 'mental' or 'psychological' may be helped, the general mental health scene in any one country is that practitioners of different types work in parallel and the clients choose one or other type – or both or several – at the same time. However, it is (Western) psychiatry that dominates the scene in terms of governmental support in most, if not all, countries and it is the Western concept of illness, with its methods of 'treatment', that is sponsored and promoted – and this applies in most, if not all countries of the world and not just those thought of as 'Western'. Then, is there no space for a meeting of the ways or, at least, collaboration between various systems? A major hindrance to such a vision being realised is the block to progress resulting from racism (which includes cultural arrogance); another is the fact that the worldviews on which the various systems are based are very different – and that the differences are complicated by value judgements linked to perceptions of what is 'scientific' and what is not. Finally, there is an inherent contradiction that must be addressed in pursuing cultural relativity and psychological universalism simultaneously (Kakar, 1984). After examining the concept and practice of 'collaboration' in a general way, this section will note a few instances where attempts at practical collaboration have been attempted between practitioners versed in psychiatry and those of other systems.

Collaboration between systems requires, first and foremost, a mutual respect for each other by the people who work – or try to work – together. And this 'respect' must be built into the structure of the programme or joint system that is evolved, otherwise the more powerful or prestigious system is likely to override the other(s) and collaboration becomes a means of imposing one on the other. In ensuring that the collaborative process does not have this result, both short- and long-term effects of the collaboration on the psychiatric/healing systems, and on the society as a whole, must be considered. Collaborative structures must be examined at a very basic level, with genuine understanding of the political forces that keep Western interests on top and with in-built anti-racist measures to counteract the devaluation of anything that is seen as not being 'white'. Otherwise, collaborative ventures in the mental health field, as in any other, are likely to become a mere tool for the imposition of Western thinking, reinforcing the concept of Western, white superiority.

One of the earliest attempts by a psychiatrist using his Western training to work in conjunction with a non-Western indigenous system was described in *The Lancet* (1964). In 1954, Adeoye Lambo founded a day hospital at Aro in western Nigeria which developed into a unique system of 'boarding out' patients in the neighbouring villages, and thence to the use of traditional therapy available in the community; 'nothing could more tellingly illustrate Lambo's use of traditional elements in Yoruba culture than his collaboration with native healers – more commonly known as witch-doctors'. Unfortunately, this tender plant of collaboration between an African indigenous system and (Western) psychiatry appears to have withered over the years. Similar attempts were pioneered by Tigani El-Mahi in the Sudan (*Lancet*, 1964) but again did not develop. Ayurvedic and Western practitioners work in geographical proximity to each other in Bangalore (India) but, apparently, do not collaborate. In modern, Western-type Chinese hospitals, herbal medicines and acupuncture are used concurrently with Western psychotropic drugs; Ratnavale (1973) observed that in one such hospital, the Shanghai Psychiatric Institute, Western drugs are used in relatively low dosages when combined with herbal therapies and that the use of acupuncture may have virtually abolished the use of electroplexy (ECT). This may represent collaboration between practitioners versed in two different systems of medicine but raises the question of cross-cultural portability of techniques discussed in Chapter 7.

Although it is difficult to envisage close cooperation between practitioners of Western and other systems because of the conceptual gulf between Western psychiatric theory and that of the older cultures, this does not mean that an individual patient or family does not move around between different types of healers, or use different systems of psychiatry concurrently. In non-Western countries such mobility is probably the rule, rather than the exception. Lorna Amarasingham (1980), an anthropologist, has described and analysed the case of a Sri Lankan patient being taken to a number of healers in seeking treatment for 'madness'. Two fortune-tellers were consulted first, then practitioner of spiritual therapy who conducted a special type of exorcism; next, an Ayurvedic physician was consulted and made a diagnosis of 'wind-bile madness'. His treatment of a decoction, headpack, etc., resulted in a lessening of symptoms but the family continued their efforts to help her by making a propitiation to 'the gods' at an important temple. Later, when an apothecary (pharmacist) gave the patient some pills that helped even further, the relatives took her to a Western-type hospital. She was admitted to hospital, diagnosed as suffering from paranoid schizophrenia, and treated with phenothiazine medication. She was discharged improved but was said to 'retain ideas of a culture-bound nature'. The view of the family was that both Western medicine and astrological forces were powerful in effecting a recovery. They felt that hospital treatment worked 'because a ritual had already been held'. Amarasingham makes the following comments:

> All the healers, with the exception of the Western physicians, share a method in which the confirmation or disconfirmation of the diagnosis rests with the patient. While the diviners, exorcist and Ayurvedic physician are all recognised as having the power to detect causes unknown to the family, the family can recognise or reject these causes. The 'burden of proof' rests on the healer to make his description of the situation 'match' the actual situation of the family.

Although the Western hospital 'presented a system of medicine which is hidden from the patient's understanding', both the patient and her family were pragmatic in their approach, taking from each system, including the Western one, whatever suited them.

The case described above is far from unique; the author is aware that this type of shopping around by users of services and their relatives is the norm in many parts of Sri Lanka. He is also aware of anecdotal evidence of benefit from spiritual therapies and Ayurveda (without Western medicine being involved at all) for people with problems that fall within the realm of 'psychoses' and 'neuroses' in the psychiatric nomenclature. The case reported by Amarasingham shows how a type of 'collaboration' was effected by the consumer – in this case the sufferer's family, who made the initial 'diagnosis' of 'madness' and searched around for sources of help. It is clear that if the practitioners concerned had collaborated in the first place a system of 'health care' may have been available that was both coordinated and cost-effective – and (most importantly) client-centred. However, for this to happen there has to be the political will to challenge the dominance of Western 'scientific' psychiatry, the recognition of the importance of consumer choice, and a move towards a relativistic approach to mental health services.

The first step towards establishing a 'collaborative system' of the type envisaged in the previous paragraph may be to develop a pragmatic approach whereby alternative systems are promoted to develop side by side, in (say) a multicultural area of a Western society. Over the past 20 years ethnic minorities in the UK, especially in London, have developed non-governmental (voluntary) agencies providing alternative systems of culturally sensitive mental health care for people with mental health problems (see Fernando, 1995). The result of this has been that in some districts there has been a movement towards a choice being available for the multicultural populations of these areas. However, as an extension of this, attempts were made to develop projects where statutory agencies (with a traditional Western approach) formed partnerships with these voluntary agencies. Unfortunately some of these were not successful for the very reasons discussed earlier in this section, but the concept of partnership – albeit partnerships between equals – has not been discarded.

Conclusions

In the earlier part of the book, psychiatry is envisaged as being composed of a discipline and a group of practices that have developed within a Western medical tradition. This chapter attempts to address the reality that the majority of people who need 'mental health care' may well consult practitioners from very different traditions. Knowledge and practices appertaining to mental health, relief of mental distress and curing of 'mental illness' (as understood in Western idioms) are considered in this chapter by describing some Asian and African approaches to these matters, irrespective of their seeming origin in medical, religious or social systems. When seen through the eyes of a dominant Western culture many of these systems are distorted by the imposition of Western methods of analysis and the value judgements derived from racism. Whenever psychiatry is considered, its adherence to a Western worldview and its racist history must not be forgotten or ignored; but similarly ethnocentricity and bias can well affect other systems of knowledge and be evident in practices based on Asian and African cultural traditions too if these are studied fully from the points of view of the users of the services. The comments on collaboration between practitioners from diverse systems – or rather the lack of such collaboration – suggest a way forward that may be most feasible in a multicultural setting of a Western country.

Western 'scientific' medicine has undoubtedly brought major benefits to human beings the world over in dealing with non-psychiatric illnesses, such as diabetes, epilepsy, pneumonia and countless other diseases. A major aspect of its 'scientific' nature is the use of a 'medical model' whereby an illness is delineated, investigated and treated as a specific entity, more or less separate from the person suffering the illness. The usefulness of the medical model in the limited Western context may be questioned but can be justified by the fact that it is clearly a part of a culture – Western culture – and cannot be considered in isolation from other aspects of Western culture. But psychiatry is not a part of non-Western cultures, and the usefulness of the 'medical model' in dealing with feelings, emotions, fears, anxieties, aggressiveness, isolation and all the other reasons that impel people to seek help, or communities to devise ways of control, is not established in a world context.

The fact that systems of knowledge or therapy akin to (Western) psychiatry have not developed in other cultures is significant. The so-called 'Tibetan psychiatry' described by Clifford (1984) is very different in many respects from (Western) psychiatry: in the Tibetan approach, a religious viewpoint predominates; the concept of individual illnesses with individual biological causes does not underpin the thinking; and herbal therapies are not geared to illnesses but to underlying disharmonies within the individual concerned. By adhering to a biological illness model, psychiatry has gained the prestige associated with the 'scientific' label. It is therefore considered to be superior to other ways of dealing with people, such as the approaches within Asian and African cultural traditions. Racism, too, plays a part in that psychiatry is seen as being superior to other approaches to madness and the relief of emotional distress because of its association with 'white' people. It is not surprising, therefore, that attempts to amalgamate psychiatry with other, non-Western ways of dealing with people who may be seen as having mental health problems or 'mentally ill' have been largely unsuccessful. Clearly, there are serious problems in bringing together systems which are fundamentally different but, even if the differences of approach are accepted, any getting together must confront the question of power, prestige and influence of the various systems and their practitioners. In the view of the author collaboration between different sections of a multicultural society – or multicultural world – is not just possible but something that is necessary – and not just in the field of mental health. The challenge for the world of mental health is to face up to the need for change and in doing so to face up to cultural difference and racism.

7

Technologies for Mental Health

The application of psychiatry across the world as a total package is clearly ill conceived and its imposition globally is referred to (in Chapter 5) as 'psychiatric imperialism'. It is equally unwise, of course, to think that other ways of dealing with emotional stress and/or maintaining mental health, some of which were described in Chapter 6, can be applied *in toto* outside the cultures that they grew up in – a matter that is easily accepted because they, unlike Western ways, are seen, erroneously and for racist reasons, as inferior to psychiatry. This chapter discusses the transcultural portability of fragments of cultural systems in the shape of technologies concerned with mental health. The term 'technology', broadly speaking, means 'any tool or technique, any product or process, any physical equipment or method of doing or making, by which human capability is extended' (Schon, 1967); in the present context (of mental health) it refers to ways of handling stress, 'psychiatric treatments' and means of promoting spiritual development. The chapter considers the feasibility of defining and cutting out 'bits' of a cultural system as technologies extracted from their cultural roots, and the practicality of transplanting such bits into other cultures. It should be seen as a prelude to Chapter 8 where ideas of unity and amalgamation across racial and cultural barriers are taken further.

It must be acknowledged at the outset that this chapter may appear to contradict two contentions seemingly implicit in earlier parts of this book. First, that a culture being an integral whole, cultural systems, such as a system of 'psychiatry', within any one culture hang together with other systems within that culture and cannot be dealt with piecemeal; and secondly, that, since the cross-cultural imposition of concepts and models (of illness and treatment) are not viable, in a culturally alien 'setting', ways of dealing with illness should not be applied cross-culturally. However, the author believes that the teaching of earlier chapters must be tempered by certain realities: cultures are not static entities but are changing all the time and this applies particularly to the different cultures – or subcultures – within multicultural societies; the world is becoming smaller in terms of human interaction and hence of cross-cultural influences although, admittedly, the overall effect at present is Westernisation because of the power structure in the world coupled with racism; and finally, it is not possible, in the world of today, to think and plan in terms of totally separate development of cultural systems nor realistic to assume that practices within a culture that affect mental health will not be copied by people from other cultures. This chapter therefore takes a pragmatic approach in attempting to face a vital question of practical significance and immediate importance: if the interchange of cultural practices (that help to maintain mental health) is taking place how best can this be managed? The aim of this chapter is not to create a 'new' form of psychiatry by combining deculturalised fragments from various sources but to determine, if possible, the principles that should govern the cross-cultural interchange of practical techniques for promoting mental health. For example, under what conditions is it justifiable to take out from one culture a method of healing, a technique for treating 'mental illness', or a means employed for 'spiritual liberation' and then apply it in another very different cultural setting? How would such methods or techniques travel and would they require modification? And, most importantly, what would the application of such 'foreign' technology do to the indigenous modes of help available in the recipient society?

The basic principle that needs to be accepted if cross-cultural interchange or transfer of this type is to take place concerns the need to counteract the force of racism at all levels. This means an open-minded and anti-racist approach in the evaluation of cultures and their constituents, whenever a technology is examined or a system evaluated. The first stage in identifying a technique for transfer cross-culturally is to examine cultures and their approaches to mental health on the lines indicated in Chapters 2 and 6. The cultures that are examined and the techniques identified must be analysed and understood from within each culture, because an outsider's view is very likely to be contaminated by preconceptions about the culture or technique, often based on racist ideas. Once a technique for promoting mental health is identified and its function within its own culture of origin understood, the question of its transfer and integration into a different culture could be considered as a second stage. Clearly, a technique that is alien to a culture will initially have a 'mystical' or magical air about it – and indeed may well have an attraction because of its novelty – but eventually it has to become absorbed and/or integrated into the new culture if it is to serve a long-term function. This is the scenario for considering cross-cultural transfer of techniques that aim to maintain mental health.

Although psychiatry as a total system is too much a part of its home culture to be plucked out and transferred into other cultures as it stands, it has within it modules of theory and practice that may be usefully offered to people of all nations, races and cultures. It has, after all, amassed, over the past 300 years, a mountain of knowledge – however ethnocentric it may be and however racist its viewpoint: it has developed ways of managing people deemed to be mentally ill or emotionally disturbed, whether by confining them in institutions or with systems of 'community care', 'crisis intervention', 'home treatment' and suchlike; it has developed medicines, 'talking therapies' and techniques of modifying behaviour aimed at the relief of human suffering. And it has refined over the years its own ways of observing human beings and examining their behaviour and thinking with complex techniques of measurement and analysis. Further, psychiatry is a part of a Western culture which has latterly developed a humanitarian tradition epitomised by (for example) the unchaining of lunatics in France in the nineteenth century and the legal safeguarding of human rights embodied in the current British Mental Health Act (Her Majesty's Stationery Office, 1983).

The ancient cultures of the East and of Africa having survived, to varying extents, the onslaught of Western spoilage, still contain within them a store of knowledge and understanding of the human condition and ways of dealing with human problems, although their systems of medicine and healing have been underdeveloped and often suppressed. It is difficult to distinguish within Asian and African traditions particular techniques that can be identified as 'psychiatric' in the way that such techniques are understood in the West. But, when viewed in a global context, the maintenance or achievement of mental health is not just about psychiatry. Methods of exorcism, meditation, acupuncture and yoga practised in African and Eastern cultures are on a par, as technologies, with Western treatments like electroplexy, family therapy and psychoanalysis – although, of course, the contexts in which they function are very different; and forms of psychotherapy (in a broad sense) are practised in all cultures. Methods of diagnosis and assessment in psychiatry and ways of evaluating people in terms of suitability for healing or 'liberation' may be designated as technologies too.

Technologies for mental health may be identifiable within cultural systems but none of these technologies is intelligible unless seen in relation to the culture in which it has grown up and remains embedded. And before even thinking of transporting a technology cross-culturally, it must be properly understood in terms of its meaning and use within its own culture, taking care to avoid racist value judgements in doing so. Then, in transporting 'bits' of a culture, such as a 'religious' technique for spiritual improvement or a 'treatment' for 'endogenous depression', the cultural context of its origin, as well as the process by which it can be fitted into the host culture, must be appreciated. And, of course, the host culture too must be understood. As Alan Watts (1962), an outstanding Western interpreter of Buddhism, states, in comparing Western psychotherapy with Eastern methods of spiritual liberation, 'we can borrow things from other cultures but only to the extent that they serve our own needs'.

The question of extracting techniques from a total system, such as psychiatry or divination, is a difficult matter for two reasons: first, there is the problem of defining the limits of a technique as distinct from its context – of separating its form from its content. For example, does a technique of exorcism include all the rituals that go with it or only some? Can electroplexy be transported without taking with it the concept of 'endogenous depression' and, more importantly, the concept of dealing with certain problems as illness? Secondly, there is the problem of evaluating the effectiveness of a technique when the aim of using it may be different in the host culture from that in its culture of origin. For example, the aim of Western psychotherapy is often conceptualised in terms of a person becoming self-reliant and independent while, in a different culture, such qualities may be seen as a sign of deviance or even illness. Spiritual growth through self-denial may be valued in one culture but seen as non-productive and maladaptive in a different society. The problem may be even more complex and serious: for instance, a process of exorcism that is concerned with elimination of evil influences may be seen in a Western culture as a sign of illness in the exorcist; the use of electric shocks or powerful 'psychotropic' drugs may be seen in an African or Asian tradition as unethical – and even evil – interference with spiritual experiences or beliefs. On the whole, it is easier to delineate and conceptualise the transport of predominantly physical techniques such as drug or herbal therapy, compared to methods that involve psychological or spiritual matters, although the difference is one of degree only, for in the case of mental health the psyche–soma division of a person is essentially an artificial one.

It must be admitted that the subject matter of this chapter is full of pitfalls and that compromises need to be made in practice. Unfortunately, there is no reliable literature to fall back on in the discussion. There are reports of Eastern techniques, such as meditation, being used in Western psychotherapy (Carrington, 1982) and psychiatry (West, 1979) and of Eastern ideas being used to develop a special type of psychotherapy, namely transpersonal psychotherapy (Vaughan and Boorstein, 1982), but no real discussion of the difficulties inherent in integrating one process or system with another. The author is aware of anecdotal reports that Asian Ayurvedic physicians and African herbalists use Western drugs as a part of their remedial mixtures, but has no knowledge of any meaningful discussion of their doing so. The author is therefore acutely conscious of the limitations of the discussions to follow and presents them as a tentative approach rather than as conclusive ideas. In doing so, individual techniques will not be described in detail or considered in depth; only a few chosen aspects will be considered. Since the book is for a mainly Western readership, 'bits' of Western psychiatric treatments, divided into the traditional physical and psychological categories, will be considered, followed by a brief reference to some aspects of assessment used in psychiatry and the legal framework of mental health legislation. Then, after a short discussion of the transportation of herbal remedies, Chinese acupuncture, Indian yoga and more recently developed Japanese psychotherapies, various healing techniques and methods of 'liberation' will be discussed. The emphasis throughout will be on the question of transporting technologies from their cultures of origin for application elsewhere. Much of the discussion will be speculative, looking to a way forward into an era where cultural interchange for the promotion of mental health replaces the 'unhealthy' tendency to impose Western ideas and techniques willy-nilly for largely political and racist reasons.

Psychiatric techniques

There are various problems in analysing the content of psychiatry in order to extract from it those aspects within it, of both theory and practice, that may be of universal relevance. First, there is doubt about the basic system used by psychiatry for diagnosing illness and about the relevance of its ways of measuring human functioning by, for example, using the 'mental state examination' and designating 'mental illness'. Secondly, the ethos of psychiatry is bound up with that of the culture in which it has grown and whatever is hived off may carry that ethos with it. Thus, wherever they are applied, Western cultural views on human existence may be an inherent part of most types of 'psychotherapy' and Western ideals on correct behaviour a part of 'behaviour therapy'. And, most importantly, racist conceptions of people and their cultures are deeply embedded in Western methods of psychiatric assessment. Hence, specific attempts must be made to minimise the effects of these drawbacks inherent in the transfer of Western technology cross-culturally.

In considering the cross-cultural transfer of Western techniques of treatment, it is necessary, first and foremost, to remove the present system of diagnosis and assessment in psychiatry in order to get at those aspects of psychiatric practice and theory that may be portable. But there is one exception: psychiatry can contribute significantly, with few reservations, to useful global knowledge in the identification of 'mental illness' caused by organic pathology – in line with the obvious advantages of Western medicine in general. In the case of so-called 'functional' illness, once diagnosis has been excluded from the scene, knowledge about the personal distress caused to individuals by specific problems and evaluation of the disturbance to society arising from people's behaviour can be looked at pragmatically; and the use of drugs or other forms of 'treatment' to alleviate symptoms, change behaviour or bring people under 'control' can be assessed. Further, all treatment techniques should be examined as methods directed at particular forms of distress or at particular modes of behaviour causing problems. But great care must be taken to fix the definition of a problem, behaviour or treatment in a cultural context free of racist bias. In general, the cultural content of all treatment must be geared to the culture of the individual patient, although the experience of Western psychologists and psychiatrists in the application of broad principles may be useful in some situations, if freed from racist value judgements. Finally, an important message that can be usefully extracted from practices that have become an integral part of psychiatry for transfer to a global scene concerns human rights. The controls exercised over lunatics in many parts of the world have been the subject of much discussion in the West because of their alleged violation of individual human rights. The legal framework for safeguarding the rights of people seen as 'mad' or 'mentally ill' is relatively well developed in some Western countries – particularly Britain – apart from the failure to address questions of race and culture. Although the legal safeguards incorporated into some Western psychiatric systems may have to be adapted to suit cultural differences and to deal with racist assumptions, they can be the basis for reform that should be extended universally.

The knowledge within psychiatry about organic disorders, unlike the knowledge about so-called 'functional disorders', is based on objective observations of a physical nature. It is therefore likely to be applicable in large measure across cultures and races, for any distortions caused by cultural and racial biases can be checked out and removed quite easily. In the case of 'functional disorders', however, such biases are too well integrated into the culture of the subject to be amenable to such action (Fernando, 1988). The organic disorders in psychiatric nosology are the diseases caused by physical, structural or biochemical factors, the major ones being chronic brain syndrome (various forms of dementia), epilepsy, nutritional disorders that may cause emotional disturbance and endocrine dysfunction. But it is the psychiatry of non-organic, 'functional' illness that this section is mainly concerned with. And for these, psychiatry uses both physical and psychological methods of therapy.

Physical treatment

Psychiatry has experience in the use of a large number of drugs and other physical treatment such as electroplexy. They are generally used empirically, i.e. their use is based on knowledge from experience alone. In preparing these techniques for transportation cross-culturally, each treatment has to be analysed in terms of its effect on particular forms of distress rather than in terms of ethnocentric 'illness' models; they must be seen as being directed at particular perceptions, such as hearing 'voices', biological functions, such as sleep and appetite, and behaviour, such as excitement or excessive

slowness. In general, techniques of 'physical treatment' are interventions that may be used for suppressing and/or distorting various
human experiences, modalities and behaviour. Once analysed in
this way, the specific circumstances, if any, in which each intervention is needed in the 'new', host culture can be evaluated. The aim is
to match a particular intervention to a type of perception, biological
dysfunction or behaviour and then to match its use to the relief of
distress in individuals or communities seen as integral units within
the host cultures. Clearly, the use of the item of treatment in the host
culture may be very different from its use in the culture of origin.

The above approach to Western psychiatric techniques of physical treatment means that they are not transported cross-culturally
as 'treatment' of (diagnosed) 'illness' but as interventions in specific
situations. In this way, it is conceivable that most of the psychotropic
drugs, and even electroplexy, may be used pragmatically across
cultures for the alleviation of distress, control of behaviour or suppression of perceptual experiences. But, as they become established
in a host culture, their use should be incorporated into the total
(host) culture without discounting the value of other forms of intervention, and without interfering with culturally consonant practices
or treatment techniques. By avoiding the process of diagnosis, the
'alien' physical technologies of psychiatry can thus diffuse into the
host culture and become incorporated into it to be used as, and if,
the need arises. In summary, since physical treatments are generally
used empirically anyway, they are usable without the need for a
diagnostic rationale for their use. As such, they can be transported
cross-culturally, once they are evaluated in terms of their individual
effects rather than in terms of treating 'illness'.

Psychological therapies

Western psychotherapies are geared to cultural needs in the West,
but are based on ways of working with human beings. Raymond
Prince (1980) argues that the common theme in all psychotherapy is
the mobilising of 'healing forces within the patient'. In examining
Western psychotherapy for universally useful concepts and procedures that are related to this basic theme, certain broad principles
may be extracted. The emphasis in Western psychotherapy on the
client gaining 'insight' should be discarded as a culture-bound phenomenon that is unlikely to have much meaning in other cultures;

but the importance of the 'therapeutic relationship' established between the therapist and client is a concept that may be universally useful – but not if it is conceptualised in terms of 'transference', since this, too, has a meaning specific to (Western) psychoanalytic psychotherapy. Clearly, the qualities in this relationship that are therapeutic must be culture-specific, but its importance in therapy is likely to be universally valid. The minutiae of psychoanalytic theory, such as the oedipal complex, are unlikely to be applicable universally in the highly ethnocentric form that they are used, although some aspects of the general approach of the (Western) psychoanalyst in evaluating infantile behaviour may be useful in the understanding of adult behaviour in other cultures also. Certain aspects of behaviour therapy may be extractible for use across cultures; but here too, they must be integrated into the cultural system of the patient and behaviour judged in terms of that culture. And, as in the case of interventions with drugs and other physical 'treatments', the 'psychological therapies' also should be used pragmatically according to personal and/or community need rather than 'treatment' for 'illness'.

Various systems of family therapy have developed recently in Europe. This phenomenon may be a corrective reaction to the emphasis on the single individual that developed in psychiatry because of its adherence to a biomedical model of illness – a problem that may not be applicable to indigenous systems of therapy in other cultures. For it is nothing new for healers in Africa and Asia to involve the family and to take a wide view of problems presented to them as illness. Although the family therapies in the West are geared to Western models of family structure and functioning, it is possible that certain ways of analysing families may be transportable across cultures. But great care is needed. Annie Lau (1986), a practitioner of transcultural family therapy, recommends the clarification of cultural assumptions about families before applying the basic approach of a Western family therapist: while accepting the assumption that an individual's problems can be helped by treating the entire family as a unit, the therapist must reinforce what is considered to be competent family functioning and discourage patterns of behaviour that are dysfunctional. As in the case of individual 'psychotherapy', the basic ethos of (Western) family therapy, namely, that family interactions matter, can be transported cross-culturally; but this is hardly necessary, since this view is already prevalent in most cultures outside the West.

Data analysis and legal framework

It has been noted earlier (Chapter 5) that psychiatric systems for analysing people through diagnosis of illness are not just of limited use cross-culturally, but may well be very destructive if imposed on to other cultures. However, some aspects of (Western) methodology used for collecting, quantifying and analysing data may well be usable universally, once valid observations sensitive to culture and free of racist bias have been made. Thus, ways of ordering some types of data and statistical techniques, such as those used in psychology research, may be useful in analysing the effectiveness of specific types of intervention for mental health generally. Also, the emphasis on objectivity characteristic of the Western, scientific approach may be applicable cross-culturally in limited ways in evaluating specific matters related to mental health. But great care needs to be taken to ensure that 'objective' criteria in a Western sense are not applied to questions of feeling, belief and spiritual values, and that the Western reductionist approach is not allowed to distort the knowledge about ways of working for mental health in other cultures.

It must be admitted that the rights and welfare of people are not always dependent on laws and regulations. However, a legal framework is generally an essential prerequisite for fair and humane treatment of people who are seen as deviant or 'mad' – and all societies tend to do this in one way or another. Mental health legislation in Europe and the United States may not be ideal – in particular, there is a general failure in the West to address the injustices of racism in psychiatric practice; however, the legislation, such as that embodied in the British Mental Health Act (Her Majesty's Stationery Office, 1983), does provide a basic framework for Western conditions. Hence, it is likely that the fundamental tenets of Western laws may be usefully transported cross-culturally for integration into legal systems elsewhere, although such a manoeuvre is not a simple matter. This question is relevant to a discussion of mental health but its examination is beyond the remit of this book.

Herbal remedies

Treatment with herbs may seem, at first sight, to have a similar basis to drug therapy, for after all some drugs were originally merely purified extracts of plants. But herbs are not usually used in the way that drugs are used in Western medicine and psychiatry. In Chinese medicine, for example, herbs do not target specific conditions or symptoms; the aim of herbal therapy, like all other therapies, is to rebalance disharmonies in bodily rhythms (Kaptchuk, 1983). Moreover, herbs are seldom used singly; different herbs are carefully blended in a balanced mixture to fit the precise disharmony that is diagnosed. In Tibetan medicine (which has been influenced by both Chinese and Indian medical systems), 'it is not so much the presence of one particular ingredient but the particular combination of many ingredients that provides the desired therapeutic effect' (Clifford, 1984). The oldest known system of herbal medicine is the ancient 'Vedic' system of the Indian tradition which predates Ayurveda. In describing a particular Vedic herbal remedy, Jaggi (1981) states:

> The herbs are propitiated and also appeased for being uprooted. The high cost of the medicinal preparation and the deep knowledge of the physician are emphasized upon. His closeness to the healing divinities is publicised. Lastly, after the administration of the drug, it is forcefully suggested that 'the herbs have driven away all defects of the body whatever'.

In modern Ayurveda, herbal remedies are suited to the individual who takes them, as well as being geared to the diagnosis – again in terms of imbalance rather than specific cause. They are usually combined with diet and other remedies. Sometimes, the way the herbs are grown and picked are considered important. In Tibetan medicine, the state of mind (of the physician) when preparing a medicine 'adds a crucial factor to the effectiveness of the medicine' (Clifford, 1984). Finally, herbs may be taken by mouth as pills or concoctions, inhaled after being burned, or even massaged into the body; the exact method is often as important as the herbs that are used.

Thus, when used in its original context, herbal remedies are not just individual substances for specific needs (as drugs are in Western medicine) but a part of a larger system of healing. If transported into a Western medical cultural setting and used in the way that drugs are used in the West, the basis of the treatment may be lost. It may be argued from a scientific standpoint that such a change would merely separate the therapeutic effects of the herbal remedy from 'placebo' effects. But, in the field of mental health, one cannot meaningfully dismiss 'placebo' effects as being fundamentally different from, or less important than, therapeutic effects. However, in spite of drawbacks, there may be some gain in research (of a scientific type) into the use of herbs in the setting of Western psychiatric practice, so long as the methods of combining herbs are honoured, some attempt is made to understand the use of the herbs in their original cultural context, and the use of herbal remedies is accepted as a means of balancing different emotions, rather than suppressing symptoms of 'pathological' conditions. The mere empirical use of herbs as substances which may affect the 'mind' in some way should be avoided.

Acupuncture

The use of acupuncture, and the associated technique of moxibustion, must be seen in the context of Chinese medicine based on Chinese philosophy, epitomised by the concept of a balance of *yin* and *yang* – distinctive but inseparable poles of life energy which are in dynamic balance. Acupuncture, by inserting needles at carefully selected points along a system of meridians traversing the human body, aims to rebalance those aspects of the body's *yin* and *yang* whose harmonious proportion and movement have become disordered (Kaptchuk, 1983). Chinese medicine is not concerned with cause and effect but with relationships, contexts and patterns of events. When an illness is diagnosed, the Chinese physician does not look for 'causes' but for disharmony between a person's environment, emotional attitude and way of life. Acupuncture is carried out in combination with dietary advice, physical exercise and advice on correct living. The aim of treatment is to reharmonise, not to eradicate, the cause (of the disharmony) nor to relieve symptoms. Thus acupuncture is part of a comprehensive system of medicine very different from that of the West. The points on the surface of the body at which acupuncture needles are applied (acupuncture points) are related to pathways (meridians) that carry *qi* (a type of energy, unifying all parts of the body into a harmonious whole). Therefore, the application of acupuncture must relate to disharmonies diagnosed within the Chinese system of medicine bearing no relation to disease entities or disorders recognised in the Western medical model.

Acupuncture is used in the West as a technology isolated from its cultural base and its traditional theory. Its application in the West is largely limited to its use for pain relief and anaesthesia; consequently, theories have been developed for its action in these aspects of medical practice – for example, the gate theory of pain (Melzack and Wall, 1965) which may provide a physiological explanation for its action in pain relief (Man and Chen, 1972). The possibility that acupuncture may stimulate the release of endorphins, a type of opiate naturally released in the brain (Goldstein, 1976), has also been hypothesised (Kaptchuk, 1983). But no physiological explanations for the existence of the meridians and the specificity of acupuncture points have been forthcoming. There are anecdotal reports that acupuncture can enhance 'antipsychotic' effects of Western drug therapy (Abeywardena, 1983), but no consistent evaluation of its use for the treatment of mental illness in a Western setting using Western diagnoses. Dunner and Dunner (1983) report that various psychiatric institutes in China, invariably modelled on Western lines and using American diagnostic systems and drug therapy, use electrical stimulation by acupuncture needles placed in the forehead where 'the patient sometimes responded with convulsions'; clearly a way of giving ECT rather than acupuncture! But earlier, Ratnavale (1973) had described the extensive use of acupuncture in Western-type psychiatric institutes in China. It seems that the doctors at the Shanghai Psychiatric Institute told him that acupuncture had replaced ECT:

> Psychotic and neurotic patients are given acupuncture along with other types of treatment. It is considered particularly helpful in treating syndromes characterised by excitement, anxiety, apathy, catatonic stupor, and depression. Points on the limbs and trunk have been identified for needling in psychiatric conditions; they lie along the standard *ching*, but why these points have been selected over others has still to be explained.

Clifford (1984) states that the acupuncture points recognised in Tibetan medicine for the treatment of psychiatric disorders are on the top of the skull and base of the neck. It is possible that research into the empirical use of acupuncture, based perhaps on its use in Tibetan medicine, may prove to be of advantage in the West in using acupuncture as an empirical technology. Such a use of acupuncture may be feasible but it is unlikely that it can be integrated into the psychiatric theory of disease unless the latter is greatly modified.

Yoga

Yoga, the 'way', is the term given to a form of Indian psychology as well as to systems of what might be called self-purification. Yogic

powers are no myth and they should not be seen as magical or supernatural. They arise from practices – yogic practices – that are a matter
of application and training. It is well beyond the scope of this section
to describe them, but some comments about yoga may be appropriate
in the context of mental health.

The ultimate goal of yoga is liberation and an eightfold path to
liberation has been described (Safaya, 1976): (1) abstention (*yama*),
(2) observance (*niyama*), (3) posture (*asana*), (4) regulation of
breath (*pranayama*), (5) withdrawal of the senses (*pratyahara*), (6)
contemplation (*dharana*), (7) fixed attention (*dhyana*) and (8) deep
meditation (*samadhi*). The first five are external or indirect means
or aids, while the last three are internal or direct aids. Different
teachers of yoga emphasise various aspects of this basic approach,
concentrating on particular practices. Bhakti yoga concentrates on
love and devotion, raja-yoga on meditation, karma-yoga on (good)
works, jnana-yoga on understanding and hatha-yoga on utilising
physical (somato-psychic) forces. Systems of yoga are expressed in
metaphorical, sometimes picturesque, presentations. For example,
in 'kundalini-yoga' the centre of psychic energy is depicted as a
coiled serpent resting within the human being. Here yogic practices
are designed to awaken the Kundalini which gradually unfolds to
reveal one's inner self, which is the same as the basic reality of the
universe.

In purely practical terms, a system of yoga is a discipline consisting
of exercises of the mind and body; thus, yoga as a means of keeping
mentally healthy seems to have great potential as a portable technology that may be isolated from its cultural medium. In fact it is as a
basic system of keeping healthy and fit that yogic exercises are often
practised in India in the present day (Sen, 1961). Hatha-yoga has
already been taken up in the West as a system for keeping physical
health and clearly has a future for integration into psychiatry. It may
be considered (in Western terms) as a somato-psychic therapy – a
way of influencing the mind by training the body. However, as with
other Eastern techniques, (Western) psychiatry has to be redefined
to some extent in order to incorporate yoga into its fold.

Japanese psychotherapies

Various forms of religious psychotherapy – as distinct from religious
practice per se – which have emerged during the twentieth century

in Japan have been written about in the English language literature. Some are seen as cults – for example, *Gedatsukai* or 'a society for deliverance' or the 'Salvation Cult' (Lebra, 1982) – but others which are more acceptable to psychiatry, such as Morita therapy (Kora and Sato, 1958; Murase and Johnson, 1974) and *naikan* therapy (Murase, 1982), are recognised as 'treatment'. Clearly, all Japanese psychotherapies have roots in Zen Buddhism and Shintoism but seem to be less 'mystical' and exotic to Western thinking than are Indian and African healing systems – for both racial and cultural reasons (as noted below). From a Western psychological viewpoint, they appear to be based on 'self reconstruction' of personality, although meditation, possession rituals and the consumption of health foods are all used.

Morita therapy was developed in the 1920s in a Western medical model of 'illness' but emphasising Japanese cultural traditions. It has undergone some change over the years and is now used in Japan entirely for a narrowly defined personality type, the *shinkeishitsu* type, who might be seen as suffering from *shinkeishitsu* neurosis. There are two steps in Morita therapy: first, absolute bedrest, and secondly, gradual adaptation to outer reality by physical work in groups (Fujita, 1986). Correspondence with the therapist by means of a written diary which is corrected by the therapist is an important part of the highly structured regime in Morita therapy. *Naikan* therapy uses meditation for 'observing oneself' for guilt and gratitude and it is carried out under the direction of an interviewer who visits the client periodically. According to Murase (1982): 'The role of the interviewer is quite different to that of the ordinary professional counselor or therapist. His primary function is to directly supervise the client in a very specific routine of concentration on his past. His main concern is that the client follows instruction and reflects successfully on the topics assigned for self-examination.' The basic ethos of both *naikan* therapy and Morita therapy is 'accepting things as they are' – summarised by the Japanese word *sunao*, which implies 'a harmonious and natural state of mind *vis-à-vis* oneself and others' (Murase, 1982).

Morita therapy has been transported to the United States and utilised in an educational model rather than a medical one; it is used on an outpatient basis, without bedrest, for the treatment of 'a broad spectrum of clients – from the neurotic to the normal, and some borderline psychotics and depressed clients as well' (Reynolds, 1988). If the efficacy of the modified version of Morita therapy is shown to be useful in a Western setting, a model may be set for transporting cross-culturally other systems of psychotherapy, such as psychoanalysis. It is significant that after transportation from its cultural roots, it is the practical methodology of Morita therapy that is used and not the explanatory model underlying the system. Further, it is a Japanese system of 'psychotherapy', not an Indian or African one, that has taken root in American psychiatry. The significance may lie in the fact that as Japan has become industrialised and, more importantly, 'Americanised' since the end of the Second World War, the Japanese have been increasingly seen as 'Western' and 'white'. This is epitomised by the (white) racist government of South Africa designating people of Japanese descent as racially 'white', as distinct from those of African, Indian and Chinese descent. Thus Morita therapy, not being blocked by a racist value judgement as inferior, has been able to get into mainstream Western culture. Perhaps racism is the main barrier to other systems being transported for application in the West.

Healing and liberation techniques

People around the world use various means – therapies – for dealing with problems that affect them. These may be social and/or interactional involving other people – for example, in exorcism rituals – or they may be for the individual to practise alone – such as meditation (although the latter may involve other people as teachers, facilitators or gurus). The self-help, healing methods considered in this chapter are those regarded, at least in their original forms, as being derived from the culture of the society they belong to. Prince (1976) argues that all people everywhere have certain 'endogenous' healing capacities of a self-help type and that healing techniques, whatever they consist of, are all 'simply manipulations and elaborations of these endogenous healing mechanisms'. In other words, healing procedures tune into or stimulate capacities for self-healing that are inherent in human beings or in the human condition. Prince suggests that the most important healing mechanisms of an individual, self-help type involve altered states of consciousness – as in dreams, dissociated states, a variety of religious experiences, mystical states and psychotic reactions. This section aims to consider first, the question of meditation as a possible technology for psychiatric healing. Secondly, dreams and trance states will be discussed briefly in the same context; and finally, some comments will be made about exorcism.

The attainment of a mystical experience through meditation is a therapeutic venture that is attained by practice and training. States of 'ecstasy' and trance states are similar, although the means for reaching them may be different. One of the most universal of self-help techniques for achieving mystical experience, and one that has been avidly taken on by Western 'scientific' authorities for investigation and use, is meditation. Exorcism is also universally seen in various religious contexts; it is the kind of procedure that is particularly associated with the activity of shamans or priests of various cultures. Trance states may be induced or occur (seemingly) spontaneously; and dreams, though more clearly spontaneous, may be seen as vehicles of divine communication and/or means of healing. Although healing and (spiritual) liberation characterise much of 'psychiatry' in many parts of the world and in diverse cultures, most of the literature on their techniques refer to practices in Eastern cultures; inevitably, much of this section is about practices in these traditions.

Meditation

All the major religions, except Zoroastrianism, appear to have religious practices that may be subsumed under the general rubric of meditation techniques (Prince, 1976). Although meditation is particularly associated with Buddhism, 'the belief that the higher spiritual life can be lived only in and through meditation' is applicable to the traditions of the Hindus, Taoists, Sufis and Christian contemplatives (Conze, 1959), as well as those of pre-Columbian North America (Freuchen, 1959) and Africa (Katz, 1973). In all these traditions, the experience of an altered state of consciousness induced by meditation is not an end in itself but closely linked to the attainment of what can be loosely described as 'liberation' or 'enlightenment'. There is a considerable body of written information on meditation in the Buddhist tradition in which various techniques (of meditation) are practised. In presenting these for Western readers, Edward Conze (1959) notes that the psychological constitution of the subject must be suited to the technique chosen. Further, there are progressive steps to be followed leading to meditation, such as the restraint of the senses (holding back from attachment to sense objects), moderation in eating and avoidance of sleep: 'With your senses turned inward, unmoved and well-controlled, with your mind undistracted, you should walk about or sit down at night.' Then, with a 'mindfulness' of all activities, the subject goes into 'seclusion'; 'sitting cross-legged in some solitary spot, hold your body straight, and for a time keep your attention in front of you... then force your wandering mind to become wholly occupied with one object'. This 'object' may be a 'mantra' (word of power) suited to the individual.

Zen meditation emphasises the importance of sitting while meditating to deal with repentance and destruction of sins. It may use a type of riddle or paradox to which there is no answer in the ordinary sense, called a *koan* – such as, 'what is the sound of one hand clapping'. The teaching is that 'the practice is the enlightenment' – but this should not be taken to mean that meditation is purposeless. Nor, of course, has it got a purpose in the ordinary sense of the word. In Zen meditation, the 'Buddha-nature' has to be *realised* not attained or awaited (Conze, 1959). In general, 'being without thoughts is the object of Zen meditation; the control of body and mind is only a method of reaching it. When body and mind have been controlled, then from the ensuing absence of thoughts, are born naturally and rightly brilliant understanding'; the ultimate state is one of 'perfect Buddha-wisdom, reading of the scriptures and devotion, asceticism and austerities' (Amakuki, 1959).

In ascribing the use of meditation according to the type of person who meditates, Buddhist theory has a complex way of evaluating 'types'. Conze (1959) quotes a teacher of meditation, Buddhaghosa, as delineating six types of persons for this purpose, each identified by a dominant quality. Thus there are people dominated by greed, hate, delusion, faith, intelligence and discursiveness. These dispositions are determined by the person's postures, attitudes and behaviour as well as 'the kind of mental Dharmas which are found in him'. Certain mental states are supposed to be found in particular types of people. For example, the 'hate-type' is characterised by anger, grudges, belittling the worth of others, etc., the 'delusion-type' by sloth, worry, perplexity, obstinacy and tenacity; the person ruled by discursiveness shows excessive talkativeness, fondness for society and a dislike of wholesome practices, and those ruled by faith are generous and are desirous of seeing holy men and hearing the dharma (teaching). The content of the meditation and the way it is carried out are geared to 'counteract some given fault', or to be 'particularly beneficial to some given type'. Thus, the 'greed-type' person may have to meditate on ten repulsive things (i.e. ten aspects of decomposing corpses) and to recollect what belongs to the body, and those ruled by discursiveness are instructed to be mindful of respiration and concentrate on 'a small kasina-object'.

The approaches to meditation, as described (very briefly) above, have been translated into Western 'exercises' or 'clinical tools'. As such, they have achieved a vogue in some circles, including psychiatric ones. In the practice of mantra meditation, 'the practitioner is generally taught to maintain awareness of the mantra excluding other thoughts, external influences and desires' (West, 1979). Transcendental meditation, or TM, a 'standardised form of mantra meditation which has been adapted for Western use', emphasises the repetition of the mantra without calling on the subject to make any effort at concentrating or preventing attention wavering and thoughts intruding (ibid.). Zen meditation, which has received much attention in the West as a technique separated from its philosophical and cultural base, is seen as the (mere) practice of 'zazen' (sitting meditation) maintaining 'a quiet awareness' (Watts, 1962).

Writing in a Western idiom in the book *The Newer Therapies*, Patricia Carrington (1982) describes meditation as a psychotherapeutic tool 'simplified and divested of esoteric trappings and religious overtones'. She compares the effect of meditation as treatment with the aims of Western psychotherapy:

> As a therapeutic intervention, meditation differs in several important respects from conventional psychotherapy, which seeks to pinpoint conflicts (often of an unconscious nature) and then attempts to bring into play the conscious integrative functions of the ego. Unlike psychotherapy, meditation does not provide any 'conceptual handle' with which to reorganise one's cognitions of self. The rational elements of the psychodynamic psychotherapies and/or cognitive therapies are conspicuously absent in meditation, and the interpersonal elements take a back seat as well. In a fundamental sense, one is alone with oneself during meditation, while simultaneously removed from the verbal–conceptual world.

Carrington goes on to emphasise what she sees as the lack of purpose in meditation: 'the meditator allows thoughts to drift through his/her mind with *no goal* whatever. The thoughts need serve no purpose, and there is usually no attempt to contemplate their meaning.' This description of meditation is a striking illustration of the loss of meaning that may be incurred when a technique is transferred cross-culturally. Of course, meditation is integrated with meaning about the meaning of life when it is in its original context; but if uprooted from a culture that gave it meaning, to be transplanted into a soil that does not nourish it and give it new – perhaps different – meaning, it appears bare and useless. Thus, when meditation is separated from its cultural roots and examined as a form of psychotherapy (as described by Carrington), it is seen as a purposeless indulgence or, at best, a technique for inducing a special type of mental state – 'a special kind of mood'; then, enjoying the mood or experience is the aim rather than being the *means* to an end. In the medical model of psychiatry, this mental state, the 'altered state of consciousness' induced by meditation, is a *treatment* equivalent to a drug or electroplexy, or a course of psychotherapy. Even when it is not practised as *treatment*, it is perceived and used as a way of counteracting undesirable feelings. Used in this way, meditation may serve a limited purpose – but a very different one from its original purpose in Buddhist tradition.

Although meditation is usually used in the West as a technique for treating specific symptoms, such as insomnia, or for 'psychoneurosis' in general (West, 1979), some Western psychotherapists have tried to incorporate meditation into a psychoanalytic theoretical framework (Shafi, 1972): 'Meditation is conceptualised as a temporary and controlled regression in the service of the ego. This regression helps the individual to experience reunion with his earlier love object in a preverbal and preconscious level. In the silence of meditation, the cumulative traumas of early childhood are reexperienced beyond verbalization and cognitive awareness.' In terms of behavioural psychology, meditation may be seen as a form of 'desensitisation' (Tart, 1971); in reviewing (Western) psychophysiological and personality studies on meditation, West (1979) concludes that 'meditation practice is associated with decreases in arousal and anxiety, and the limited work which has been carried out to assess the usefulness of meditation as a therapy has provided grounds for cautious optimism'.

Clearly, there is a vast difference at a very basic level between meditation as treatment in a Western medical model and its place in the Buddhist tradition, as a process used for healing or liberating. Prince (1980) sees meditation techniques as 'institutionalised forms of psychotherapy, whose aim is to release the therapeutically potent mystical experience'. In transporting it across into Western society from other cultures, it must be integrated into the former in order to fulfil a function, for when used in isolation from a function, it is unlikely to serve a purpose in a meaningful way. It is conceivable that meditation *can* be incorporated into Western culture if taken on its own merits as a process for self-understanding, rather than as a psychological or psychiatric 'treatment' as such. But for this to happen, the strict illness model of emotional distress must be abandoned; spiritual needs and ethical considerations must be a part of the process of achieving liberation or cure. It cannot be used in isolation but only in concert with insights from Chinese and Indian philosophies, which underlie the use of mystical states. It is such insights that have given rise to 'new' approaches in psychotherapy, such as 'transpersonal psychotherapy' (Vaughan and Boorstein, 1982), 'psychosynthesis' (Assaglioli, 1975) and 'enlightenment intensive' (Graham, 1986).

Trance states, ecstasy and dreams

Unlike the case with mystical states, full memory is usually not retained of experiences under a trance state, although there may be a hazy recollection of what happens during it. In Western culture, and hence in psychiatry, such states are seen as being associated with loss of 'ego control'; and they are seen as pathological because domination by the conscious 'ego' – commonly called self-control – is important in that culture. In many other cultures, dissociation states are used for psychotherapeutic purposes. Prince (1976) delineates two broad patterns: in one, the healer alone dissociates and in the other the client, or both healer and client, dissociates. When the healer alone dissociates, the power of the healer is affected by suggestion, the power being greatly augmented when a supernatural spirit is seen to speak through the healer. Field (1960) describes healing at an Ashanti shrine in Ghana where many of the 'patients', healed by this sort of technique, were identifiable in Western terms as suffering from 'depression'. Although, in that instance, self-curative, 'endogenous' healing mechanisms may be being tapped, this may not always be the case in situations where dissociation is used for healing. Fuchs (1964) has described a healing technique among the Balahis of central India in which the 'Barwa' (a shaman), becoming possessed by a superhuman power or spirit, 'announces the disease of which the patient is suffering, mentions the name of the deity or spirit that caused the illness, and enumerates the offerings that have to be made to ensure a cure'. However, this basic 'magic' is a process in which the patient's family participates and in the course of which much advice is given to all and sundry – a community treatment process that is in tune with cultural beliefs and expectations.

'Shamanic ecstasy' is the name given by Prince (1980) to a type of consciousness that is different in his view from trance states, although similar to them. He describes the shamanic traditions of Siberia and America in producing states of 'ecstasy'.

> Fundamental is the belief that during ecstasy the shaman voyages to the upper world of the spirits or to the underworld of demons to obtain information about illness or misfortune or in quest of the kidnapped souls of the patient. An important variant is the belief that during his ecstasy the shaman may command his spirit assistants to make the voyage.

This is a dying art because of ideological and political suppression by 'Westernisation'. Singing, drumming and dancing are used usually, culminating in 'shamanic ecstasy':

> The distinction between shamanic ecstasy and a dissociated state should be noted here. In the ecstasy there is loss of motor power but intense subjective experience of a visionary nature that can subsequently be remembered and reported on by the shaman. On the other hand, in the dissociated state the subject engages in highly coordinated motor activity but has amnesia for the period of the altered state. (ibid.)

Prince (1980) states that similar healing ceremonies are practised in South East Asia, Korea, Taiwan and the Pacific Islands, 'but [they are] much more likely to take on a mediumistic or spirit possession flavour'. The ceremonies in North America are also similar to those in Siberia, but in the southern part of the Americas drug-induced ecstasies are carried out in the course of healing ceremonies. The plants and fungi that are used for this purpose contain various hallucinogens including mescaline, D-lysergic acid and psilocybin (Schultes, 1969). Dobkin De Rios (1972) describes one such ceremony in north-east Peru in which the visions experienced by the patients are interpreted by the therapist (shaman) who may take the drugs himself. In reviewing the available information about the 'great shamanic tradition' of the Americas, Prince (1980) describes the 'democratization of shamanism'; by this he means that among some indigenous American groups, contact with the 'spirit-world' through dreams or induced visions becomes a part of everyday practice in order to keep (mentally) healthy – akin to the use of yoga in India.

The use of dreams for therapeutic purposes is a part of the Western psychiatric tradition. Prince (1980) believes that 'dreams are related to illness and its cure in a variety of peripheral ways in many cultures'. He states that in 8 out of 15 cultures referred to in the book *Magic, Faith and Healing* by Kiev (1964), dreams were related to illness, although involved in the healing process in only three, namely, the Ndembu of Central Africa, indigenous Australians, and people of the northern part of Sierra Leone (West Africa). The tradition of healing by 'temple incubation', widespread in ancient Egypt and Greece, involved sleeping in a room (of a temple) in order to have dreams with healing powers; a remnant of this tradition persists in Morocco, according to Prince (1980). But it is in north-east America, among the Iroquois, that dream fulfilment is described as having been a complex and important healing process even into the eighteenth century, and still surviving in some form today (Wallace, 1958).

Exorcism

Various types of exorcism are carried out all over the world by practitioners called by the general term 'shamans', although they are carried out within the Judaeo-Christian and other religious traditions by priests. Exorcism in the South Asian context has been subsumed within 'spiritual healing' (Chapter 5). Usually, the process of exorcism in non-Western cultures is examined from outside the culture and therefore seen as sorcery or 'magic' – or, at least, as non-comprehensible. The following account by Fuchs (1964) of exorcism in central India is an example:

> The manner of exorcism varies slightly, depending on the nature of the spirit or deity that is supposed to 'possess' the sufferer. The exorcism of a *churel* (the spirit of a woman who has died in childbirth), for instance, is more complicated and difficult than that of any other spirit, because a *churel* is considered to be the most dangerous among the evil spirits. It is the spirit of a woman who has had to die in the prime of her youth and at a moment when she was fulfilling her most cherished vocation, bringing forth new life.

In many cultures possession is attributed to something evil or at least unwanted – usually a demon or spirit – akin to 'conflicts' or deeper disturbances of the psyche or noxious biochemical events postulated in Western psychology and psychiatry. The process of removing the unwanted demon or influence is, broadly speaking, a form of exorcism. Hence, if there is a belief in illness being caused by the possession of a person by one or more forces, be they extrinsic or intrinsic, counteracting the malign (pathological) factor by exorcism may be as logical as 'treatment' involved in counteracting psychopathology with psychotherapy or medication carried out in the interests of the afflicted person. Thus a shaman may be perceived as performing similar functions to those of a psychologist or psychiatrist.

Terry Clifford (1984) believes that the 'demons' recognised by Tibetan lamas as causing mental illness represent a 'wide range of forces and emotions which are normally beyond conscious control and all of which prevent well-being and spiritual development'. She sees the lama–doctor–exorcist as 'a spiritual wizard who understands that he is purifying the demons of his own mind, as it were, the powerful "independent" forces of the unconscious as well as the negative forces in the outer world'. Exorcism is 'not some spiritual weirdness draped in cruel and ritual veils (as it is pictured in the movies). It is a spiritual operation performed with the instruments of bodhiccita and compassion.' In the Tibetan tradition, there are many types of ritual exorcism used to clear away 'demons, evil forces, and hindrances which are either obstructing Dharma practice or interfering with good health'. Offerings and ritual *pujas* may be performed in order to persuade the demons to go away; an effigy of the person afflicted may be used in some rituals. In 'destructive exorcism', burying, burning and throwing are used in rituals by which 'the consciousness of the demon is transferred by the lama to another realm in which it may hear Dharma and enter the path of liberation'. All kinds of exorcism practised by Tibetan lamas are underpinned by an understanding of 'emptiness and compassion for the spirits'.

Each technique for exorcism is deeply involved in the cultural roots that gives it form and meaning. It is difficult to see how any particular type of exorcism can be extracted from its culture to be applied as a technology in a different culture. However, compromises may be possible in the case of people who maintain their own cultures in predominantly Western societies. Here, exorcism rituals may have to be adapted to become acceptable to the wider society. This is not a matter of cross-cultural transfer of a technique but the elaboration and development of cultural forms to deal with changes in society. How this is done is likely to vary from society to society but assumes an acceptance of many cultural forms without racist value judgements being attached to them.

Conclusions

This chapter takes a pragmatic approach in trying to dissect from (Western) psychiatry culturally transportable 'bits' of the discipline, and to extract from other cultures those techniques that may be concerned with the maintenance of mental health (in a wide sense) or counteracting problems that are seen (in Western terms) as 'mental illness' for transport to a Western context. Clearly, racist thinking underlies much of the reluctance of Western nations to appreciate the fact that the psychiatry developed in the West does not measure up to the standards of Eastern and African views of mankind. It is also because of racist arrogance that Eastern and African wisdom about mental health is not taken seriously in the West. The speculations in this chapter are presented as possible ways forward. But one major corollary of these ideas is the loosening or abandonment of ways of thinking in Western culture that tend to identify mental illness. Another is the suppression of racism. The overall aim is to promote the interchange of cultural information on an equal basis between the North and South, the East and West.

In considering psychiatric technologies in isolation from their cultural bases and applying them in other 'alien' cultures, two drawbacks are noteworthy. First, the technology may lose its very essence, the core reason for its effectiveness, by being plucked out of context; and secondly, its introduction into another culture may destroy or interfere with aspects of the host culture that are important, resulting in an overall imbalance within that culture. Thus, the introduction of a powerful drug that suppresses the perception of hallucinatory experiences may interfere with the power of exorcism ceremonies that are already available in the culture for dealing with people who experience them; the overall result may be to cause dysfunction of the balance within the society. Similarly, the use of antidepressant medication may interfere with mourning processes that are culturally effective in dealing with sadness; the practice of mantra meditation by a Western person who is absorbed in fantasies (possibly deemed 'psychotic') without the spiritual preparation that goes with meditation in Buddhist culture, may well complicate the psychiatric treatment he/she may well respond to.

Notwithstanding the drawbacks and problems, the argument in this chapter is that sometimes a technology may be portable across cultures if uprooted carefully and with an understanding of its place in the home culture, and transplanted with an equally sympathetic understanding of its place and need in the host culture. It is important that a technology introduced into a culture fits into it and is absorbed by it; and such a transplanted technology should be given time to grow and become incorporated (or rejected). Some technologies are more portable than others. In general, yoga and acupuncture from Eastern systems of medicine may be integrated into (Western) psychiatry without too much difficulty; similarly, drug therapy and possibly ECT from (Western) psychiatry may be portable for integration into other systems of healing. However, a medical model of illness in Western terms is a hindrance to cross-cultural sharing of techniques and ideas, and if psychiatry is to acquire and use techniques from non-Western cultural sources, *and* vice versa, it must move away from its present position on defining illness.

8

Mental Health for All

Whatever the meaning of mental health – and it has many interpretations (Chapter 2) – maintaining mental health is not just a medical or psychological problem but also one that has religious, ethical and spiritual dimensions. While ideas about mental health are largely determined by culture, racism has distorted Western knowledge about other cultures and the ways in which mental health is perceived in non-Western traditions. But human beings the world over are not all that different in terms of their basic individual needs, their tendency to live in groups or communities, and their propensity to relate to each other through language. It is the culturally determined ways of looking at human existence and the historically determined ways of judging people as distinct races that have imposed some (at least) of the problems arising from cultural and racial differences. Today, people of different races and ethnic groups increasingly have to interact with each other and to learn to live together; and cultures have become intertwined as never before. Yet racism is not dead and the adherence to ethnic identities with racial connotations appears to be growing in strength all over the world.

A general approach to mental health in such a context needs to emphasise universally valid themes as much as it needs to recognise differences between peoples. But the content of knowledge about mental health cannot be taken at face value. Concepts about mental health developed in one culture may be very different from those in another. Moreover, in aiming to develop a way of understanding mental health that is globally applicable, questions of race and culture must be confronted; racist views of cultures and people must be avoided and 'health' must be seen in the context of culture. And deviations from 'health' must be evaluated by procedures that incorporate culture and race, and not in a manner that excludes culture from 'illness' and denies or ignores the effects of racism – as is the case, for example, in the research into 'mental illness' conducted by the World Health Organisation (WHO) and described in Chapter 5.

Three key imperatives should be followed concurrently – not consecutively – if mental health care is to have relevance to people everywhere, of all cultures and all races. First and foremost, biased conceptions of cultural forms and habits must be challenged. This entails an honest, non-racist, open-minded approach to cultural, religious and medical practices all over the world that are to do with the maintenance of mental health – from family systems to idioms of distress, from beliefs in deities to religious ceremonies, from definitions of illness to exorcism rituals. An anti-racist stance is required in all mental health work, in anthropology, in sociology and, most of all, in psychiatry. Secondly, all aspects of mental health must be seen as cultural matters to be considered in relation to other aspects of culture. Clearly, a medical viewpoint has a part to play, for in all cultures the world over, some forms of human distress and 'madness' are seen as illness. But it is necessary to recognise that medicine, too, is a part of culture and not a system with a life of its own outside the culture in which it lives – as it seems to be considered in Western thinking. Admittedly, the development of a secular medical science that attempts to be objective and purely biological has promoted the progress of medical knowledge, but such an approach is a drawback in the case of understanding mental health. Finally, close attention must be paid to the spiritual needs of people, their social experiences and their economic situations seen in their cultural and political contexts, since the mental health of human beings the world over is fashioned – sometimes in very different ways – by these factors as much as by their biological and genetic make-up.

Although different approaches to mental health and to ways of alleviating mental distress (which includes conditions identified as 'mental illness') have arisen in different cultures (Chapters 2 and 6), there must be a unity of purpose underlying all if, as it must be when commonalities can be identified across cultures, they all serve a function in each of their respective societies. The function may not be the same in all cases; (Western) psychiatry, for example, has an important role in social control, while, for instance, in most Asian cultural systems appertaining to mental health the concern is largely with spiritual development. However, the common theme that runs through all systems is the part they play in the field of mental health of individual people living in families, communities, etc. This fact highlights the damaging effects of racism that instil artificial barriers of misunderstanding, prejudice and mutual hostility between them.

The purpose of this final chapter is to develop a viewpoint where the issues of race and culture are fully confronted in a movement for mental health that is universally applicable as well as culturally valid. It is an attempt at getting beyond the long-standing conflict between concepts of cultural relativism and concepts of universality in questions of mental health, while facing up to the reality of racism, ethnic loyalties and the many social and political issues that complicate the picture. Although the task is considerable, its enormity must not prevent a start being made. The matter is urgent because of the political conditions in the world today – particularly the suppression of Asian and African cultures by 'Westernisation' and the imposition of Western models of mental health and illness across the world; the pervasive influence of institutional and individual racism; and the risks inherent in the apparent need of many people to identify themselves as belonging to ethnic groups. Also, the recognition of the dangers arising from some reactions against Western domination, such as the revival of militant Islamic fundamentalism, and from the rise of reactionary forces in Europe, represented by extreme right-wing political parties in many European countries, adds to the urgency for action to bring about understanding between peoples of different cultures and races.

The whole field of mental health requires realignment in terms of race and culture. But the cards are stacked against a remodelling of thinking on mental health designed to take an anti-racist stance and incorporate the wisdom and experience of Asia and Africa. A revision of current thinking would challenge the cultural arrogance and racist ideology incorporated in many of the assumptions of the West, reflected (for example) in that of (Western) psychiatry in propagating its 'scientific knowledge' about mental health. The question of power is crucial. A new approach to mental health must stand apart from the power structure in the world today: it must accept the fact that most of the world is neither culturally Western nor racially white; it must take on the validity of the black experience in a white-dominated world; it should acknowledge the importance of concepts about human life from Asia and Africa and the relativity of all 'knowledge' in a subject that encompasses human feelings, beliefs and behaviour. The situation in multicultural and multiracial societies is of special concern: white domination of black people promotes, and often imposes, a cultural domination so that ways of thinking, family life, and patterns of mental health and mental health care that are identified as 'European' in tradition, or 'white' by racial origin, are seen as superior to others. This must be overcome if mental health is to have a real meaning in all cultures and to people of all races.

Psychiatry and psychology give precedence to objectivity over subjectivity. A result of this has been a communication gulf between, on the one hand, these disciplines emphasising 'objectivity' and, on the other, people whose lived experience is first and foremost 'subjective'. Further, both disciplines tend to see a clear distinction between the 'inner world' and the 'outer world' but to most people these are felt as one – perhaps somewhat like mirror images of each other. If psychiatry and psychology are to make real connection with the people that psychiatrists and psychologists are supposed to understand and help, the disciplines must bring into their domain sensitivity to what subjectivity means and develop a holistic approach that encompasses both internal and external worlds. Spirituality (discussed later in this chapter) is a dimension of human beings that psychiatry and psychology tend to avoid or even dismiss as 'unscientific'; yet, it is something that many people feel is important to them as human beings – perhaps central to their subjective experience of living. So if these disciplines are to reach out to people then spirituality must be addressed, taking on board the fact that introducing a spiritual dimension to psychiatry and psychology is not a reversal to a pre-scientific era but progress from nineteenth-century science to that of the twentieth and twenty-first.

Earlier chapters of this book consider mental health in the context of a world in which racial and cultural differences between people are realities that must be taken into account in both theory and practice. Chapter 7 moves towards bringing cultures together by attempting to define conditions under which cross-cultural transfer of techniques for mental health may be justified. This final chapter goes further along the same line; an attempt is made to point the way towards a vision of mental health and an approach to mental health care that go beyond race and culture and so have universal relevance. It is not an attempt to provide a blueprint for change; that is too massive an undertaking and unrealistic given the present power of vested interests. The question of redefining the (Western) concepts of mental illness is examined as a practical proposition, not just a theoretical concept; some ideas for restructuring the thinking about mental health at international, national and personal levels, are discussed. They may be about aspirations rather than real expectations, but they are not merely theory – rather, practical suggestions that are entirely feasible. Some proposals are made for tuning mental health promotion so that cultural and racial realities are addressed. Finally, this chapter attempts to indicate ways in which a spiritual dimension can be built into psychiatry and psychology by discussing the nature of spirituality in the context of mental health for the twenty-first century. The general approach in this chapter is fashioned by pragmatism and realism – practical necessity and the realities of life in a rapidly globalising world. It is an attempt at pointing a way forward to realisable alternatives to the current approach to mental health.

Redefining mental illness

Western thinking about mental health is dominated by psychiatry and propagated throughout the world as a 'scientific' approach. And mental illness and mental health are generally seen as two sides of the same coin. Further, the province of psychiatry is much wider than situations defined in terms of 'mental illness' per se; sexual and marital difficulties, family conflicts and many other forms of human distress or misbehaviour in general seem to fall within the purview of psychiatric expertise. And inevitably, the medical aura carried by psychiatry means that problems in all these fields are implicitly, if not explicitly, medicalised into being conceptualised and acted upon in terms of illness, even if problems are not actually designated as such. Many forms of human distress and misbehaviour, seen through Western eyes as 'illness', are not medicalised in other cultures – at least not unless Western models have been imposed. But in every culture, there appear to be certain problems that are accepted as illness, presumably because it is through an illness model that they are traditionally handled within the culture. However, an illness model in one culture may not be the same as that in another. Similarly, all cultures appear to recognise 'madness', roughly – but only roughly – translated into the Western idea of 'psychosis', although here, too, the definitions may not be identical across cultures.

The fact that both 'illness' and 'madness' are concepts that seem to be recognised the world over across cultures appears to mean that some agreement may be possible on what is, and is not, essentially illness or madness. But when the WHO attempted to develop a common language for defining mental illness that cuts across culture – as in its International Pilot Study of Schizophrenia (IPSS) described in Chapter 5 – what actually happened was that real cultural differences were ignored and, even more importantly, Western ideas were imposed across the world with racist perceptions dominating the process. In any case, illness in non-Western cultures is not always dealt with by treatment as understood in the West nor is madness always considered as an illness. An explanatory model for the genesis of illness is not necessarily bound up with the concept of illness; and a condition can be an illness or madness and be dealt with by (seemingly) religious manoeuvres or medical treatment – or a mixture of the two. For all these reasons, a search for a common language for defining mental illness across cultures – or even for a universally applicable theory or model for analysing questions of illness and health, such as, say, 'systems theory' which was suggested by Capra (1982) for this purpose, must be abandoned. And attempts to standardise treatment (for 'mental illness') cross-culturally must be seen as unattainable and possibly undesirable. However, some cross-cultural communication on concepts of mental health and the definition of common aims in this field with universal and cross-cultural relevance are necessary if only because human beings are united by a common ancestry and have to live together on one small planet.

In popular Western thinking, an illness is generated by one or more causes arising from biological or psychological change, i.e. a cause–effect model is generally adhered to. In other cultures, all changes are seen as relative – as in the thinking of modern physics – and illnesses are seen as resulting from imbalances of various types. It is possible that Western ideas in psychiatry, which emphasise biological 'causes', can be incorporated into a model that gets beyond the impasse inherent in the argument between cultural relativism and universality (Chapter 2). It would mean reinterpreting much of the information about mental illness that is available – not an impossible task. Thus, if a genetic predisposition is postulated for psychosis, it is a genetic balance/imbalance that should be looked for rather than a genetic determinant or cause. It is not biochemical causes but the balances of biochemical influences that are significant. But more than that, biochemical, genetic and other influences must be seen as being in dynamic balance/imbalance with other influences – social, spiritual and cosmological. The importance and significance of the various influences would depend on the society, the culture and the person concerned, as well as the knowledge available.

A flexible approach to (Western) conceptions about 'mental' illness would be the first step towards opening it up and improving communication with other ways of thinking. This would lead to a fluidity of thought (about illness) that is culture-sensitive and flexible – and free of racist ideology. In practice, it is a way forward that is being proposed, not a comprehensive theory. The final vision is that a concept of illness may well remain but it will be a very different one from the present one, and one that will not be fixed in firm categories that are supposed to be universally applicable. Different societies will develop variations on what may be, eventually, one or more universal themes; and culture will be an integral part of the way that 'illness' will be defined and recognised. The explanatory models will vary with the culture, again each and every model incorporating culture into its fabric. Any one type of explanation will not be seen as superior to another because they will all be embedded within their cultures but understandable on the basis of universal themes – and hence, not 'culture-bound'. There will be diversity within unity; perhaps a culturally relativistic view integrated into a universalist approach.

Restructuring mental health

Strategies for changing attitudes and practices in order to bring about a universal understanding of mental health must be directed at the international – global – scene and the national scene, as well as being concerned with personal (individual or family) matters. And such strategies must face and overcome racism at all these levels. Anti-racist strategies need to be devised worldwide, suited to each individual situation – particularly in Western countries and in global organisations. (This is not to deny the existence of various abhorrent ideologies and practices, apart from racism, that disturb harmony between peoples and interfere with mental health. Nor is it to ignore the many practical problems inherent in providing services to combat mental ill health.) Anti-racist strategies for personal change, usually called racism-awareness training or anti-racism training, must be accompanied by action against racism at institutional and political levels. This section presents some ideas for a restructuring of attitudes and practices in the mental health field. It is not a plan for radical changes or a new approach but a beginning for changes in the future.

Although mental health is as much to do with cultural and social issues as it is to do with 'health' as the obverse of illness, it is the gospel according to (Western) psychiatry that underpins and fashions the work of most health systems throughout the world. This is, first, a biological, secular teaching where concepts of illness are paramount and ethical and spiritual values discounted; and second, its theory and practice are permeated by racist ideology current in Western society. On the whole, psychiatry fails to address racial injustice and, even more importantly, its ethos suits the marketing of Western drugs produced by multinational companies. It is now over 20 years since the WHO voiced its aim of promoting 'traditional medicine' in Asia and Africa (WHO, 1978). But the shift towards implementing this aim in the mental health field is hardly discernible at grass roots, although the author is aware of individuals within the organisation attempting to move the WHO forward in this way. In this context, it is not surprising that many governments in Asia and Africa, seduced by advice from 'experts' in 'scientific psychiatry', unwittingly take on models and therapies of psychiatry, lock, stock and barrel and import large quantities of psychotropic drugs. The result is that indigenous systems for maintaining mental health continue to be underdeveloped and given a low status – as they were in colonial times.

The first strategy at an international level is to influence the WHO to change its ways of working so that the unholy – although possibly unwitting – alliance between the WHO and Western economic interests may be broken. Unfortunately, the attitude of some Western nations towards the United Nations Organisation itself may not augur well for such a change. As it is, the WHO has serious problems in pursuing policies that interfere with the economic interests of Western pharmaceutical, tobacco and baby milk firms. It is necessary to bear in mind the significance of the events leading to the 'fall' of UNESCO as an effective agency of the United Nations as a result of withdrawal of funding by Britain and the United States, fully described by Nihal Singh (1988):

> The long-term Western objective was to separate peace from disarmament and disarmament from development, reduce the scope of 'studies' on peace and international understanding and exorcise the 'orders' proposed by the Third World . . . [which] . . . work against the West insofar as the demand for redistributive justice are often aimed at Western interests and values.

Clearly, the WHO has to be cautious but must reorientate its projects, including its research, in the mental health field. It can set the scene for a change of direction by, for example, controlling the indiscriminate sale of powerful psychotropic drugs, which are presented by commercial interests as the 'scientific' approach to establishing mental health, and by introducing proper standards for assessing their usefulness in countries of the Third World. The practical projects undertaken by the WHO in the mental health field should be aimed primarily at identifying and alleviating stress, rather than diagnosing and 'treating' mental illness based on Western concepts, and mental health promotion must take into account indigenous systems of therapy and care using local experts in the field, supported where necessary by Western expertise in organisation. Research promoted by the WHO should be directed at evaluating ways of helping people that are culturally consonant and tuned to the real needs of the people in the countries concerned. And, most importantly, the WHO must eliminate racial bias at all levels with careful regulation of its research projects, selection of 'experts' who provide consultative advice and organise the delivery of services, and staffing of the organisation itself. Obviously, if WHO takes on both anti-racism and cultural sensitivity, many ways of promoting universal mental health would emerge. It is essentially a political will that is needed to begin with.

Changes at a national level must take place in both the rich Western countries – the developed world – and the poor, developing 'Third World'. In general, the former provide 'aid' in various forms to the latter. Over the past 40 years, Western technology has built dams, factories, irrigation works, etc. in the Third World, but vast numbers of people in those countries still cannot earn a living. Schumacher (1973) has pointed out that Western 'high technology' is actually exacerbating the plight of the world's poor by distorting their economies and misusing their resources. Applying this view to the mental health field, current Western intervention in the Third World may, on the one hand, be creating mental ill health through its economic and political pressures, and, on the other, be failing to promote mental health by encouraging and supporting 'high tech' psychiatry that uses inappropriate methods of diagnosis and treatment. Further, the imposition of psychiatry may actually cause cultural damage by medicalising human suffering and tying 'remedies' to the purchase of expensive drugs from Western countries. Thus, Western 'aid' in the mental health field must be geared to address the needs of the people it is supposed to help. The following principles enunciated by Schumacher for an 'intermediate technology' to replace 'high technology' in aid programmes may be usefully applied in the mental health field: first, aid programmes must be located in villages and towns, where most of the poor live; secondly, the programmes should not require much financial capital invest-ment and be sustainable within the resources available; thirdly, new training should be minimal; and finally, maximum use should be made of local talent and resources.

A change in the policies of aid-giving countries must be matched by changes in the attitudes of governments and mental health pro-fessionals in the Third World. The assumption of Western superior-ity in *everything* – an attitude that is rife in many parts of Asia and Africa – must be seriously confronted and changed in a realistic fashion. The baby should not be thrown out with the bathwater by attempting to deny, say, the real advantages to African and Asian countries that accrue from, say, obtaining Western help for indus-trial development or the improvement of medical services. But the limitations of Western expertise in the field of mental health care and in particular the ethnocentricity of Western psychiatric practice must be faced. The sort of change in the ethos and structure of 'aid' indicated here would lead to (Western) psychiatry becoming involved in the Third World on the basis of mutual benefit with a give and take of knowledge about mental health, rather than (the present) involvement as an 'expertise'. And so a sense of mutual respect may emerge between rich and poor, Western and non-West-ern, black and white. An exchange of technology on such a basis must be underpinned by an acceptance that ideas about mental health and methods of dealing with mental ill health are strongly influ-enced by culture (though not 'bound' by culture) – as is the concept of illness itself.

The restructuring of mental health at a personal level must be concerned with developing a universal psychology that is sufficiently flexible and free of racism to understand mental health and ill health cross-culturally. But if such a psychology is to be devised, the aim is not to build bridges between culturally distinct psychological –philosophical systems that are for ever separate but to evolve strategies to promote interaction (between cultures) that result in a better understanding *on both sides*, so that culture will be a part of that understanding and not something that divides people. However, there is some indication that a truly universal psychology is possible on a basis of the similarity of concepts and ideas in modern physics, on the one hand, and the traditional ways of thinking of India and Africa, on the other. For this to happen, it is necessary to think in terms of a coming together of *Ancient Wisdom and Modern Science*, to quote the title of a book edited by Stanislav Grof (1984). But this is a vision for the distant future and this section is concerned with the here and now.

At the practical level of working together, it could be envisaged, as Welwood (1979) believes, that a combination of 'the experiential, holistic, and enlightenment-oriented traditions of the East with the precision, clarity, skepticism, and independence of Western methods could lead to a new kind of psychology that transcends cultural limitations'. But Welwood (1979) warns: 'Many Westerners seem to assume that they understand Eastern ideas if they can use the correct jargon and key phrases, while underestimating the radical changes in one's life orientation that the Eastern paths are pointing to.' He quotes Harvey Cox (1977) as seeing the danger of Eastern ideas falling prey to Western 'consumer mentality' and greed for new experience: 'It could pervert them into Western mental-health gimmicks and thereby prevent them from introducing the sharply alternative vision of life they are capable of bringing to us.' Medard Boss (1979), a Swiss psychiatrist, describes a visit to India where he met European seekers after Eastern wisdom who 'had merely inflated their very limited egos with Indian formulas of wisdom instead of with large bank accounts or other means of power'. Eastern psychotherapies are essentially ways of contemplative awareness but much of Western psychotherapy is directed towards problem solving or decision-making, reflecting the value given in Western thinking to personal self-sufficiency and control of events. What is called neurosis – an illness – can be a path to enlightenment for a Buddhist. An amalgamation seems unthinkable but Welwood (1979) outlines the basis for one:

In short, such a new approach in psychology, based on self-knowledge disciplines, would include the whole range of human consciousness in the study of human behaviour; from the automatic responses that behaviourism has studied, to the unconscious patterns that psychoanalysis brought to light, to the farthest reaches of human possibility that Maslow called self-transcendence. Such an encompassing approach might provide a meaningful context and framework for interpreting and guiding research in experimental and clinical psychology. It might also provide a secular framework in which people might begin to glimpse the possibility for a meaningful life beyond the confines of the isolated ego, and to realize a

more ecological relationship with the world around them. This approach would
not be a substitute for traditional spiritual paths, but might serve as a bridge to
them, as well as a neutral meeting ground where practitioners of different self-
knowledge disciplines could come together and work out common understandings of human development as a conscious process.

Racism, both in its individual form and as institutionalised racism, is
a barrier to the development of universal understanding; and, in this
sense, strategies aimed at counteracting personal racism are more
important than those that may promote a universal (personal) psychology. But dealing with racism is not a matter, primarily, of developing theories or bringing people together – although there may be
a place for both these manoeuvres. Racism has to be dealt with
systematically and deliberately. Strategies must be aimed at both
the practices that are racist and the thinking that underlies them.
Attempts to change racist attitudes must go hand in hand with
the implementation of strict codes of practice to counteract racism
in behaviour; racism-awareness training must be carried out in a
context of anti-racist practices, for, not only does one feed into, or
feed on, the other, but to separate thinking from behaviour is unrealistic. Racism-awareness training without anti-racist practices being
strictly implemented may worsen an individual's racism by reinforcing a dissociation of an 'intellectual' attitude – often seen in lip service
to anti-racism – from a real conviction reflected in behaviour. And
there is the issue of institutional racism. Facing up to this aspect of
racism – a subtle but very pernicious variety – requires careful planning with long-term strategies. Anti-racism in this context may be
more about building up strengths of black people and changing
power structures as much as anything else.

Welwood's approach to the amalgamation of systems of psychology might be applied to the field of psychiatric research and theory.
Self-knowledge may replace objective understanding as the basis of
research and psychiatry may take on the study of consciousness,
including altered states of consciousness, without identifying some
states as pathological. Thus, for example, people who hear 'voices'
or have intensely meaningful experiences will no longer be seen as
pathologically 'hallucinated' or 'suffering' from symptoms of 'passivity
feelings'; illness will relate to disturbances of balance – within individuals, families and societies in a context of their relationship with
the universe. Religion and psychiatry will not be considered in
separate compartments, but as one system that deals with all aspects
of human existence.

In applying fundamental principles from theory to practical appli-cations in the mental health field, all cultures must be seen as equally valid and important and communication between peoples must be freed from the barriers arising from racism and the power structure in the world. A system of defining individual mental health in terms of balance must be accepted; a much 'loosened' psychiatric diagnostic system can be a special ethnocentric variant of this, but other systems too must be accepted as equally valid. Once this is done, the need for ethnocentric practices should be faced because, in practical terms, the world will continue to consist of a plurality of cultures, all hybrid and subject to continuous change – but yet equal in value. As communication is opened up and the interchange of ideas and methods of help-giving and help-seeking is promoted, the pragmatism of people the world over will make itself evident; people will give and take to evolve an approach – or more likely a variety of approaches – to mental health, or even perhaps a univer-sal 'psychiatry' very different from the present (Western) one, that is culturally flexible and racially neutral. All this, of course, is an ideal. Its realisation depends not on the goodwill of practitioners alone, but on the will and ability of powerful vested interests to recognise the need for systemic institutional changes. Until some of the changes envisaged here come about and international organisa-tions, such as the WHO, become truly globally sensitive, there is little likelihood of a major shift towards a new age in the field of mental health, although minor changes could well set the stage on which a new vision could eventually be played out.

Mental health promotion

Mental health as a concept has been discussed in various parts of this book. Earlier sections of this chapter attempt to address changes of a general nature aimed at establishing an understanding of mental health that may have universal relevance. In devising a practical approach to its promotion, mental health must be seen as a matter applicable to people – in terms of helping individuals (seeking mental health), developing healthy families or communities, or promoting healthy attitudes, healthy values, healthy behaviour, etc. Thus, mental health promotion may be about mental functioning of the individual person but also about questions of personal rela-tionships, stability of communities, relationships between groups of people and even matters of international peace and harmony. It is not proposed here to draw any firm lines between these different 'aims'.

Mental health promotion as a practical proposition may be considered at two levels, the 'mega' level of international or national policies and the 'micro' level of the individual and the family. These two overlap when communities wider than the family are considered. But questions of health cannot be considered in isolation from economic and political matters, and this applies particularly to the Third World; the continuing exploitation of peoples and resources of Asia, Africa and most of America for the benefit of the West must be thrown into the discussion. In the case of mental health, the damage caused by exploitation is compounded by the damage caused by racism. The psychological effects of racism prevail in most countries, damaging individuals and societies. At a personal level, racism has an adverse effect on the self-confidence of people seen as racially inferior, while undermining the self-respect and psychological stability of those on the other side. At a social level, it is seriously divisive in multiracial and multicultural communities, and a barrier to social harmony generally. The eradication of racism is a sine qua non of any mental health programme.

Although the concept of mental health in both theory and practice has major problems when compared to that of physical health, primary health care (PHC) is generally conceptualised as being directed towards mental well-being, in addition to physical and social well-being. And mental health promotion at a national level may be seen as a problem of PHC. In *Practising Health for All* (Morley *et al.*, 1983), two clear lessons are drawn by the authors:

> First, the *mobilisation* of the community's human, financial, and material resources for PHC [primary health care] activities is highly desirable – not just to ease government resource constraints but to help the community achieve a sense of responsibility. Second, this sense of responsibility will develop only if the community is involved in *every* stage of the project – the initial assessment and definition of problems, planning, implementation, and evaluation. In these ways the members of the community gain more *control* over the social, political, economic, and environmental factors affecting health.

Three principles for success in PHC are defined, based on the experience of workers in the field. These may be applied to mental health as much as to physical health, with certain safeguards discussed below. First, a political commitment to social equity is 'an essential starting point for a successful PHC programme'. It seems that 'universal coverage by health services and the integration of health with other sectors of development' are more important than high capital investment or technical sophistication. Secondly, community participation is necessary at all stages, so that the people affected by health care systems have an effective voice in decision-making, with women being 'in the front line'. Thirdly, a 'technical fit' is required between the health care that is provided and the community affected. Projects need to be based on epidemiological analyses so that they focus on 'important conditions for which affordable solutions exist'. And technology has to be appropriate to the society and the task at hand.

The principles given above were developed with the Third World in mind; issues of race and culture must be addressed when they are applied. The need for cultural sensitivity at all stages is obvious but the need to address questions of racism may be less so. First, racist ideology may be manifest in judgements that are made or imposed from without. It is all too easy for Western aid-giving agencies or Western experts to allow their preconceptions to affect the judgement of, say, who forms the 'community' that is listened to. Political commitment may be compromised by governments which have to bow to pressures for maintaining Western systems of health care because they are judged as superior for racist reasons alone and/or promoted for reasons of economic gain of, say, Western drug companies. 'Epidemiological analyses' may be forced into models determined by Western experts bringing over concepts, such as 'depression' and 'schizophrenia' that may be irrelevant to the cultural setting concerned; the result would be an imposition of Western models of health and health care with consequent damage to indigenous ways of coping and caring.

Mental health promotion programmes in the Third World must start off with clear policies on their aims *before* seeking help or advice from Western countries. And the basis for any programme should be the evaluation and development of culturally consonant systems of care based on an understanding of how their own people perceive mental health needs. Once this is done, help may be sought for planning ways and means of carrying out the programme. However, in the present circumstances, countries of the Third World should steer clear of any involvement with Western drug firms and multinationals with an interest in the manufacture of drugs. This is not to imply that drug usage should be excluded as one means of perhaps alleviating mental stress, but mental health programmes should be safeguarded from the pressures that economic interests may exert. Experts from the West should not be shunned but must be carefully monitored for their ability to keep to the primary aims of the mental health programme. And they should at all times work under the supervision of local experts with a knowledge of the culture and an ability to tease out racist viewpoints.

Although the discussion about mental health promotion as a part of PHC has focused on the Third World, the same basic principles (outlined above) apply elsewhere. Further, cultural sensitivity and an awareness of the effects of racism are important in the West, too, especially in countries with multicultural populations. Racist notions are very likely to distort mental health programmes because of the value judgements placed on varying cultural practices of people and communities, some being considered less 'advanced' than others (for racist reasons). Therefore, any mental health programme should contain within it a strong anti-racist component. Also, some people or whole communities may easily miss out unless targeted positively; so, mental health programmes should be culturally sensitive in terms that suit the communities they are directed at.

Mental health promotion at a 'micro' level, compared to that at a 'macro' level, is primarily involved with basic needs of individuals and families in terms of adequate housing, food, gainful employment for adults and proper education for children, etc., harmonious relationships within families and communities, and a sense of fulfilment and feelings of ethical and spiritual well-being in the individual person. The provision of a 'healthy' environment, free of pollution, discrimination and undue pressure, must be accompanied by prospects of correcting disharmony in relationships and personal 'ill health', if and when required. Finally, structures to counteract racism must be in place. Thus the promotion of mental health at this level overlaps with primary health promotion considered above, but also includes the need for personal services for preserving mental health – whether this is seen as treatment, counselling, liberation or spiritual enlightenment. Clearly, considerations of race and culture are paramount at this level in order to ensure a 'healthy' environment. The systems of help that a person has access to must be indigenous to her/his culture and sensitive to issues of racism. But health promotion at a 'micro' level must reach beyond culture and race to be geared to the needs of the individual and family. These needs would naturally vary according to place and time but also according to the person –

for example, someone in a big city: there are differences between, say, the needs of an African in Nairobi, a European in London and a Native American in Washington – assuming that a native of America can get to its capital city. But it is equally important to realise that, although focused on the individual, mental health promotion at the 'micro' level cannot and must not ignore the overall social, economic and political aspects of the society in which the person lives. For example, while the needs of an African may be different from those of a European, the needs of an African in South Africa would be very different from those of a white person at the same place and at the same time.

Spirituality and mental health

Spirituality is not something that can be understood by reviewing written accounts or studying organised religion. Yet, it is true to say that stated wisdom, whether oral or written, may guide one to an understanding of spirituality and spirituality may well form the basis – the 'spiritual basis' – of all religious systems and traditions. The aim of this section is to explore the meaning of spirituality in the context of mental health considered in a West European and American setting that is significantly multicultural (in the sense described earlier in this book), drawing from traditions across the world as much as possible.

The meaning of spirituality in everyday work in the mental health field is often unclear – and perhaps can never be clear. First, spirituality should be distinguished from spiritualism, which refers to a belief in, or practice of contacting, 'spirits' – non-physical beings with human characteristics. Activities such as the identification of 'spirit possession', exorcism (of spirits) and communication with spirits during seances are bound up with spiritualism. Second, spirituality should not be equated with religion as such – at least not with religion as understood in Western thinking – although it must be admitted that 'being religious' and 'being spiritual' are similar and may well be identical within non-Western worldviews. A Western scholar of Eastern traditions, Edward Conze (1957), refers to Buddhism as an 'Eastern form of spirituality.... Its doctrine, in its basic assumptions, is identical with many other teachings all over the world, teachings which may be called "mystical"' (1957: 11). Yet, Buddhism, like Hinduism, is a system for understanding the human condition that is akin to (Western) psychology rather than (Western) ideas of religion. In Western thinking (e.g. within anthropology) spirituality is not usually distinguished from spiritualism and is often identified and dismissed as a belief system – religious ideas concerned with the soul or spirits. And traditional psychology and psychiatry take a similar approach. In their book *Zen Buddhism and Psychoanalysis*, Erich Fromm *et al.* (1960) propose that psychoanalysis emerged as an attempt (in European thinking) to find a solution to 'Western man's spiritual crisis' (1960: 80) – a crisis attributed by them to Europe's 'abandonment of theistic ideas in the nineteenth century' with 'a big plunge into objectivity' (1960: 79). Cultures in Asia and Africa did not undergo this change – at least not at that time – and, although undoubtedly influenced later by Western ideas, appear to have maintained a spiritual dimension to their thinking in many ways until the present. Thus, it can be assumed that non-Western ways of thinking accept spirituality as central to human experience, different from 'belief' or 'cognition' or even an emotional state.

In the mental health field, many people conceptualise the 'spirit' as a concept similar to the 'mind' but yet different. When people talk of being 'spiritual' they generally mean a feeling of connectedness, the personal being connected to others – the 'I and I' as Rastafarians would say – the 'community' (a 'community spirit') or even wider to the land or environment (an 'ecological' spirit?), the earth and the sky – the cosmos (a unity with *atman* the Hindu godhead?). Lack of spirituality may be experienced as an impoverishment of the spirit – a sense of emptiness. Prayer and meditation may then be a way of replenishing this lack; joint action in a group setting may equally well do the same.

Ross (1992) writes about indigenous (first nations) Americans undergoing spiritual observance in preparing to embark on a task such as making a journey or venturing on a hunting expedition. Nobles (1986) believes that the integration of mind, body and spirit is characteristic of the worldviews derived from African thinking, and Richards (1985) makes a case for this spirituality having survived the transatlantic slave trade to continue in an African-American spirituality. Indeed Du Bois (1903) in his classic *The Souls of Black Folk* saw 'Spiritual Strivings' as a characteristic of the cultural ideal of black (African) Americans. Ninety years later, bell hooks (1994) writing in *Outlaw Cultures*, regrets the 'spiritual loss' of modern African-American communities in the USA and advocates the need for political movements that can effectively address the 'needs of the spirit' (1994: 247). It is the experience of the author that a major demand from users of mental health services in the UK is that the disciplines of psychiatry and psychology should incorporate a spiritual dimension. This section may help to clarify what this means and indicate how it may be brought about.

Conclusions

The ideas presented in this chapter are tentative suggestions for changing traditional ways of thinking about mental health – whether seen in relativist or universalist terms – so that an understanding of the subject may have truly universal relevance as well as cultural validity free of racism. Ways of progressing to a new definition of mental illness are proposed and ideas are presented for a new understanding of mental health that is part of a general move towards greater understanding between people. Also, some suggestions are given for mental health promotion, both in a local and a global context. The importance of culture and race emphasises a general point: although mental health is a very personal matter in the sense that it can never be defined in exactly the same terms for any two people, it is also never purely personal or entirely ethnocentric, since it is impossible to formulate the mental health of an individual in terms of the person concerned alone or that of a society isolated from contact with all other groups of people. In broad terms, the concept of mental health is not unlike that of happiness or sorrow; it is not a matter that can be defined in isolation from its context. What is mentally healthy for an individual in one situation may be different (for that person) if (s)he is in a different context vis-à-vis family, social setting, political climate, etc. And similar arguments apply to social, cultural and political groups. Mental health promotion as a practical proposition is not just about individuals, families and communities but also about society in general, international relations and universal harmony.

An understanding of race and culture is necessary for a discussion of mental health on a global scale, but human beings are really of one race and their diverse cultures may be seen as different paths taken by them for the same basic reasons – in order to live together in relative peace, in communion with one another and in harmony with the environment and within each person. Spirituality is a theme that is concerned intimately with lives of all human beings and possibly involves their connection with aspects of the universe that is thought of sometimes as 'inert' or 'non-living' – such as the earth and the air, the stars and the planets. Understanding the meaning of spirituality is about understanding the interconnection of all these elements and understanding the significance of subjectivity for human beings.

Basic human needs and concerns are probably similar, if not the same, the world over. The concluding message of this chapter is of the unity of humankind, beyond all cultural differences between communities and all divisions imposed on the human race by racism. But, in order to understand this unity, a realistic approach must be taken to the problems arising from differences in culture and the divisions arising from racism. The paradox that mental health is different because of culture and race and yet the same irrespective of culture and race is the reality.

Bibliography

Aakster, C. W. (1986) 'Concepts in Alternative Medicine', *Social Science and Medicine*, **22**: 265–73.

Abeywardena, J. S. P. (1983) Personal communication.

Adams, G. L., Dworkin, R. J. and Rosenberg, S. D. (1984) 'Diagnosis and Pharmacotherapy Issues in the Care of Hispanics in the Public Sector', *American Journal of Psychiatry*, **141**: 970–4.

Adebimpe, V. R., Chu, C. C., Klein, H. E. and Lange, M. H. (1982) 'Racial and Geographic Differences in the Psychopathology of Schizophrenia', *American Journal of Psychiatry*, **139**: 888–91.

Ademuwagun, Z. A., Ayoade, J. A. A., Harrison, I. and Warren, D. M. (eds) (1979) *African Therapeutic Systems* (Waltham, Mass.: Crossroads Press).

Akbar, N. (1981) 'Mental Disorders among African Americans', *Black Books Bulletin*, **7**(2): 18–25, cited by Nobles (1986).

Allon, R. (1971) 'Sex, Race, Socio-economic Status, Social Mobility, and Process-reactive Ratings of Schizophrenia', *Journal of Nervous and Mental Disease*, **153**: 343–50.

Allport, G. (1954) *The Nature of Prejudice* (New York: Doubleday).

Amakuki, S. (1959) 'Zen Meditation' in E. Conze (ed.) *Buddhist Scriptures*, trans. E. Conze (Harmondsworth: Penguin) pp. 134–44.

Amarasingham, L. R. (1980) 'Movement among Healers in Sri Lanka: a Case Study of a Sinhalese Patient', *Culture, Medicine and Psychiatry*, **4**: 71–92.

American Psychiatric Association (1980) *Diagnostic and Statistical Manual of Mental Disorders, DSM-III*, 3rd edn (Washington: APA).

American Psychiatric Association (1987) *Diagnostic and Statistical Manual of Mental Disorders. DSM-III-R*, 3rd edn revised (Washington: APA).

American Psychiatric Association (1994) *Diagnostic and Statistical Manual of Mental Disorders. DSM-IV*, 4th edn (Washington: APA).

Anon (1851) 'Startling Facts from the Census', *American Journal of Insanity*, **8**(2): 153–5.

Ardrey, R. (1967) *The Territorial Imperative* (London: Collins)

Argyle, M. (1975) *Bodily Communication* (London: Methuen).

Asante, M. K. (1985) 'Afrocentricity and Culture', in M. K. Asante and K. W. Asante (eds) *African Culture: The Rhythms of Unity* (Westport, Conn.: Greenwood Press) pp. 3–12.

Asante, M. K. and Asante, K. W. (1985) 'Preface', in M. K. Asante and K. W. Asante (eds), *African Culture: The Rhythms of Unity* (Westport, Conn.: Greenwood Press) pp. ix–x.

Assaglioli, R. (1975) *Psychosynthesis: A Manual of Principles and Techniques* (New York: Hobbs Dorman) cited by Graham (1986).

Ayoade, J. A. A. (1979) 'The Concept of Inner Essence in Yoruba Traditional Medicine', in Z. A. Ademuwagun, J. A. A. Ayoade, I. Harrison and D. M. Warren (eds) *African Therapeutic Systems* (Waltham, Mass.: Crossroads Press) pp. 49–55.

Babcock, J. W. (1895) 'The Colored Insane', *Alienist and Neurologist*, **16**: 423–47.

Bagley, C. (1971) 'Mental Illness in Immigrant Minorities in London', *Journal of Biosocial Science*, **3**: 449–59.

Banton, M. (1987) *Racial Theories* (Cambridge: Cambridge University Press).

Banton, M. and Harwood, J. (1975) *The Race Concept* (London: David & Charles) cited by Husband (1982).

Barker, M. (1990) 'Biology and the New Racism,' Chapter 2 in D. T. Goldberg (ed.) *Anatomy of Racism* (Minneapolis: University of Minnesota Press) pp. 18–37.

Barzun, J. (1965) *Race: A Study of Superstition* (New York: Harper & Row) cited by Husband (1982).

Bayer, R. (1981) *Homosexuality and American Psychiatry: The Politics of Diagnosis* (New York: Basic Books).

Bean, R. B. (1906) 'Some Racial Peculiarities of the Negro Brain', *American Journal of Anatomy*, **5**: 353–415.

Bebbington, P. E. (1978) 'The Epidemiology of Depressive Disorder', *Culture, Medicine and Psychiatry*, **2**: 297–341.

Beiser, M. (1987) 'Commentary on Culture-bound Syndromes and International Disease Classifications', *Culture, Medicine and Psychiatry*, **II**: 29–33.

Ben-Tovim, G., Gabriel, J., Law, I. and Stredder, K. (1986) *The Local Politics of Race* (London: Macmillan).

Benedict, P. K. and Jacks, I. (1954) 'Mental Illness in Primitive Societies', *Psychiatry*, **17**: 377–84.

Benedict, R. (1942) *Race and Racism* (London: Routledge & Kegan Paul).

Bernal, M. (1987) *Black Athena: The Afroasiatic Roots of Classical Civilisation*, Vol. 1 (London: Free Association).

Berreman, G. D. (1960) 'Caste in India and the United States', *American Journal of Sociology*, **66**(2): 120–7.

bhabha, homi (1994) *The Location of Culture* (London: Routledge).

Bhugra, D., Leff, J., Mallett, R., Der, G., Corridan, B. and Rudge, S. (1997) 'Incidence and Outcome of Schizophrenia in Whites, African-Caribbeans and Asians in London', *Psychological Medicine*, **27**: 791–8.

Biko, S. (1971) 'Some African Cultural Concepts', paper given at a conference at the Ecumenical Training Centre, Natal, reprinted in A. Stubbs (ed.) *Steve Biko. I Write What I Like. A Selection of his Writings* (Harmondsworth: Penguin) pp. 54–61.

Biko, S. (1972) White Racism and Black Consciousness', in H. W. van der Merwe and D. Welsh (eds), *Student Perspectives on South Africa* (Cape Town: David Philip), reprinted in A. Stubbs (ed.) *Steve Biko. I Write What I Like. A Selection of his Writings* (Harmondsworth: Penguin) pp. 75–86.

Billig, M. (1979) *Psychology, Racism and Fascism* (Birmingham: A. F. and R. Publications).

Bleuler, E. (1950) *Dementia Præcox or the Group of Schizophrenias*, trans. J. Zitkin (New York: International Universities Press). Originally published in 1911.

Bloch, S. and Reddaway, P. (1984) *The Shadows over World Psychiatry* (London: Gollancz).

Blumenbach, J. F. (1865) *The Anthropological Treatises of Johann Friedrich Blumenbach* (London: Anthropological Society of London).

Bohm, D. (1980) *Wholeness and the Implicate Order* (London: Routledge & Kegan Paul).

Bolton, P. (1984) 'Management of Compulsorily Admitted Patients to a High Security Unit', *International Journal of Social Psychiatry*, **30**: 77–84.

Boss, M. (1979) 'Eastern Wisdom and Western Psychotherapy' in J. Welwood (ed.) *The Meeting of the Ways* (New York: Schocken Books) pp. 183–96.

Brittan, A. and Maynard, M. (1984) *Sexism, Racism and Oppression* (Oxford: Blackwell).

Brody, E. B. (1964) 'Society, Culture and Mental Illness', *Journal of Nervous and Mental Diseases*, **139**: 62–73.

Bromberg, W. and Simon, F. (1968) 'The "Protest" Psychosis. A Special Type of Reactive Psychosis', *Archives of General Psychiatry*, **19**: 155–60.

Brown, C. (1984) *Black and White Britain. The Third PSI Survey* (London: Heinemann).

Brown, D. and Pedder, J. (1979) *Introduction to Psychotherapy. An Outline of Psychodynamic Principles and Practice* (London: Tavistock).

Brown, G. W. and Harris, T. (1978) *Social Origins of Depression. A Study of Psychiatric Disorder in Women* (London: Tavistock).

Browne, A. (2000) 'The Last Days of a White World', *The Observer*, 3 September, 17.

Buenzod, J. (1967) *La Formation de la Pensée de Gobineau et 'l'Essai sur l'Inégalite des Races Humaines'* (Paris: Nizet) cited by Banton (1987).

Busfield, J. (1986) *Managing Madness: Changing Ideas and Practice* (London: Hutchinson).

Bynum, W. F. Jr (1981) 'Rationales for Therapy in British Psychiatry, 1780–1835', in A. Scull (ed.) *Madhouses, Mad-doctors and Madmen: The Social History of Psychiatry in the Victorian Era* (London: Athlone Press) pp. 35–57.

Campling, P. (1989) 'Race, Culture and Psychotherapy', *Psychiatric Bulletin*, **13**: 550–1.

Capra, F. (1982) *The Turning Point. Science, Society, and the Rising Culture* (London: Wildwood House).

Caraka (1983) *Caraka Samhita*, transl. R. K. Sharma and V. B. Dash, 2nd edn, Vols 1 and 2 (Varanasi: Choukhamba Sanskrit Series Office).

Carothers, J. C. (1947) 'A Study of Mental Derangement in Africans and an Attempt to Explain Its Peculiarities, More Especially in Relation to the African Attitude to Life', *Journal of Mental Science*, **101**: 548–97.

Carothers, J. C. (1951) 'Frontal Lobe Function and the African', *Journal of Mental Science*, **97**: 12–48.

Carothers, J. C. (1953) *The African Mind in Health and Disease: A Study in Ethnopsychiatry*, WHO Monograph Series No. 17 (Geneva: WHO).

Carpenter, L. and Brockington, I. F. (1980) 'A Study of Mental Illness in Asians, West Indians and Africans in Manchester', *British Journal of Psychiatry*, **137**: 201–5.

Carrington, P. (1982) 'Meditation Techniques in Clinical Practice', in L. E. Abt and I. R. Stuart (eds) *The Newer Therapies: A Sourcebook* (New York: Van Nostrand Reinhold) pp. 60–78.

Carruthers, J. H. (1986) 'The Wisdom of Governance in Kemet', in M. Karenga and J. H. Carruthers (eds) *Kemet and the African Worldview* (Los Angeles: University of Sankore Press) pp. 3–30.

Cartwright, S. A. (1851) 'Report on the Diseases and Physical Peculiarities of the Negro Race', *New Orleans Medical and Surgical Journal*, May: 691–715; reprinted in A. C. Caplan, H. T. Engelhardt and J. J. McCartney (eds) *Concepts of Health and Disease* (Reading, Mass.: Addison-Wesley, 1981).

Cashmore, E. E. and Troyna, B. (1983) *Introduction to Race Relations* (London: Routledge & Kegan Paul).

Castaneda, C. (1968) *The Teachings of Don Juan: A Yaqui Way of Knowledge* (Berkeley: University of California Press, 1968; Harmondsworth: Penguin, 1970).

Castel, R. (1985) 'Moral Treatment; Mental Therapy and Social Control in the Nineteenth Century', in S. Cohen and A. Scull (eds) *Social Control and the State* (Oxford: Blackwell) pp. 246–66.

Clarke, J. H. (1985) 'African American Historians and the Reclaiming of African History', in M. K. Asante and K. W. Asante (eds) *African Culture: The Rhythms of Unity* (Westport, Conn.: Greenwood Press) pp. 157–71.

Clarke, K. B. and Clarke, M. P. (1947) 'Racial Identification and Preference in Negro Children', in T. M. Newcombe and E. L. Hartley (eds) *Readings in Social Psychology* (New York: Holt, Rinehart and Winston) pp. 169–78.

Clifford, T. (1984) *Tibetan Buddhist Medicine and Psychiatry: The Diamond Healing* (York Beach, Main, USA: Samuel Weiser).

Clough, B. (1999) *Clough's Sinhala English Dictionary*. Second New and Enlarged Edition for Sri Lanka (New Delhi: Asian Educational Services).

Cochrane, R. (1977) 'Mental Illness in Immigrants to England and Wales', *Social Psychiatry*, **12**: 25–35.

Cohen, Phil (1999) *New Ethnicities, Old Racisms?* (London: Zed Books).

Coleman, W. (1964) *George Cuvier, Zoologist: A Study in the History of Evolution Theory* (Cambridge, Mass.: Harvard University Press) cited by Banton (1987).

Connolly, C. J. (1950) *External Morphology of the Primate Brain* (Illinois: Springfield) cited by Carothers (1953).

Conze, E. (1957) *Buddhism. Its Essence and Development*, 3rd edn (Oxford: Bruno Cassirer).

Conze, E. (1959) 'Meditation', in E. Conze (ed.) *Buddhist Scriptures* (Harmondsworth: Penguin) pp. 98–144.

Cooper, J. E., Kendall, R. E., Garland, B. J., Sharpe, I., Copeland, J. R. M. and Simon, R. (1972) *Psychiatric Diagnosis in New York and London*, Maudsley Monograph No. 20 (Oxford: Oxford University Press).

Cooter, R. (1981) 'Phrenology and British Alienists ca. 1825–1845', in A. Scull (ed.) *Madhouses, Mad-doctors and Madmen: The Social History of Psychiatry in the Victorian Era* (London: Athlone Press) pp. 58–104.

Coulter, J. (1979) *The Social Construction of Mind: Studies in Ethnomethodology and Linguistic Philosophy* (London: Macmillan).

Cox, H. (1977) *The Promise and Peril of the New Orientation* (New York: Simon & Schuster).

Cox, O. C. (1948) *Caste, Class and Race: A Study in Social Dynamics* (Detroit, Ill.: Wayne State University Press) cited by Cashmore and Troyna (1983).

Dalal, F. (1988) 'The Racism of Jung', *Race and Class*, **29**(3): 1–22.

D'Andrade, R. G. (1984) 'Cultural Meaning Systems', in R. A. Shweder and R. A. LeVine (eds) *Culture Theory: Essays on Mind, Self and Emotion* (Cambridge: Cambridge University Press) pp. 88–119.

Darwin, C. R. (1871) *The Descent of Man* (London: Murray).

Darwin, C. (1872) *The Expression of the Emotions in Man and Animals* (New York: Appleton) reprinted (London: University of Chicago Press, 1965).

Davis, A. (1982) *Women, Race and Class* (London: The Women's Press).

Dawkins, R. (1976) *The Selfish Gene* (New York: Oxford University Press).

Dean, G., Walsh, D., Downing, H. and Shelley, E. (1981) 'First Admissions of Native-born and Immigrants to Psychiatric Hospitals in South-East England, 1976', *British Journal of Psychiatry*, **139**: 506–12.

Demerath, N. J. (1942) 'Schizophrenia among Primitives', *American Journal of Psychiatry*, **98**: 703–7.

Devereux, G. (1939) 'Mohave Culture and Personality', *Character and Personality*, **8**: 91–109.

Diop, C. A. (1967) *Antériorité des Civilisations Nègre: Mythe ou Vérité Historique?* (Paris: Présence Africaine) transl. M. Cook *The African Origin of Civilization: Myth or Reality?* (Westport, Conn.: Lawrence Hill, 1974).

Dobkin De Rios, M. (1972) *Visionary Vine: Psychedelic Healing in the Peruvian Amazon* (San Francisco: Chandler).

Dobzhansky, T. (1971) 'Race Equality', in R. H. Osborne (ed.) *The Biological and Social Meaning of Race* (San Francisco: Freeman) pp. 13–24.

Down, J. L. M. (1866) 'Observations on an Ethnic Classification of Idiots', *Lectures and Reports from the London Hospital for 1866*, reprinted in C. Thompson (ed.) *The Origins of Modern Psychiatry* (Chichester: Wiley, 1987) pp. 15–18.

Du Bois, W. E. B. (1903) *The Souls of Black Folk* (Chicago: McClurg) reprinted (New York: Dover Publications, 1994).

Dummett, A. (1973) *A Portrait of English Racism* (Harmondsworth: Penguin) republished (Manchester: Manchester Free Press, 1984).

Dunner, D. L. and Dunner, P. Z. (1983) 'Psychiatry in China: Some Personal Observations', *Biological Psychiatry*, **18**: 799–801.

Eagleton, T. (2000) *The Idea of Culture* (Oxford: Blackwell).

Edgerton, R. B. (1980) 'Traditional Treatment for Mental Illness in Africa: A Review', *Culture, Medicine and Psychiatry*, **4**: 167–89.

Ellenberger, H. F. (1974) 'Psychiatry from Ancient to Modern Times', in S. Arieti (ed.) *American Handbook of Psychiatry*, 2nd edn (New York: Basic Books) pp. 3–27.

Elling, R. H. (1978) 'Medical Systems as Changing Social Systems', *Social Science and Medicine*, **12**: 107–15.

Engel, G. L. (1977) 'The Need for a New Medical Model: A Challenge for Biomedicine', *Science*, **196**: 129–36.

Estroff, S. E. and Zimmer, C. (1994) 'Social Networks, Social Support, and Violence among Persons with Severe, Persistent Mental Illness', Chapter 11 in J. Monahan and H. J. Steadmen (eds) *Violence and Mental Disorder. Developments on Risk Assessment* (Chicago: University of Chicago Press) pp. 259–95.

Evarts, A. B. (1913) 'Dementia Precox in the Colored Race', *Psychoanalytic Review*, **14**: 388–403.

Eysenck, H. J. (1952) *The Scientific Study of Personality* (London: Routledge & Kegan Paul).

Eysenck, H. J. (1971) *Race, Intelligence and Education* (London: Temple Smith).

Eysenck, H. J. (1973) *The Inequality of Man* (London: Temple Smith).

Fabrega, H. Jr (1989) 'Cultural Relativism and Psychiatric Illness', *Journal of Nervous and Mental Disease*, **177**: 415–25.

Faculty of Community Medicine (1986) *Health for All by the Year 2000: Charter for Action* (London: Faculty of Community Medicine).

Fanon, F. (1952) *Peau Noire, Masques Blancs* (Paris: Editions de Seuil) transl. C. L. Markmann, *Black Skin, White Masks* (New York: Grove Press, 1967).

Fanon, F. (1961) *Les Damnés de la Terre* (Paris: Maspero) transl. C. Farrington *The Wretched of the Earth* (New York: Grove Press, 1965).

Favazza, A. R. (1985) 'Anthropology and Psychiatry', in H. I. Kaplan and B. J. Sadock (eds), *Comprehensive Textbook of Psychiatry*, Vol. 1, 4th edn (Baltimore: Williams & Wilkins) pp. 247–65.

Fernando, S. (1986) 'Depression in Ethnic Minorities', in J. L. Cox (ed.) *Transcultural Psychiatry* (London: Croom Helm) pp. 107–38.

Fernando, S. (1988) *Race and Culture in Psychiatry* (London: Croom Helm).

Fernando, S. (1989a) 'Schizophrenia in Ethnic Minorities', *Psychiatric Bulletin*, **13**: 250–1.

Fernando, S. (1989b) 'Schizophrenia in Ethnic Minorities', *Psychiatric Bulletin*, **13**: 573–4.

Fernando, S. (1991) 'Black Europeans', *Openmind*, **54**: 15.

Fernando, S. (ed.) (1995) *Mental Health in a Multi-ethnic Society* (London: Routledge).

Fernando, S., Ndegwa, D. and Wilson, M. (1998) *Forensic Psychiatry, Race and Culture* (London: Routledge).

Field, M. J. (1960) *Search for Security: An Ethnocentric Study of Rural Ghana* (Evanston, Ill.: Northwestern University Press).

Fitzpatrick, P. (1990) 'Racism and the Innocence of Law', In D. T. Goldberg (ed.) *Anatomy of Racism* (Minneapolis: University of Minnesota Press) pp. 247–62.

Flaherty, J. A. and Meagher, R. (1980) 'Measuring Racial Bias in Inpatient Treatment', *American Journal of Psychiatry*, **137**: 679–82.

Flaherty, J. A., Naidu, J., Lawton, R. and Pathak, D. (1981) 'Racial Differences in Perception of Ward Atmosphere', *American Journal of Psychiatry*, **138**: 815–17.

Folkman, S. and Lazarus, R. S. (1988) 'The Relationship between Coping and Emotion: Implications for Theory and Research', *Social Science and Medicine*, **26**(3): 309–17.

Foote, R. F. (1858) 'The Condition of the Insane and the Treatment of Nervous Diseases in Turkey', *Journal of Mental Science*, **4**: 444–50.

Foucault, M. (1967) *Madness and Civilization. A History of Insanity in the Age of Reason* (London: Tavistock) Originally published in French as *Histoire de la Folie* (Paris: Libraire Plon, 1961).

Foucault, M. (1977) *Discipline and Punish. The Birth of the Prison*. Translated by Alan Sheridan (London: Allen Lane). Reprinted 1991 (Harmondsworth: Penguin Books). First published as *Surveiller et punir: Naissance de la prison* by Editions Gallimard (1975).

Foucault, M. (1988) *Politics Philosophy Culture. Interviews and Other Writings 1977–1984* (ed. L. D. Kritzman) (London: Routledge).

Frank, J. D. (1963) *Persuasion and Healing* (New York: Schocken Books).

Freuchen, P. (1959) *The Book of the Eskimos* (New York: Fawcett) cited by West (1979).

Freud, S. (1913) *Totem and Taboo* (Vienna: Hugo Heller) transl. and publ. in English (London: Routledge & Kegan Paul, 1950).

Freud, S. (1915) 'Thoughts for the Times on War and Death', *Imago*, **4**(1): 1–21, transl. J. Strachey in *The Standard Edition of the Complete Psychological Works of Sigmund Freud*, Vol. 14 (London: Hogarth Press) pp. 273–300.

Freud, S. (1917) 'Mourning and Melancholia', transl. J. Strachey in *The Standard Edition of the Complete Works of Sigmund Freud*, Vol. 14 (London: Hogarth Press, 1957) pp. 243–58.

Freud, S. (1930) 'Civilization and Its Discontents', in J. Strachey (ed.) transl. J. Riviere, *The Standard Edition of the Complete Works of Sigmund Freud*, Vol. 21 (London: Hogarth Press, 1961) pp. 57–145.

Fried, M. H. (1968) 'The Need to End the Pseudoscientific Investigation of Race', in M. Mead *et al.* (eds), *Science and the Concept of Race* (New York: Columbia University Press) cited by Thomas and Sillen (1972).

Fromm, E., Suzuki, D. T. and de Martino, R. (1960) *Zen Buddhism and Psychoanalysis* (London: George Allen and Unwin).

Fryer, P. (1984) *Staying Power: The History of Black People in Britain* (London: Pluto Press).

Fuchs, S. (1964) 'Magic Healing Techniques among the Balahis of Central India', in A. Kiev (ed.) *Magic, Faith and Healing: Studies in Primitive Psychiatry Today* (New York: Free Press of Glencoe) pp. 121–38.

Fujita, C. (1986) *Morita Therapy* (Tokyo: Igaku Shoin) cited by Reynolds (1988).

Fuller, C. E. (1959) 'Ethnohistory in the Study of Culture Change in Southeast Africa', in W. R. Bascom and M. J. Merskovits (eds) *Continuity and Change in African Cultures* (Chicago: University of Chicago Press) pp. 113–29.

Gaines, A. D. (1982) 'Cultural Definitions, Behaviour and the Person in American Psychiatry', in A. J. Marsella and G. M. White (eds) *Cultural Conceptions of Mental Health and Therapy* (Dordrecht: Reidel) pp. 167–92.

Galton, F. (1865) 'Hereditary Talent and Character', *MacMillan Magazine*, 157–66.

Galton, F. (1869) *Hereditary Genius: An Inquiry into Its Laws and Consequences* (London: Macmillan).

Gauron, E. F. and Dickinson, J. K. (1966) 'Diagnostic Decision Making in Psychiatry: Information Usage', *Archives of General Psychiatry*, **14**: 225–32.

Gelfand, M. (1964) *Witch Doctor. Traditional Medicine Man of Rhodesia* (London: Harvill Press).

Gilroy, P. (1993) *Small Acts. Thoughts on the Politics of Black Cultures* (London: Serpent Tail).

Glover, G. (1988) 'Psychiatric Illness among British Afro-Caribbeans', *British Medical Journal*, **296**: 1538–9.

Glover, G. and Malcolm, G. (1988) 'The Prevalence of Depot Neuroleptic Treatment among West Indians and Asians in the London Borough of Newham', *Social Psychiatry*, **23**: 281–4.

Gobineau, Le Compte de (1853) *Essai sur l'inegalité des Races Humaines* (Paris: Firmin-Didot) cited by Banton (1987).

Goldstein, A. (1976) 'Opoid Peptides (Endorphins) in Pituitary and Brain', *Science*, **193**: 1081–6.

Gottesman, I. I. (1991) *Schizophrenia Genesis. The Origins of Madness* (New York: Freeman).

Gould, S. J. (1981) *The Mismeasure of Man* (Harmondsworth: Penguin).

Graham, H. (1986) *The Human Face of Psychology: Humanistic Psychology in its Historical, Social and Cultural Contexts* (Milton Keynes: Open University Press).

Green, E. M. (1914) 'Psychoses among Negroes – a Comparative Study', *Journal of Nervous and Mental Disorder*, **41**: 697–708.

Grof, S. (1984) *Ancient Wisdom and Modern Science* (Albany, NY: State University of New York Press).

Grounds, A. (1987) 'On Describing Mental States', *British Journal of Medical Psychology*, **60**: 305–11.

Guglielmino-Matessi, C. R., Gluckman, P. and Cavalli-Sforza, L. L. (1979) 'Climate and the Evolution of Skull Metrics in Man', *American Journal of Physical Anthropology*, **50**(4): 549–64.

Gutman, H. (1976) *The Black Family in Slavery and Freedom 1750–1925* (New York: Pantheon Books) cited by A. Davis (1982).

Hacker, A. (1992) *Two Nations. Black and White, Separate, Hostile and Unequal* (New York: Random House).

Haldipur, C. V. (1984) 'Madness in Ancient India: Concept of Insanity in Charaka Samhita (1st Century A. D.)', *Comprehensive Psychiatry*, **25**: 335–43.

Hall, G. S. (1904) *Adolescence: Its Psychology and Its Relations to Physiology, Anthropology, Sociology, Sex, Crime, Religion and Education*, Vol. II (New York: D. Appleton).

Hall, S. (1978) 'Racism and Reaction', in Commission for Racial Equality (ed.) *Five Views of Multi-Racial Britain* (London: CRE) pp. 23–35.

Hall, S. (1992) 'New Ethnicities', in J. Donald and A. Ratansi (eds) *'Race', Culture and Difference* (London: Sage) pp. 252–9.

Hall, S., Critcher, C., Jefferson, T., Clarke, J. and Roberts, B. (1978) *Policing the Crisis: Mugging, the State, and Law and Order* (London: Macmillan).

Harris, M. (1968) *The Rise of Anthropological Theory* (New York: Crowell) cited by Thomas and Sillen (1972).

Harrison, G., Ineichen, B., Smith, J., and Morgan, H. G. (1984) 'Psychiatric Hospital Admissions in Bristol II: Social and Clinical Aspects of Compulsory Admission', *British Journal of Psychiatry*, **145**: 605–11.

Harrison, G., Owens, D., Holton, A., Neilson, D. and Boot, D. (1988) 'A Prospective Study of Severe Mental Disorder in Afro-Caribbean Patients', *Psychological Medicine*, **18**: 643–57.

Harrison, G., Glazebrook, C., Brewin, J., Cantwell, R., Dalkin, T., Fox, R., Jones, P. and Medley, I. (1997) 'Increased Incidence of Psychotic Disorders in Migrants from the Caribbean to the United Kingdom', *Psychological Medicine*, **27**: 799–806.

Harrison, P. (1979) *Inside the Third World: The Anatomy of Poverty* (Harmondsworth: Penguin).

Her Majesty's Stationery Office (1983) *Mental Health Act 1983* (London: HMSO).

Herrnstein, R. J. and Murray, C. (1994) *The Bell Curve: Intelligence and Class Structure in American Life* (New York: Free Press).

Highwater, J. (1981) *The Primal Mind: Vision and Reality in Indian America* (New York: New American Library).

Hilliard III, A. G. (1986) 'Pedagogy in Ancient Kemet', in M. Karenga and J. Carruthers (eds) *Kemet and the African Worldview: Research, Rescue and Restoration* (Los Angeles: University of Sankore Press) pp. 131–48.

Hochschild, A. (1999) *King Leopold's Ghost. A Story of Greed, Terror and Heroism in Colonial Africa* (Basingstoke: Macmillan).

Hodge, J. L. and Struckmann, D. K. (1975) 'Some Components of the Western Dualist Tradition', in J. L. Hodge, D. K. Struckmann and L. D. Trost (eds) *Cultural Bases of Racism and Group Oppression* (Berkeley: Two Riders Press) pp. 122–95.

Home Department (1999) *The Stephen Lawrence Inquiry. Report of an Inquiry by Sir William Macpherson of Cluny* (London: Stationery Office).

Home Office Statistical Bulletin (1986) *The Ethnic Origin of Prisoners: The Prison Population on 30 June 1985 and Persons Received July 1984 to March 1985*, Statistical Bulletin No. 17/86, Issue No. 17/86 (Surbiton: Government Statistical Service).

hooks, bell (1994) *Outlaw Culture. Resisting Representations* (New York: Routledge).

Hunt, J. (1863) *On the Negro's Place in Nature* (London: Trubner) cited by Fryer (1984).

Hunter, R. A. and MacAlpine, I. (1963) *Three Hundred Years of Psychiatry 1535–1860: A History Presented in Selected English Texts* (London: Oxford University Press).

Husband, C. (1982) '"Race", the Continuity of a Concept', in C. Husband (ed.) *Race in Britain: Continuity and Change* (London: Hutchinson) pp. 11–23.

Ineichen, B., Harrison, G. and Morgan, H. G. (1984) 'Psychiatric Hospital Admissions in Bristol: 1. Geographical and Ethnic Factors', *British Journal of Psychiatry*, **145**: 600–4.

Ingleby, D. (1982) 'The Social Construction of Mental Illness', in P. Wright and A. Treacher (eds) *The Problem of Medical Knowledge: Examining the Social Construction of Medicine* (Edinburgh: Edinburgh University Press) pp. 123–43.

Jablensky, A., Schwarz, R. and Tomov, T. (1980) 'WHO Collaborative Study on Impairments and Disabilities Associated with Schizophrenic Disorders', *Acta Psychiatrica Scandinavica*, **62**, Suppl. 285, 152–63.

Jaco, E. G. (1960) *Social Epidemiology of Mental Disorders: A Psychiatric Survey of Texas* (New York: Russell Sage Foundation).

Jaggi, O. P. (1981) *Ayurveda: Indian System of Medicine*, Vol. 4, 2nd edn (Delhi: Atma Ram).

Jahoda, G. (1961) 'Traditional Healers and Other Institutions Concerned with Mental Illness in Ghana', *International Journal of Social Psychiatry*, **7**(4): 245–68.

James, G. G. M. (1954) *Stolen Legacy: The Greeks Were Not the Authors of Greek Philosophy, But the People of North Africa, Commonly Called the Egyptians* (New York: Philosophical Library).

Janzen, J. M. (1978) 'The Comparative Study of Medical Systems as Changing Social Systems', *Social Science and Medicine*, **12**: 121–9.

Janzen, J. M. (1979) 'Pluralistic Legitimation of Therapy Systems in Contemporary Zaire', in Z. A. Ademuwagun, J. A. A. Ayoade, I. R. Harrison and D. M. Warren (eds) *African Therapeutic Systems* (Waltham, Mass.: Crossroads Press) pp. 208–16.

Jarvis, E. (1852) 'On the Supposed Increase of Insanity', *American Journal of Insanity*, **8**: 333–64.

Jayatilleke, K. N. (1984) 'Buddhism and the Scientific Revolution', in B. P. Kirthisinghe (ed.) *Buddhism and Science* (Delhi: Motilal Banarsidas) pp. 8–20.

Jensen, A. R. (1969) 'How Much Can We Boost IQ and Scholastic Achievement?', *Harvard Educational Review*, **39**: 1–123.

Jewkes, R. (1984) *The Case for South Africa's Expulsion from International Psychiatry, United Nations Centre against Apartheid. Notes and Documents* (New York: United Nations).

Jilek, W. G. (1971) 'From Crazy Witch Doctor to Auxiliary Psychotherapist: The Changing Image of the Medicine Man', *Psychiatrica Clinica*, **4**: 200–20.

Johnson, T. M. (1987) 'Premenstrual Syndrome as a Western Culture-specific Disorder', *Culture, Medicine and Psychiatry*, **11**: 337–56.

Jones, J. S. (1981) 'How Different are Human Races?', *Nature*, **293**: 188–90.

Jones, W. H. S. (1823) *Hippocrates with an English Translation* (London: Heinemann).

Jordan, W. D. (1968) *White over Black: American Attitudes towards the Negro, 1550–1812* (Baltimore: Penguin) cited by Fryer (1984).

Jung, C. G. (1921) *Psychologische Typen, Psychologische Typen* (Zurich: Rascher Verlag) transl. H. G. Baynes as *The Psychology of Individuation* (London: Kegan Paul); revised R. F. C. Hull, *Psychological Types. Collected Works of C. G. Jung*, Vol. 6 (London: Routledge & Kegan Paul, 1971).

Jung, C. G. (1930) 'Your Negroid and Indian Behaviour', *Forum*, **83**(4): 193–9.

Jung, C. G. (1939a) 'The Dreamlike World of India', *Asia* (New York), **39** (1): 5–8, reprinted in H. Read, M. Fordham and G. Adler (eds) *Civilization in Transition. Collected Works of C. G. Jung*, Vol. 10 (London: Routledge & Kegan Paul, 1964) pp. 515–24.

Jung, C. G. (1939b) 'What India Can Teach Us', *Asia* (New York), **39**(2): 97–8, reprinted in H. Read, M. Fordham and G. Adler (eds), *Civilization in Transition. Collected Works of C. G. Jung*, Vol. 10 (London: Routledge & Kegan Paul, 1964) pp. 525–30.

Kabbani, R. (1986) *Europe's Myths of Orient: Devise and Rule* (London: Macmillan).

Kakar, S. (1984) *Shamans, Mystics and Doctors: A Psychological Inquiry into India and its Healing Tradition* (London: Unwin Paperbacks).

Kalikow, T. J. (1978) 'Konrad Lorenz's "Brown Past": A Reply to Alec Nisbett', *Journal of the History of the Behavioral Sciences*, **14**: 173–80.

Kamin, L. J. (1974) *The Science and Politics of IQ* (London: Wiley).

Kapferer, B. (1991) *A Celebration of Demons. Exorcism and the Aesthetics of Healing in Sri Lanka*, 2nd edn (Washington: Berg Publishers and Smithsonian Institute Press).

Kaptchuk, T. J. (1983) *Chinese Medicine* (London: Century Paperbacks).

Kapur, R. L. (1987) 'Commentary on Culture Bound Syndromes and International Disease Classification', *Culture, Medicine and Psychiatry*, **11**: 43–8.

Kardiner, A. and Ovesey, L. (1951) *The Mark of Oppression: A Psychosocial Study of the American Negro* (New York: Norton).

Karenga, M. (1982) *Introduction to Black Studies* (Los Angeles: Kawaida Publications).

Karno, M. (1966) 'The Enigma of Ethnicity in a Psychiatric Clinic', *Archives of General Psychiatry*, **14**: 516–20.

Karpf, A. (1988) 'Why We Get Bad Health by Media', *The Guardian*, 11 May: 21.

Katz, M. M., Marsella, A., Dube, K. C., Olatawura, M., Takahashi, R., Nakane, Y., Wynne, L. C., Gift, T., Brennan, J., Sartorius, N. and Jablensky, A. (1988) 'On Expression of Psychosis in Different Cultures: Schizophrenia in an Indian and in a Nigerian Community', *Culture, Medicine and Psychiatry*, **12**: 331–55.

Katz, R. (1973) *Preludes to Growth: An Experimental Approach* (New York: Free Press of Glencoe) cited by West (1979).

Kendell, R. (1975) *Role of Diagnosis in Psychiatry* (Oxford: Blackwell).

Kiev, A. (1964) *Magic, Faith and Healing. Studies in Primitive Psychiatry Today* (New York: Free Press of Glencoe).

King, M., Coker, E., Leavey, G., Hoar, A. and Johnson-Sabine, E. (1994) 'Incidence of Psychotic Illness in London: Comparison of Ethnic Groups', *British Medical Journal*, **309**: 1115–19.

Kleinman, A. (1977) 'Depression, Somatization and the "New Cross-cultural Psychiatry"', *Social Science and Medicine*, **11**: 3–10.

Kleinman, A. (1978) 'Concepts and a Model for the Comparison of Medical Systems as Cultural Systems', *Social Science and Medicine*, **12**: 85–93.

Kleinman, A. (1980) 'Major Conceptual and Research Issues for Cultural (Anthropological) Psychiatry', *Culture, Medicine and Psychiatry*, **4**: 3–13.

Kleinman, A. (1987) 'Culture and Clinical Reality: Commentary on Culture-bound Syndromes and International Disease Classifications', *Culture, Medicine and Psychiatry*, **11**: 49–52.

Kluckholm, C. (1944) *Mirror for Man* (New York: McGraw-Hill).

Knox, R. (1850) *The Races of Men: A Fragment* (London: Renshaw) cited by Banton (1987).

Kora, T. and Sato, K. (1958) 'Morita Therapy: A Psychotherapy in the Way of Zen', *Psychologia*, **1**: 219–25.

Kovel, J. (1984) *White Racism: A Psychohistory*, 2nd edn (New York: Columbia University Press) reprinted (London: Free Association Books, 1988).

Kraepelin, E. (1899) *Psychiatrie: ein Lehrbuch fur Studirende and Artze*, 6th edn (Leipzig: Verlag von Johann Ambrosius Barth).

Kraepelin, E. (1904) 'Vergleichende Psychiatrie', *Zentralblatt Nervenheilkunde und Psychiatrie*, **27**: 433–7, transl. H. Marshall in S. R. Hirsch and M. Shepherd (eds) *Themes and Variations in European Psychiatry* (Bristol: Wright, 1974) pp. 3–6.

Kraepelin, E. (1913) *Manic Depressive Insanity and Paranoia*, translation of *Lehrbuch der Psychiatrie*, R. M. Barclay, 8th edn, Vols 3 and 4 (Edinburgh: Livingstone).

Kraepelin, E. (1920) 'Die Erscheinungsformen des Irreseins', *Zeitschrift für die gesamte Neurologie and Psychiatrie*, **62**: 1–29, transl. H. Marshall; reprinted as 'Patterns of Mental Disorder' in S. Hirsch and M. Shepherd (eds) *Themes and Variations in European Psychiatry* (Bristol: John Wright, 1974) pp. 7–30.

Kraepelin, E. (1921) *Manic-depressive Insanity and Paranoia*, transl. and edited R. M. Barclay and G. M. Robertson (Edinburgh: Livingstone).

Lambo, A. (1964) 'Patterns of Psychiatric Care in Developing African Countries', in A. Kiev (ed.) *Magic, Faith and Healing: Studies in Primitive Psychiatry Today*, Part 4 (New York: Free Press of Glencoe) pp. 443–53.

Lambo, A. (1969) 'Traditional African Cultures and Western Medicine', in F. N. L. Poynter (ed.) *Medicine and Culture* (London: Wellcome Institute of the History of Medicine) pp. 201–10.

Lancet, The (1964) 'The Village of Aro', *The Lancet*, no. 2, pp. 513–14.

Lau, A. (1986) 'Family Therapy across Cultures', in J. L. Cox (ed.) *Transcultural Psychiatry* (London: Croom Helm).

Lawrence, E. (1982) 'In the Abundance of Water the Fool is Thirsty: Sociology and Black "Pathology"', in Centre for Contemporary Cultural

Studies (ed.) *The Empire Strikes Back: Race and Racism in 70s Britain* (London: Hutchinson) pp. 95–142.

Lawson, E. T. (1984) *Religions of Africa: Tradition and Transformation* (San Francisco: Harper & Row).

Lawson, W. B., Yesavage, J. A. and Werner, P. D. (1984) 'Race, Violence and Psychopathology', *Journal of Clinical Psychiatry*, **45**: 294–7.

Lazarus, R. S., Averill, J. R. and Opton, E. M. Jr (1970) 'Toward a Cognitive Theory of Emotions', in M. Arnold (ed.) *Feelings and Emotions* (New York: Academic Press) pp. 207–32.

Lazarus, R. S., Kanner, A. D. and Folkman, S. (1980) 'Emotions: A Cognitive–Phenomenological Analysis', in R. Plutchnik and H. Kellerman (eds) *Emotion: Theory, Research and Experience*, Vol. 1, *Theories of Emotion* (New York: Academic Press) pp. 189–217.

Lazlo, E. (1972) *Introduction to Systems Philosophy* (London: Gordon & Breach) cited by Capra (1982).

Lebra, T. S. (1982) 'Self-reconstruction in Japanese Religious Psychotherapy', in A. J. Marsella and G. M. White (eds) *Cultural Conceptions of Mental Health and Therapy* (Dordrecht: Reidel) pp. 269–83.

Leff, J. (1973) 'Culture and the Differentiation of Emotional States', *British Journal of Psychiatry*, **123**: 299–306.

Leff, J. (1977) 'The Cross-cultural Study of Emotions', *Culture, Medicine and Psychiatry*, **1**: 317–50.

Leighton, A. H. and Hughes, J. M. (1961) 'Cultures as Causative of Mental Disorder', *Millbank Memorial Fund Quarterly*, **39**(3): 446–70.

Lévi-Strauss, C. (1963) *The Sorcerer and His Magic in Structural Anthropology* (New York: Basic Books).

Levy-Bruhl, L. (1923) *Primitive Mentality*, transl. L. A. Clare (London: Allen & Unwin).

Lewis, A. (1965) 'Chairman's Opening Remarks', in A. V. S. De Rueck and R. Porter (eds) *Transcultural Psychiatry* (London: Churchill) pp. 1–3.

Lewis, G. (1986) 'Concepts of Health and Illness in a Sepik Society', in C. Currer and M. Stacey (eds) *Concepts of Health, Illness and Disease: A Comparative Perspective* (Leamington Spa: Berg) pp. 119–35.

Lewis, N. (1989) *The Missionaries* (London: Arena).

Lewis, N. D. C. (1974) 'American Psychiatry from Its Beginnings to World War II', in S. Arieti (ed.) *American Handbook of Psychiatry*, 2nd edn, Vol. 1 (New York: Basic Books) pp. 28–42.

Linnaeus, C. (1758–59) *Systema Naturae per Regina Tria Naturae*, 10th edn (Stockholm: Laurentius Salius) cited by Fryer (1984).

Linton, R. (1956) *Culture and Mental Disorders* (Springfield, Ill.: Thomas).

Littlewood, R. and Cross, S. (1980) 'Ethnic Minorities and Psychiatric Services', *Sociology of Health and Illness*, **2**: 194–201.

Littlewood, R. and Lipsedge, M. (1981) 'Acute Psychotic Reactions in Caribbean-born Patients', *Psychological Medicine*, **11**: 303–18.

Littlewood, R. and Lipsedge, M. (1987) 'The Butterfly and the Serpent: Culture, Psychopathology and Biomedicine', *Culture, Medicine and Psychiatry*, **11**: 289–335.

Littlewood, R. and Lipsedge, M. (1988) 'Psychiatric Illness among British Afro-Caribbeans', *British Medical Journal*, **296**: 950–1.

Long, E. (1774) *History of Jamaica* (London: Frank Cass) cited by Fryer (1984).

Loring, M. and Powell, B. (1988) 'Gender, Race and DSM-III: A Study of the Objectivity of Psychiatric Diagnostic Behavior', *Journal of Health and Social Behavior*, **29**: 1–22.

Lucas, J. O. (1948) *The Religion of the Yorubas* (Lagos: CMS Bookshop) cited by Diop (1967).

Lutz, C. (1985) 'Depression and the Translation of Emotional Words', in A. Kleinman and B. Good (eds) *Culture and Depression: Studies in the Anthropology and Cross-Cultural Psychiatry of Affect and Disorder* (Berkeley: University of California Press) pp. 63–100.

McClintock, A. (1995) *Imperial Leather. Race, Gender and Sexuality in the Colonial Contest* (New York: Routledge).

McDougall, W. (1921) *Is America Safe for Democracy?* (New York: Scribner).

McGovern, D. and Cope, R. (1987) 'The Compulsory Detention of Males of Different Ethnic Groups, with Special Reference to Offender Patients', *British Journal of Psychiatry*, **150**: 505–12.

McQueen, D. V. (1978) 'The History of Science and Medicine as Theoretical Sources for the Comparative Study of Contemporary Medical Systems', *Social Science and Medicine*, **12**: 69–74.

Mama, A. (1995) *Beyond the Masks* (London: Routledge).

Man, P. L. and Chen, C. H. (1972) 'Mechanism of Acupunctural Anesthesia: The Two-gate Control Theory', *Diseases of the Nervous System*, **33**: 730–5.

Marfleet, P. (1999) 'Europe's Civilising Mission', Chapter 2 in P. Cohen (ed.) *New Ethnicities, Old Racisms* (London: Zed Books) pp. 18–36.

Marsella, A. J. (1978) 'Thoughts on Cross-cultural Studies on the Epidemiology of Depression', *Culture, Medicine and Psychiatry*, **2**: 343–57.

Marsella, A. J. and White, G. M. (eds) (1982) *Cultural Conceptions of Mental Health and Therapy* (Dordrecht: Reidel).

Maudsley, H. (1867) *The Physiology and Pathology of Mind* (New York: D. Appleton).

Maudsley, H. (1879) *The Pathology of Mind* (London: Macmillan).

Mbiti, J. S. (1969) *African Religions and Philosophy* (New York: Doubleday) reprinted (London: Heinemann, 1988).

Melzack, R. and Wall, P. (1965) 'Pain Mechanisms: A New Theory', *Science*, **150**: 971–9.

Mental Health Act Commission (1991) *Fourth Biennial Report 1989–1991* (London: HMSO Publications).

Mental Health Act Commission (1993) *Fifth Biennial Report 1991–1993* (London: HMSO Publications).

Mental Health Act Commission (1995) *Sixth Biennial Report 1993–1995* (London: HMSO Publications).

Meyer, A. (1905) 'Discussion on the Classification of the Melancholias', *Journal of Nervous and Mental Disease*, **32**: 112–18.

Miles, R. (1982) 'Racism and Nationalism in Britain', in C. Husband (ed.) *'Race' in Britain: Continuity and Change* (London: Hutchinson) pp. 279–300.

Molnar, S. (1983) *Human Variation: Races, Types and Ethnic Groups*, 2nd edn (Englewood Cliffs, NJ: Prentice-Hall).

Mora, G. (1961) 'Historiographic and Cultural Trends in Psychiatry: A Survey', *Bulletin of the History of Medicine*, **35**: 26–36.

Morel, B. A. (1852) *Traité des Mentales* (Paris: Masson) cited by Gottesman (1991).

Morley, D., Rohde, J. E. and Williams, G. (1983) *Practising Health for All* (Oxford: Oxford University Press).

Morrison, T. (1987) *Beloved* (London: Chatto and Windus).

Morton, S. G. (1839) *Crania Americana: Or, A Comparative View of the Skulls of Various Aboriginal Nations of North and South America* (Philadelphia and London) cited by Banton (1987).

Moynihan, D. (1965) *The Negro Family in the United States: The Case for National Action* (Washington: US Governmental Printing Office).

Mukherjee, S., Shukla, S., Woodle, J., Rosen, A. M. and Olarte, S. (1983) 'Misdiagnosis of Schizophrenia in Bipolar Patients: A Multiethnic Comparison', *American Journal of Psychiatry*, **140**: 1571–4.

Muller, M. (1888) *Biography of Words and the Home of Aryans* (London) cited by Benedict (1942).

Murase, T. (1982) 'Sunao: A Central Value in Japanese Psychotherapy', in A. J. Marsella and G. M. White (eds) *Cultural Conceptions of Mental Health and Therapy* (Dordrecht: Reidel) pp. 317–29.

Murase, T. and Johnson, F. (1974) 'Naikan, Morita and Western Psychotherapy: A Comparison', *Archives of General Psychiatry*, **31**: 121–30.

Murphy, H. B. M. (1986) 'The Historical Development of Transcultural Psychiatry', in J. L. Cox (ed.) *Transcultural Psychiatry* (London: Croom Helm) pp. 7–22.

Myrdal, G. (1964) *The American Dilemma* (New York: McGraw-Hill).

Nanajivako, Bhikkhu (1984) 'Aniccum – the Buddhist Theory of Impermanence. An Approach from the Standpoint of Modern Science and Philosophy', in B. P. Kirthisinghe (ed.) *Buddhism and Science* (Delhi: Motilal Banarsidass) pp. 21–39.

Nasr, S. H. (1980) *Living Sufism* (London: Unwin Paperbacks).

Nasser, M. (1987) 'Psychiatry in Ancient Egypt', *Bulletin of the Royal College of Psychiatrists*, **11**: 420–2.

National Institute of Mental Health (1971) *Socio-economic Characteristics of Admissions to Inpatient Services of State and County Mental Hospitals, 1969*, DREW Publication no. (HSM) 72-9048 (Washington: Superintendent of Documents, US Government Printing Office).

New Internationalist (1989) 'Third World Novels', *New Internationalist*, **191**: 12–14.

NHS Management Executive (1993) *Collecting Information about the Ethnic Group of Patients*. Letter sent October 1993. Department of Health, Leeds.

Nichter, M. (1981) 'Idioms of Distress: Alternatives in the Expression of Psychosocial Distress. A Case Study from South India', *Culture, Medicine and Psychiatry*, **5**: 379–408.

Nobles, W. W. (1986) 'Ancient Egyptian Thought and the Renaissance of African (Black) Psychology', in M. Karenga and J. H. Carruthers (eds) *Kemet and the African Worldview. Research, Rescue and Restoration*, Part 3 (Los Angeles: University of Sankore Press) pp. 100–18.

Obembe, A. (1983) 'Nigerian Psychiatry – Past, Present and Future', in S. Brown (ed.) *Psychiatry in Developing Countries* (London: Gaskell and Royal College of Psychiatrists) pp. 4–6.

Obeyesekere, G. (1977) 'The Theory and Practice of Psychological Medicine in the Ayurvedic Tradition', *Culture, Medicine and Psychiatry*, **1**: 155–81.

Obeyesekere, G. (1981) *Medusa's Hair. An Essay on Personal Symbols and Religious Experience* (Chicago: University of Chicago Press).

Obeyesekere, G. (1985) 'Depression, Buddhism, and the Work of Culture in Sri Lanka', in A. Kleinman and B. Good (eds) *Culture and Depression* (Berkeley: University of California Press) pp. 134–52.

Offer, D. and Sabshin, M. (1966) *Normality: Theoretical and Clinical Concepts of Mental Health* (New York: Basic Books).

Okasha, A. and Ashour, A. (1981) 'Psycho-demographic Study of Anxiety in Egypt: The PSE in its Arabic Version', *British Journal of Psychiatry*, **139**: 70–3.

O'Nell, T. (1989) 'Psychiatric Investigations among American Indians and Alaska Natives: A Critical Review', *Culture, Medicine and Psychiatry*, **13**(1): 51–87.

Orley, J. and Wing, J. (1979) 'Psychiatric Disorders in Two African Villages', *Archives of General Psychiatry*, **36**: 513–20.

Osborne, F. (1971) 'Races and the Future of Man', in R. H. Osborne (ed.) *The Biological and Social Meaning of Race* (San Francisco: Freeman) pp. 149–57.

Owens, D., Harrison, G. and Boot, D. (1991) 'Ethnic Factors in Voluntary and Compulsory Admission', *Psychological Medicine*, **21**: 185–96.

Pakenham, T. (1991) *The Scramble for Africa 1876–1912* (London: Abacus).

Panikkar, K. M. (1959) *Asia and Western Dominance* (London: George Allen) reprinted (USA: Collier, 1969).

Pasamanick, B. (1963) 'Some Misconceptions Concerning Differences in the Racial Prevalence of Mental Disease', *American Journal of Orthopsychiatry*, **33**: 72–86.

Pearsall, J. and Trumble, B. (1995) *The Oxford English Reference Dictionary* (Oxford: Oxford University Press).

Pearson, K. (1901) *National Life from the Standpoint of Science* (London: A. & C. Black) cited by Fryer (1984).

Pederson, P. B., Draguns, J. G., Lonner, W. J. and Trimble, J. E. (eds) (1981) *Counselling across Cultures*, revised and enlarged edn (Hawaii: University Press of Hawaii).

Penal Affairs Consortium (1996) *Race and Criminal Justice* (London: Penal Affairs Consortium).

Pertold, O. (1930) *The Ceremonial Dances of the Sinhalese. An Inquiry into Sinhalese Folk Religion* (Dehiwala, Sri Lanka: Tisara Prakasakayo).

Pierce, C. M. (1973) 'The Formation of the Black Psychiatrists of America', in C. V. Willic, B. M. Kramer and B. S. Brown (eds) *Racism and Mental Health: Essays* (Pittsburgh: University of Pittsburgh Press) pp. 525–54.

Pieterse, J. N. (1992) *White on Black. Images of Africa and Blacks in Western Popular Culture* (Yale University Press). Published in paperback 1995. Original edition published in Dutch as *Wit Over Zwart: Beelden van Afrika en Zwarten in de Westerse Populaire Cultur* (Amsterdam: Koninklijk Institut voor de Tropen, 1990).

Plummer, B. L. (1970) 'Benjamin Rush and the Negro American', *American Journal of Psychiatry*, **127**: 793–8.

Popper, K. R. and Eccles, J. C. (1977) *The Self and Its Brain* (Berlin: Springer International).

Prichard, J. C. (1835) *A Treatise on Insanity and Other Disorders Affecting the Mind* (London: Sherwood, Gilbert & Piper).

Prince, R. (1964) 'Indigenous Yoruba Psychiatry', in A. Kiev (ed.) *Magic, Faith and Healing. Studies in Primitive Psychiatry Today*, Part 2 (New York: Free Press of Glencoe) pp. 84–120.

Prince, R. (1968) 'The Changing Picture of Depressive Syndromes in Africa', *Canadian Journal of African Studies*, **1**: 177–92.

Prince, R. (1976) 'Psychotherapy as the Manipulation of Endogenous Healing Mechanisms: A Transcultural Survey', *Transcultural Psychiatric Research Review*, **13**: 115–33.

Prince, R. (1980) 'Variations in Psychotherapeutic Procedures', in H. C. Triandis and J. Draguns (eds) *Handbook of Cross-Cultural Psychology*, Vol. 6 (Boston: Allyn & Bacon) pp. 291–349.

Prince, R. (1983) 'Is Anorexia Nervosa a Culture-bound Syndrome?', *Transcultural Psychiatric Research Review*, **20**: 299–300.

Prince, R. and Tcheng-Laroche, F. (1987) 'Culture-bound Syndromes and International Disease Classifications', *Culture, Medicine and Psychiatry*, **11**: 3–19.

Pryce, K. (1979) *Endless Pressure* (Harmondsworth: Penguin).

Rack, P. (1982) *Race, Culture and Mental Disorder* (London: Tavistock).

Rama, Swami (1985) *Perennial Psychology of the Bhagavad Gita* (Honesdale, Pa.: Himalayan International Institute of Yoga Science and Philosophy of the USA).

Ramphal, S. S. (1987) 'The Development/Environment Connection', in E. Carim (ed.) *Towards Sustainable Development* (London: Panos Publications, Panos Institute) pp. 26–38.

Ratnavale, D. N. (1973) 'Psychiatry in Shanghai, China: Observations in 1973', *American Journal of Psychiatry*, **130**: 1082–7.

Rex, J. (1986) *Race and Ethnicity* (Milton Keynes: Open University Press).

Reynolds, D. K. (1988) 'Review Article', *Culture, Medicine and Psychiatry*, **12**: 257–8.

Richards, D. (1985) Asante and K. W. Asante (eds) *African Culture: The Rhythms of Unity* (Westport, Conn.: Greenwood Press) pp. 207–31.

Richards, Graham (1997) *'Race', Racism and Psychology. Towards a Reflexive History* (London: Routledge).

Richardson, J. and Lambert, J. (1985) *The Sociology of Race* (Ormskirk, Lancs: Causeway Press).

Rinbochay, L. and Napper, E. (1980) *Mind in Tibetan Buddhism* (New York: Snow Lion Publications).

Rinpoche, R. and Kunzang, J. (1973) *Tibetan Medicine* (London: Wellcome Institute of the History of Medicine).

Rogers, J. A. (1972) *World's Great Men of Color*, Vol. 1 (New York: Macmillan) cited by Karenga (1982).

Rose, Steven, Lewontin, R. C. and Kamin, Leon (1984) *Not In Our Genes. Biology, Ideology and Human Nature* (Harmondsworth, UK: Penguin).

Rosen, G. (1968) *Madness in Society* (New York: Harper & Row).

Rosenthal, D. and Frank, J. D. (1958) 'The Fate of Psychiatric Clinic Outpatients Assigned to Psychotherapy', *Journal of Nervous and Mental Disease*, **127**: 330–43.

Ross, R. (1992) *Dancing with a Ghost. Exploring Indian Reality* (Markham, Ontario: Reed Books Canada).

Roy, C., Choudhuri, A. and Irvine, D. (1970) 'The Prevalence of Mental Disorders among Saskatchewan Indians', *Journal of Cross-Cultural Psychology*, **1**(4): 383–92.

Royal College of Psychiatrists (1989) *Report to Council of the Special Committee on Psychiatric Practice and Training in a British Multi-Ethnic Society* (London: Royal College of Psychiatrists).

Ryle, G. (1949) 'Descartes' Myth', in G. Ryle, *The Concept of Mind* (New York: Hutchinson); reprinted in H. Morick (ed.) *Introduction to the Philosophy of Mind* (Atlantic Highlands, NJ: Humanities Press).

Sabshin, M. (1967) 'Psychiatric Perspectives on Normality', *Archives of General Psychiatry* (Chicago), **17**: 258–64.

Sabshin, M., Diesenhaus, H. and Wilkerson, R. (1970) 'Dimensions of Institutional Racism in Psychiatry', *American Journal of Psychiatry*, **127**: 787–93.

Safaya, R. (1976) *Indian Psychology* (New Delhi: Munshiram Manoharlal).

Said, E. W. (1994) *Culture and Imperialism* (London: Vintage).

St Clair, H. R. (1951) 'Psychiatric Interview Experiences with Negroes', *American Journal of Psychiatry*, **108**: 113–19.

Sampath, H. M. (1974) 'Prevalence of Psychiatric Disorders in a Southern Baffin Island Eskimo Settlement', *Canadian Psychiatric Association Journal*, **19**: 363–7.

Sartorius, N. (1988) 'Experience from the Mental Health Programme of the World Health Organisation', *Acta Psychiatrica Scandinavica*, **78**, Supplementum 344: 71–4.

Sartorius, N., Jablensky, A., Gulbinat, W. and Ernberg, G. (1980) WHO Collaborative Study: Assessment of Depressive Disorders', *Psychological Medicine*, **10**: 743–9.

Sartorius, N., Jablensky, A., Korten, A., Ernberg, G., Anker, M., Cooper, J. E. and Day, R. (1986) 'Early Manifestations and First-contact Incidence of Schizophrenia in Different Cultures: A Preliminary Report on the Initial Evaluation Phase of the WHO Collaborative Study on Determinants of Outcome of Severe Mental Disorders', *Psychological Medicine*, **16**: 909–28.

Sartre, J. P. (1948) *Antisemite and Jew* (New York: Schocken Books).

Sashidharan, S. P. (1986) 'Ideology and Politics in Transcultural Psychiatry', in J. L. Cox (ed.) *Transcultural Psychiatry* (London: Croom Helm) pp. 158–78.

Schon, D. A. (1967) *Technology and Change: The New Heraclitus* (Oxford: Pergamon Press).

Schultes, R. E. (1969) 'Hallucinogens of Plant Origin', *Science*, **163**: 245–54.

Schumacher, E. F. (1973) *Small is Beautiful: A Study of Economics as if People Mattered* (London: Blond & Briggs).

Scull, A. (1979) *Museums of Madness: The Social Organization of Insanity in Nineteenth-Century England* (London: Allen Lane).

Select Committee on Race Relations and Immigration (1977) *The West Indian Community* (London: Her Majesty's Stationery Office).

Sen, K. M. (1961) *Hinduism* (Harmondsworth: Penguin).

Senghor, L. S. (1965) *Prose and Poetry*, transl. by J. Reed and C. Wake (London: Heinemann).

Shafi, M. (1972) 'Adaptive and Therapeutic Aspects of Meditation', *International Journal of Psychoanalytic Psychotherapy*, **2**: 364–82.

Shaikh, A. (1985) 'Cross-cultural Comparison: Psychiatric Admission of Asian and Indigenous Patients in Leicestershire', *International Journal of Social Psychiatry*, **31**: 3–11.

Schweder, R. A. and Bourne, E. J. (1982) 'Does the Concept of the Person Vary Cross-culturally?', in A. J. Marsella and G. M. White (eds) *Cultural Concepts of Mental Health and Therapy* (Dordrecht: Reidel) pp. 97–137.

Shweder, R. A. and Levine, R. A. (eds) (1984) *Culture Theory. Essays on Mind, Self and Emotion*, Ch. 3 (Cambridge: Cambridge University Press) pp. 88–119.

Simmons, W. S. (1986) *Spirit of the New England Tribes: Indian History and Folklore, 1620–1984* (Hanover, NH: University Press of New England).

Simon, B. (1978) *Mind and Madness in Ancient Greece. The Classical Roots of Modern Psychiatry* (London: Cornell University Press).

Simon, B. and Weiner, H. (1966) 'Models of Mind and Mental Illness in Ancient Greece', *Journal of the History of the Behavioural Sciences*, **2**: 303–14.

Simon, R. I. (1965) 'Involutional Psychosis in Negroes', *Archives of General Psychiatry*, **13**: 148–54.

Simon, R. J., Fleiss, J. L., Gurland, B. J., Stiller, P. R. and Sharpe, L. (1973) 'Depression and Schizophrenia in Hospitalised Black and White Mental Patients', *Archives of General Psychiatry*, **28**: 509–12.

Singer, K. (1975) 'Depressive Disorders from a Transcultural Perspective', *Social Science and Medicine*, **9**: 289–301.

Singh, S. N. (1988) *The Rise and Fall of Unesco* (Ahmedabad: Allied Publishers Private).

Sivanandan, A. (2000) 'Refugees from Globalism', *CARF Campaigning Against Racism and Fascism*, August/September: 10–12.

Skultans, V. (1979) *English Madness. Ideas on Insanity 1580–1890* (London: Routledge and Kegan Paul).

Skultans, V. (1980) 'The Management of Mental Illness among Maharashtrian Families: A Case Study of a Mahanubhav Healing Temple', *Man (N.S.)*, **22**: 661–79.

Soloff, P. H. and Turner, S. M. (1981) 'Patterns of Seclusion: A Prospective Study', *Journal of Nervous and Mental Disease*, **169**: 37–44.

Special Hospitals Service Authority (SHSA) (1993) *Report of the Committee of Inquiry into the Death in Broadmoor Hospital of Orville Blackwood and a Review of the Deaths of Two Other Afro-Caribbean Patients: 'Big, Black and Dangerous?'* (Chairman Professor H. Prins) (London: SHSA).

Spuhler, J. N. and Lindzey, G. (1967) 'Racial Differences in Behaviour', in J. Hirsch (ed.) *Behaviour-Genetic Analysis* (New York: McGraw-Hill) pp. 367–414.

Steadman, H. J. (1983) 'Dangerousness among the Mentally Ill: Art, Magic and Science', *International Journal of Law and Psychiatry*, **6**: 381–90.

Steinberg, M. D., Pardes, H., Bjork, D. and Sporty, L. (1977) 'Demographic and Clinical Characteristics of Black Psychiatric Patients in a Private General Hospital', *Hospital and Community Psychiatry*, **28**: 128–32.

Stott, D. H. (1983) *Issues in the Intelligence Debate* (Windsor: NFER-Nelson Publishing).

Stubbs, A. (1988) 'Martyr of Hope: A Personal Memoir', in A. Stubbs (ed.) *Steve Biko. I Write What I Like. A Selection of His Writings* (Harmondsworth: Penguin) pp. 174–239.

Susruta (1963) *Susruta Samhita*, ed. and transl. K. S. Bhisagratne (Varanasi: Chowkambra Sanskrit Series Office).

Swartz, L., Ben-Arie, O. and Teggin, A. F. (1985) 'Subcultural Delusions and Hallucinations. Comments on the Present State Examination in a Multi-cultural Context', *British Journal of Psychiatry*, **146**: 391–4.

Tajfel, H. (1982) 'The Social Psychology of Minorities', in C. Husband (ed.) *'Race' in Britain: Continuity and Change* (London: Hutchinson) pp. 216–58.

Tart, C. T. (1971) 'A Psychologist's Experience with Transcendental Meditation', *Journal of Transpersonal Psychology*, **3**: 135–40.

Thomas, A. and Sillen, S. (1972) *Racism and Psychiatry* (New York: Brunner/Mazel).

Thomas, W. I. (1904) 'The Psychology of Race Prejudice', *American Journal of Sociology*, **9**: 593–611.

Tischler, G. L. (1987) *Diagnosis and Classification in Psychiatry. A Critical Appraisal of DSM-III* (Cambridge: Cambridge University Press).

Torda, C. (1980) *Memory and Dreams: A Modern Physics Approach* (Chicago: Walters).

Torrey, E. F. (1973) 'Is Schizophrenia Universal? An Open Question', *Schizophrenia Bulletin*, **7**: 53–7.

Torrey, E. F. (1987) 'Prevalence Studies of Schizophrenia', *British Journal of Psychiatry*, **150**: 598–608.

Tourette, Gilles de la (1885) 'Etude sur une affection nerveuse caracterisée par l'incoordination motrice accompagnée d'écholalie et de coprolalie', *Archives Neurology* (Paris), **9**: 158–200.

Transcultural Psychiatry Society (1985) *The Constitution of the TCPS (UK)* (London: TCPS).

Tseng, W. and McDermott, J. F. (1981) *Culture, Mind and Therapy. An Introduction to Cultural Psychiatry* (New York: Brunner/Mazel).

Tuke, D. H. (1858) 'Does Civilization Favour the Generation of Mental Disease?' *Journal of Mental Science*, **4**: 94–110.

Vaughan, F. and Boorstein, S. (1982) 'Transpersonal Psychotherapy', in L. E. Abt and I. R. Stewart (eds) *The Newer Therapies: A Sourcebook* (New York: Van Nostrand Reinhold) pp. 118–34.

Wallace, A. F. C. (1958) 'Dreams and the Wishes of the Soul: A Type of Psychoanalytic Theory among Seventeenth Century Iroquois', *American Anthropologist*, **60**: 234–48.

Warner, R. (1985) *Recovery from Schizophrenia. Psychiatry and Political Economy* (London: Routledge & Kegan Paul).

Watson, P. (1973) 'Psychologists and Race: The "Actor Factor"', in P. Watson (ed.) *Psychology and Race* (Harmondsworth: Penguin) pp. 13–19.

Watts, A. (1962) *The Way of Zen* (London: Pelican Books).

Waxler, N. E. (1979) 'Is Outcome for Schizophrenia Better in Non-industrial Societies? The Case of Sri Lanka', *Journal of Nervous and Mental Disease*, **167**: 144–58.

Wellman, D. (1977) *Portraits of White Racism* (Cambridge: Cambridge University Press).

Welwood, J. (ed.) (1979) *The Meeting of the Ways: Explorations in East/West Psychology* (New York: Schocken Books).

West, Cornel (1994) *Race Matters* (New York: Vintage Books).

West, M. (1979) 'Meditation', *British Journal of Psychiatry*, **135**: 457–67.

Westermeyer, J. (1989) 'Paranoid Symptoms and Disorders among 100 Hmong Refugees: A Longitudinal Study', *Acta Psychiatrica Scandinavica*, **80**: 47–59.

White, G. M. (1982) 'Ethnographic Study of Cultural Knowledge of "Mental Disorder"', in A. J. Marsella and G. M. White (eds) *Cultural Concepts of Mental Health and Therapy* (Dordrecht: Reidel) pp. 69–95.

WHO (World Health Organisation) (1973) *Report of the International Pilot Study of Schizophrenia*, Vol. 1 (Geneva: WHO).

WHO (1975) *Schizophrenia: A Multinational Study. A Summary of the Initial Evaluation Phase of the International Pilot Study of Schizophrenia* (Geneva: WHO).

WHO (1977) *Apartheid and Mental Health Care* (Geneva: WHO).

WHO (1978) *The Promotion and Development of Traditional Medicine*, Technical Report Series 622 (Geneva: WHO).

WHO (1979) *Schizophrenia: An International Follow-up Study* (London: Wiley).

WHO (1986) 'A Report on the Collaborative Study in Determinants of Outcome of Severe Mental Disorders', unpublished manuscript cited by Katz *et al.* (1988).

WHO (1993) *The ICD-10 Classification of Mental and Behavioural Disorders. Diagnostic Criteria for Research* (Geneva: WHO).

WHO (2000) *The World Health Report 2000. Health Systems: Improving Performance* (Geneva: WHO).

Wijesekera, N. (1989) *Deities and Demons Magic and Masks*, Part 2 (Colombo: Gunasena).

Williams, B. (1976) *The Destruction of Black Civilizations* (Chicago: Third World Press) cited by Clarke (1986).

Wilmore, G. S. (1973) *Black Religion and Black Radicalism* (Garden City, NY: Anchor Books).

Wilson, D. C. and Lantz, E. M. (1957) 'The Effect of Culture Change on the Negro Race in Virginia, as Indicated by a Study of State Hospital Admissions', *American Journal of Psychiatry*, **114**: 25–32.

Wimby, R. (1986) 'The Unity of African Languages', in M. Karenga and J. H. Carruthers (eds) *Kemet and the African Worldview: Research, Rescue and Restoration* (Los Angeles: Sankore Press) pp. 151–66.

Wing, J. K. (1978) *Reasoning about Madness* (Oxford: Oxford University Press).

Wing, J. K. (1985) 'The PSE in Different Cultures', *British Journal of Psychiatry*, **147**: 325–6.

Wing, J. K. Cooper, J. E. and Sartorius, N. (1974) *Measurement and Classification of Psychiatric Symptoms* (London: Cambridge University Press).

Wirz, P. (1954) *Exorcism and the Art of Healing in Ceylon* (Leiden: E. J. Brill).

Wise, T. A. (1845) *Commentary on the Hindu System of Medicine* (London: Smith Elder).

Yamamoto, J., James, Q. C., Bloombaum, M. and Hattem, J. (1967) 'Racial Factors in Patient Selection', *American Journal of Psychiatry*, **124**: 630–6.

Yamamoto, J., James, Q. C. and Palley, N. (1968) 'Cultural Problems in Psychiatric Therapy', *Archives of General Psychiatry*, **19**: 45–9.

Yancey, W. L., Erickson, E. P. and Julian, R. N. (1976) 'Emergent Ethnicity: A Review and Reformulation', *American Sociological Review*, **41**: 391–402.

Young, A. (1986) 'Internalising and Externalising Medical Belief Systems: An Ethiopian Example', in C. Currer and M. Stacey (eds) *Concepts of Health, Illness and Disease: A Comparative Perspective* (Leamington Spa: Berg) pp. 137–60.

Young, R. M. (1987) 'Racist Society, Racist Science', in D. Gill and L. Levidow (eds) *Anti-Racist Science Teaching* (London: Free Association Books) pp. 16–42.

Zilborg, G. (1941) *A History of Medical Psychology* (New York: Norton).

Index

233